Dream Careers

HOW TO QUICKLY BREAK INTO A FAB JOB!

Tag and Catherine Goulet
with Jennifer James

DREAM CAREERS
How to Quickly Break Into a Fab Job!
by Tag and Catherine Goulet with Jennifer James

Cover design by George Foster

Library and Archives Canada Cataloguing in Publication

Goulet, Therese
Dream Careers : How to Quickly Break into a Fab Job! /
Tag and Catherine Goulet ; with Jennifer James.

Includes bibliographical references.
ISBN-13:   978-1-894638-90-6
ISBN-10:   1-894638-90-5

1. Occupations.   2. Vocational guidance.   I. Goulet, Catherine
II. James, Jennifer   III. Title.

HF5381.G69 2006   331.702   C2006-901423-X

Important Disclaimer: Although every effort has been made to ensure this guide is free from errors, this publication is sold with the understanding that the authors, editor, and publisher are not responsible for the results of any action taken on the basis of information in this work, nor for any errors or omissions. The publishers, and the authors and editor, expressly disclaim all and any liability to any person, whether a purchaser of this publication or not, in respect of anything and of the consequences of anything done or omitted to be done by any such person in reliance, whether whole or partial, upon the whole or any part of the contents of this publication. If expert advice is required, services of a competent professional person should be sought.

About the Websites Mentioned in this Guide: Although we aim to provide the information you need within the guide, we have also included a number of websites because readers have told us they appreciate knowing about sources of additional information. Due to the constant development of the Internet, websites can change. Any websites mentioned in this guide are included for the convenience of readers only. We are not responsible for the content of any sites except FabJob.com.

FabJob Inc.   FabJob Inc.
19 Horizon View Court   4603 NE University Village #224
Calgary, Alberta, Canada T3Z 3M5   Seattle, Washington, USA 98105

To order books in bulk phone 403-949-2039
Journalists: to arrange an interview with the authors phone 403-949-4980

www.FabJob.com

About the Authors

Sisters **Tag and Catherine Goulet** are the world's leading experts on how to break into a dream career.

In 1999, they founded FabJob Inc., a publisher of career information. They are co-CEOs of this company which has published more than 75 FabJob guides (books, e-books and CDs) offering expert advice on how to break into a wide variety of dream careers. Their website **FabJob.com** has been visited by more than 50 million people and was named "the # 1 place to get published online" by *Writer's Digest*.

Tag (seated in photo), Catherine and FabJob have been featured in many media including ABC, Oprah.com, *Woman's Day*, and stories at the *Wall Street Journal* and *Entrepreneur Magazine* websites. Tag and Catherine's career columns have appeared in newspapers in the U.S., Canada, and Europe, and their career articles are published at leading sites including AOL.com, CareerBuilder.com and MSN.com.

Inspiring, encouraging and fun, Tag and Catherine love their readers, as this book clearly shows. They are like two good friends telling you "you can do it!" and showing you how.

Acknowledgements

 This book would not have been possible without FabJob Managing Editor **Jennifer James**, a fabulous woman who has edited, researched for, and contributed to more than 40 FabJob career guides. In addition to editing the manuscript for *Dream Careers*, Jen wrote much of the content for this book.

We are grateful to the many talented women who assisted in researching and writing this book. Special thanks to contributing authors **Alisa Gordaneer** and **Grace Jasmine** for their contributions. Thanks also to the other contributing authors who are (in alphabetical order): **Stephanie Afonso**, **Jill Andrew**, **Caryne Brown**, **Rochelle Clark**, **Rachel Gurevich**, **Mary Snyder**, and **Lex Thomas**. Thanks to our literary agent **Marilyn Allen** for encouraging us and helping us develop the concept for this book.

We also appreciate the talented men who made us look good, including **Dave Brandt**, who designed the inside of the book, **George Foster**, who designed the cover, **Peter Cyngot**, who provided the illustration of the thinker that appears next to the "Did You Know?" items in this book, and **Greg Fulmes**, who took our photo for the cover. Thanks also to **Margo Earl** for the author photo which appears on page *iii* and to **Brenna Pearce** for editorial assistance.

Special thanks go out to our fabulous husbands, **Clayton Warholm** (Tag's) and **Mike Harris** (Catherine's), and to our precious little ones (Amoreena, Devon, Logan, Tommy, Sunny, and Newt) for their support, encouragement, patience, and love while we spent many long hours growing our company, FabJob.com, and working on this fabulous book. This book has traveled with us to Arizona, Hawaii, Vancouver, and the Rocky Mountains. Next stop – Disneyland!

Many career experts are quoted throughout this book and we have included information about many other books, associations, and web sites. Where appropriate, some job descriptions and salary ranges come from the U.S. Department of Labor's Bureau of Labor Statistics' *Occupational Outlook Handbook*, based on data collected in May, 2004.

Contents

Part One: *Discover*

Part Two: *Choose*

6. Fab Creatives
Careers for Creative People 78

7. Fab Merchants
Careers Running Your Own Business 133

8. Fab Relaters
Careers Working with People (and Animals) 166

9. Fab Brains
Careers for Critical Thinkers

Part Three: *Create*

How to Use This Book

This book can help you have the career of your dreams. Whether you know exactly what your dream career is, whether you are having trouble choosing among several careers, or whether you have no idea what career you should choose – this book is for you.

Read Part 1 if you haven't yet chosen your dream career.

If you don't yet know which career to choose, start with Part 1. In these chapters you will discover more about yourself and find advice to help you decide which career to pursue at this point in your life. (Remember you can likely pursue some of your other career choices later in life.)

We'll act as your facilitators, asking questions and giving you exercises to help you identify for yourself what your dream career is.

Some of our quizzes have been published on the career pages of AOL.com and MSN.com. As a result, we have heard from some readers who loved the quizzes, and some who ... well, let's just say they didn't love them. What we've learned is that if you want to get maximum value from our quizzes and exercises, you should use them as a way to tap into your own intuition.

As Glinda the Good Witch said to Dorothy in *The Wizard of Oz,* "you have always had the power within you."

We do not have Ph.D.s in statistical analysis so if a score doesn't reflect your personal experience, then throw it out and trust your gut. Even if you think you are hopelessly undecided about a career, we believe you have it in you to know which career is right for you at this time. And just by doing the exercises in this book, you might be surprised at how much you realize you already know about yourself.

If, after doing these exercises, you still want quizzes written by people with Ph.D.s in statistical analysis (or something almost as impressive), you'll find some great resources at the end of the book.

Who can skip Part 1.

If you already know which of the 101+ careers in this book you want to break into, you can skip Part 1 and turn to the specific page in Part 2 that gives the scoop on your chosen career (check the table of contents for the complete list of careers in Part 2). Each career write-up includes information on *What They Do, Who Is Likely to Succeed, How to Learn the Job,* and *What It Pays.* Each write-up is an introduction to the career with resources for learning more.

Our team of researchers tracked down the latest information available at the time this book was written, but information such as average salaries and web addresses can change. To find current information, be prepared to do some additional research once you've chosen which career you want to break into. We'll recommend some resources to help you get started.

Hey, this book is already 360 pages long. If we had tried to include more than an introduction to each career this would be *The Dream Careers Encyclopedia – Volume 1.*

At the end of each chapter you will find fabulous advice on *How to Break In* that applies to all the careers in that chapter. If you have what it takes and apply this advice, it will help you land the career of your dreams. It could give you a huge advantage over people you are competing with who have not read this book.

In other words, don't miss the "How to Break In" information at the end of each chapter in Part 2. It is vital to your success.

The *How to Break In* advice at the end of each chapter in Part 2 can help you break into any career in those fields, not just those featured in this book. For example, the *How to Break In* section of the *FabEntertainers* chapter gives you advice that will help you break into any career in the entertainment industry. Among other things, you'll learn how to get professional photos, how to create a demo, and how to get an agent.

FabCreatives (people who want to work in creative careers) will learn how to create a portfolio. *FabMovers* (people who want to break into the corporate world) will be coached on office politics and how to present a professional image that can help them land the job. Plus there is specialized advice for *FabBrains* (people who want to work in analytical careers), *FabMerchants* (people who want to run their own business), and *FabRelators* (people who need people).

You will also find a sample resume in the *How to Break In* section at the end of each applicable chapter in part 2, which will show you exactly what kind of information to include in your resume to put you ahead of the competition. Through the different sample resumes included in this book, you can see the many different ways you can present yourself – including different ways to tell employers your name.

Did we mention not to miss the "How to Break In" information at the end of each chapter in Part 2?

Part 2 is so packed with practical advice to help you land your dream job that if you miss the *How to Break In* section at the end of the chapter, it could make the difference between you landing the career of your dreams or just continuing to dream about it.

In part 2, where it is applicable, we have also recommended FabJob career guides for specific dream careers, which will give you even more information and step-by-step, detailed instructions to assist you with breaking into the career of your dreams. However, we encourage you to read a variety of books about your chosen dream career, because we believe that arming yourself with additional information and knowledge about a particular career can only help you in the long run.

Part 3 will help you make it happen.

Also not to be missed is Part 3. In these chapters you will get concrete advice to help you make it happen. You will learn how to set a specific goal for achieving your dream career, how to stand out from the crowd when applying for an advertised job, how to find a job through word of mouth, and even how to "create" a job that doesn't yet exist.

How did we pick the 101+ careers for this book?

To select the careers for this book we used two criteria: (1) which careers do people *most want* to break into, and (2) which dream careers can someone break into *quickly*. Although you can get started in some careers tomorrow, in most cases it will take longer to either learn the job or land the job. However, in all cases, we have included careers that do not require you to go back to school for a degree.

If you look closely, you will note that we have also included three bonus careers. (See if you can figure out which careers we've given you as a free bonus!)

This next part is optional. It's for the FabBrainy types who always want to know "why."

To determine which careers people most want to break into, we focused on the careers that have brought more than 50 million visitors to our website, FabJob.com, and that people ask for our advice about. We use the term "dream careers" because the careers we talk about in this book are careers that many people dream about having.

Interestingly, in our research on careers, we found that the careers described as "hot" by many government agencies and career sites tend to be the jobs that are plentiful – in other words, careers where there are far more jobs available than people who want to fill them. According to one website, currently "hot" jobs include accounting, clerical, customer service, manufacturing, and retail sales.

Careers that relatively few people want aren't what we consider dream careers.

Of course any career can be a dream career to the person who wants it (we have had people ask us how to break into everything from billing to truck driving). However, the "dream careers" we include in this book are those that really are hot – typically they are so popular that there are far more people who want to break into them than there are jobs available. For this reason, dream careers tend to be highly competitive and most positions are unadvertised. It is these types of careers that people are most in need of advice about.

But what about careers that aren't covered in the book?

Remember, the fabulous advice in this book applies to many more careers than those featured in this book. If there is any chance that you will be changing careers, looking for job openings, applying for a job, going on interviews, networking, or doing anything else involved in searching for a job, you will find valuable information in this book.

So turn the page and start learning how to quickly break into your dream career.

Part One
Discover

1

Where Are You Now?

How to Determine If You Are Ready for a New Career

Imagine you have just woken up on a typical Monday morning.

Do you bounce out of bed, excited to face the day ahead?

Or does the thought of getting up and going to work make you wish you could stay snug in your bed? Maybe you roll over and hit the snooze bar to grab another 10 minutes... then another... then another... When you finally drag yourself out of bed and stumble to the bathroom, you're already dreading work — and it hasn't even started.

If you're like many working people, Monday mornings are a low point in your week. It's a time when you realize you're not doing what you want to do with your life and your heart and your gifts. Instead of feeling passionate about your work, you feel you aren't doing work that is meaningful or challenging.

You may have known this the day you were hired for your current job. If you settled on a job as a temporary "pay the bills" position until something better came along, or if you are currently unemployed, this book will help you find that better job.

On the other hand, job dissatisfaction may have snuck up on you. When you started your job, it may have seemed like the dream career you'd been looking for. You were excited about the opportunity, and enjoyed learning how to do the work. But as time went by your excitement started to wane. If you have grown bored with your formerly fabulous job, it may be a sign that it's time for you to start a new career.

Often we know what we want subconsciously before we know it consciously. In other words, you may still be mentally debating whether or not to stay at your job, while your subconscious mind has already decided it's time to quit. When that happens, most people behave in ways that are noticeably different than when they want to keep a job. Try the following checklist to see how many of the following are true for you.

Job Dissatisfaction Index

For each of the following, check off whether it is something you often, sometimes, or never experience. While the quiz will apply to most workers who are likely to purchase this book, if a statement doesn't fit, feel free to adapt it to your situation or skip it.

		Never	Sometimes	Often
1.	I find it hard to get out of bed in the morning.	❏	❏	❏
2.	I'm late for work.	❏	❏	❏
3.	Once I arrive at work, it takes me a while to actually get started working.	❏	❏	❏
4.	I sit at my desk and daydream.	❏	❏	❏
5.	I have less patience with customers or co-workers than I used to.	❏	❏	❏
6.	I spend time at work doing personal tasks.	❏	❏	❏
7.	I look at job websites on the Internet when I'm at work.	❏	❏	❏
8.	I get impatient with rules and red tape at work.	❏	❏	❏
9.	I take longer breaks than I should.	❏	❏	❏
10.	When I have to phone people as part of my job, I spend more time chatting than I need to.	❏	❏	❏
11.	I feel tired during the work day.	❏	❏	❏
12.	I don't bother mentioning concerns to the boss because it's usually a waste of time.	❏	❏	❏
13.	If I leave the office during the day, I take my time getting back to work.	❏	❏	❏
14.	I do the minimum amount of work required.	❏	❏	❏

	Never	Sometimes	Often
15. I check the time throughout the day to see how close to quitting time it is.	❏	❏	❏
16. I feel bored at work.	❏	❏	❏
17. I "kill time" during the day by chatting with co-workers or doing other non-essential tasks.	❏	❏	❏
18. I schedule medical and other personal appointments during working hours.	❏	❏	❏
19. I start getting ready to leave work before quitting time.	❏	❏	❏
20. I am out the door as soon as it is quitting time.	❏	❏	❏
21. On the weekends I look at the job classifieds or surf job sites on the Internet.	❏	❏	❏
22. I have called in sick when I actually could have worked.	❏	❏	❏
23. I complain to my friends about my job.	❏	❏	❏
24. I have trouble sleeping on Sunday nights because I'm thinking about having to go back to work.	❏	❏	❏
25. When I'm on holidays I dread going back to work.	❏	❏	❏

Interpreting Your Results

Give yourself 0 points for each "Never" answer, 1 point for each "Sometimes" answer and 2 points for each "Often" answer, then use the following scores as a starting point to measure your level of job satisfaction.

0—10 points	*Very satisfied*
11—20 points	*Somewhat satisfied*
21—30 points	*Somewhat dissatisfied*
31—40 points	*Very dissatisfied*
41—50 points	*Why are you still working there?*

While a score over 40 is a clear sign of dissatisfaction, even the most satisfied worker is likely to score some points on this quiz. For example, a night owl who prefers to sleep late might score a 2 on "I find it hard to get out of bed in the morning" even if she likes her job. Only you can decide whether you are satisfied or not with your work. (However, if you are a night owl, have you considered the fact that you could have a dream career working the hours you want?)

While you probably have a good sense of whether you are dissatisfied with your job, the questions below can help you decide whether you actually want to quit.

"Is It Quitting Time?" Quiz

Answer the following YES or NO:

		Yes	No
1.	I don't get along with my boss.	❏	❏
2.	My work is not challenging.	❏	❏
3.	I am thinking of asking for a pay raise.	❏	❏
4.	I have seriously considered taking stress leave.	❏	❏
5.	I often work late.	❏	❏
6.	I have looked into how much severance pay I would get if I left my job.	❏	❏
7.	I am reading a book about how to break into a new career.	❏	❏

Interpreting Your Results

Your answers provide solid clues to whether or not it is time to quit your job. Were any of your responses "yes"? The precise number of questions you answered "yes" to doesn't matter, because even a single one of these factors may be a sign it's time to quit your job. Here are some thoughts to consider for each one:

1. I don't get along with my boss.

A Gallup Poll of more than one million employees found that how long workers stay at companies is determined by their relationship with their immediate supervisor. You and your boss don't have to be drinking buddies, but you should at least be able to tolerate your boss.

While "bad bosses" make for good *Dilbert* cartoons, the reality is no laughing matter for most employees. Problems with a supervisor can hinder an employee's work and may even affect the employee's personal life. The result may be lost sleep, negative feelings, and physical symptoms of stress. There are some bad bosses in the world, but that doesn't mean you have to work for one.

5

2. My work is not challenging.

Having very little challenge in a job can make the days seem long and boring. Challenge is good. It's what makes work interesting, lets you use your brain, and gives you the feeling of accomplishment at the end of the day. Of course, too many challenges create stress. What we're talking about is having just enough challenge to feel good about your work.

The problem is that challenging jobs rarely stay that way. A job that was challenging when you were hired can become boring once you've mastered it. In order to stay satisfied at a job, most people need new challenges every few months or so, such as new projects to work on, new skills to master, or new things to learn. If your current employer can't provide that, it may be time to move on.

3. I am thinking of asking for a pay raise.

"Low pay" is one of the top reasons people typically give for quitting a job. While pay is usually a secondary issue if someone enjoys their work, if you don't like your job then it's highly unlikely you feel you are being paid enough to do it.

Many people who are thinking of quitting decide instead to ask for a raise to see if the extra money will make the job more bearable. Unfortunately, by the time many unhappy employees ask for a raise, their work is already suffering noticeably as a result of their dissatisfaction, making it unlikely their employer will be eager to give them a raise.

4. I have seriously considered taking stress leave.

Consider a new career that causes you less stress instead.

5. I often work late.

Whether working late is a bad thing depends on how you feel about it. Some people work late because they love their job so much they want to spend as much time doing it as they possibly can. They may even consider their job to be their favorite "hobby."

However, for most people, working late is not a reason to celebrate. It's a bad thing if you feel burdened with too much work, angry about your job cutting into your personal life, or resentful that you aren't being fairly compensated for the hours you work. Other negative feelings may range from inadequacy to frustration. And if you are seriously overworked, you probably answered "yes" to considering stress leave as well.

6. I have looked into how much severance pay I would get if I left my job.

You should probably look into finding a new career as well.

7. I am reading a book about how to break into a new career.

Of course this is a tongue-in-cheek statement, but it says something about what is going on in your mind. Even if you haven't consciously made up your mind to quit your job, your behavior can give you solid clues about your unconscious desires. At the very least, you are curious to learn if there might be something better for you out there.

To help you decide if it's time to move on, try one more exercise:

8. Choose one word that best describes how you feel about your job at this moment.

Don't analyze. Just choose the first word that pops into your mind. Yes, that word you just thought. That's the one.

If you didn't analyze your answer, but simply chose the first word that popped into your head, chances are the word you chose is an accurate representation of your overall feelings about your job. However, it's possible your feelings about your job may change from day to day.

It is normal to have mixed feelings about leaving a job. Even the worst jobs usually have something good about them. You might dislike the work you do, but have close friendships with some of the people you work with. Or you might enjoy the status you feel your job gives you.

To help you decide if and when you are ready to quit, ask yourself how you feel about your job on a regular basis. If you're the type who likes to do a lot of personal reflection about something before making a change, you might even begin to keep a journal.

In the meantime, spend some time exploring the chapters that follow. They may give you the incentive you're looking for to move on to a fabulous new career.

2

Where Have You Been?

How It Can Help You Find Your Dream Career

Did you know the greatest source of wisdom about your dream career is sitting in your chair? Yes, we mean you!

You already have a wealth of knowledge about the ideal career for you. In this chapter, we'll help you uncover that treasure with an exercise we call the:

Where You've Been Inventory

In the "Where You've Been Inventory" you will start to identify what you need in a dream career by reviewing your past experiences in the areas of:

- Work
- Volunteer activities
- Education
- Life in general

This inventory serves a dual purpose:

- It gives you a list of all your skills and experiences to choose from when selling yourself to an employer or client
- It helps you identify what you love doing

To create your "Where You've Been" Inventory, start by setting aside an hour or so when you can focus on writing without interruptions. You'll need note paper and a pen, or you can use a computer to take notes. If you have paperwork such as resumes or files with information about your activities, keep them nearby in case you need them to trigger your memory.

If you have a lot of life experiences, it will take longer than an hour to inventory them all, so feel free to continue past the hour if you want to. But don't feel like you have to finish your inventory in one session. It's okay to add items to your inventory as you remember them over the next few days, weeks, or months. Plus, your inventory will continue to grow as you have new experiences.

Work Experience

Chances are your resume includes work experience, so this can be a good place to start with your inventory. In this part of your inventory you will begin by preparing a "master resume" of everything you have ever done that might in any way interest an employer. By keeping such a record you'll ensure that you won't forget anything relevant when you're applying for a job in future.

TIP: Your master resume isn't meant to be sent out to employers. You'll use it to select the most relevant items to include on each resume you create to apply for a specific job.

For this part of your inventory, list every job you've ever held, going as far back as you can remember. Perhaps your first job involved delivering newspapers, babysitting, or asking, "Do you want fries with that?" Even those early experiences may provide valuable experience and give you insights into what you want — or want to avoid — in future jobs. You can also include any unpaid work experiences, such as internships or apprenticeships.

For each job that you've held, these are some of the things you can include about the job itself. Don't worry if you can't remember all the details from jobs you held years ago. Just include as much as you can recall.

- Job title
- Company name and location
- Dates of employment
- Responsibilities (what did you do?)
- Skills and knowledge acquired (what did you learn?)
- Results (what did you achieve?)
- Recognition (how were your achievements recognized?)

Wherever possible, your responsibilities, results, and recognition should be quantifiable, such as: supervised 3 people, made 50 phone calls a day, cut costs by 5%, etc. Instead of saying, "I sold a lot of widgets," say, "I increased widget sales by 10% the first year and 20% the second year." For the recognition category include any awards, promotions, extraordinary raises or praise that you received.

As mentioned, this information will be invaluable when you are selling yourself to future employers or clients. However, to get the most from this inventory, you should ask yourself some additional questions. Exploring your feelings about the job can help you identify if there are parts of this job that you want to include in your dream career:

- What did you enjoy most about this job?
- What did you dislike about this job?
- If you could have changed anything about this job what would it be?
- Are there any parts of this job that you want to have in your dream career?
- Are there any parts of this job that you want to avoid in future jobs?

Volunteer Experience

Just like your work experience, an inventory of your volunteer experience can be used to build your resume and identify what you want in a dream job. Your volunteer experience is any involvement you've had with an organized group or activity, such as:

- Business organizations
- Campus activities
- Charitable organizations
- Community groups
- Cultural organizations
- Ethnic groups

- Membership associations
- Political parties
- Professional associations
- Religious organizations
- School activities
- Service clubs
- Sports associations

Gathering the information for this part of your inventory will probably take more time than preparing the inventory of your work experience, because if you are like most people, you haven't kept track of every volunteer activity you have been involved with throughout your life. However, tasks such as serving on a committee, being a team captain, or canvassing door-to-door can not only help you develop job skills, they can also help you identify what you enjoy doing.

The information you gather about your volunteer experience can be similar to what you will have for work experience, such as:

- Organization name and location
- Dates of involvement
- Level of involvement (did you hold an elected or appointed position?)
- Responsibilities (what did you do?)
- Skills and knowledge acquired (what did you learn?)
- Results (what did you achieve?)
- Recognition (how were your achievements recognized?)

In addition, ask yourself what you enjoyed, disliked, would have changed, or anything else you learned about the types of activities you would like to have or avoid in your dream career.

Educational Experience

In this part of your inventory you will list every formal educational experience you have had, from high school to the present day. This might include:

- Degree programs
- Certificate programs
- Continuing education classes
- Seminars or workshops you have attended
- Personal growth courses
- Tutoring

Note the specifics of each educational experience such as:
- Name of program
- Educational institution and location
- Dates
- Courses completed
- Degree, diploma, or certificate earned
- Skills and knowledge acquired
- Achievements (e.g. scholarships and other awards, Grade Point Average, ranking in class, etc.)

As with your work and volunteer experiences, go beyond the factual information. Ask yourself which courses you enjoyed most and which you enjoyed least, and why.

Life Experience

This is the category for every significant experience that doesn't fit into one of the categories above. For example, if you have ever done missionary work, joined an expedition, or run away with the circus — but didn't do it "officially" — you can include those experiences in this part of your inventory. In this section you might include experiences related to:
- Family
- Hobbies
- Recreation
- Travel
- Self-study
- Social activities

There isn't enough space in this chapter to describe every possible human experience, so we'll list just a few to get you started. For example, your family experiences might include:
- Child care
- Closet organizing
- Cooking
- Decorating
- Elder care
- Event organizing (e.g. a family reunion)
- Hiring contractors
- Hosting guests
- Household finances

- Housekeeping
- Pet care
- Planning parties
- Selling your home
- Shopping
- Vacation planning

Instead of listing everything you have done, you can focus in this section on the activities you found most impactful, either in a positive or negative way. Questions you can ask include:

- How do you feel when you do this activity? (anxious, bored, frustrated, joyful, peaceful, proud, etc.)
- Which activities do you care about doing well?
- Which activities are "want to" and which are "have to"?
- Which activities do you find most rewarding?
- Which activities do you wish you didn't have to do?
- Which activities are you most passionate about?
- Which activities do you enjoy so much you would pay to do them?
- If money were no object, which activities would you prefer to pay someone to do for you?

As you work through the "Where You've Been Inventory" and recall your experiences, you will probably start to notice patterns in the types of activities you have found most rewarding. For example, you may discover that the experiences you loved most have involved working with people, or let you express your creativity, or challenged your intellect. Likewise, you will probably find patterns in the activities you have found to be most frustrating.

In the next chapter, you can use that knowledge to identify the types of careers that are best for you.

3

What Do You Want?

How to Narrow Down Your Career Choices

What do you want to be when you grow up?

Most kids have no problem answering: "I want to be a ballerina... a firefighter... a teacher."

But somewhere along the way to adulthood, most of us change our mind. We discover there are hundreds of careers to choose from, and what looked like an easy choice in childhood now seems almost overwhelming.

With so many careers to choose from, how do you decide? If you are dissatisfied with where you are now in your career but don't know where to go from here, this chapter will help you start to narrow down your choices.

In the next few pages, we will help you identify the types of careers that are most likely to be rewarding for you. In Part 2 of this book, you will learn more about some specific career options in those areas. If you discover that you are a creative genius, for example, you can focus on exploring careers that will allow you to express your creativity.

Identifying the types of careers that are best for you will make it easier to get what you want. Instead of wasting your energy going after careers that would be only slightly fulfilling, you can concentrate on the ones that are ideal for you.

TIP: If you're the type of person who prefers buffets to sit-down dinners, you might want to explore all your options instead of targeting one specific area. In that case, feel free to read about all the careers in Part 2. However, if you're like most people, you'll probably enjoy the experience more (and avoid getting heartburn) if you concentrate on what you want most instead of trying everything.

It's important to focus on what *you* actually want, and not on what you, your parents, friends, or spouse/partner think you should want.

One of the mistakes many people make when trying to choose a new career is to focus only on their skills. In other words, they look at what they know how to do, or what they're good at doing, and try to choose a career on that basis.

However, your skills should not be the only basis for choosing a dream career. After all, if you have a talent for filing paperwork, do you really want to spend the rest of your life as a file clerk? (On the other hand, if you enjoy filing, you could have a dream career as a professional organizer.)

While it's important to be good at what you do (as off-key singers auditioning to become idols are sometimes brutally told), most skills can be learned. In many cases, even if you have no previous experience, you can learn the skills you need to do a job well enough to get paid to do it. So why not do something that fulfills you?

The exercises that follow can help you identify what you need in a job in order to feel that it is your dream career.

Dream Career Mini-Questionnaire

For those who like to do things the easy way, we'll start with a few key questions which may help you immediately identify your dream career.

- What's the first thing that pops into your head in response to the question, "What's the best job in the world?"
- What did you dream about doing when you were a child?
- If you could do any job in the world, what would you do?
- If you could take over anyone's job for a day, whose job would you choose?

- If you had all the money you wanted, how would you choose to spend your days?

The fabulous cult classic movie *Office Space* pokes fun at the "what would you do if you had a million dollars and didn't have to work" question, with answers ranging from the innocent to the outrageous.

The question may nevertheless give you some valuable insights into your dream career. For example, if you would choose to spend your days cooking, that may be a sign that you would enjoy a career as a caterer, chef, or restaurant owner.

If you have now identified your dream career, congratulations! You can focus on doing what it takes to make your dream come true. If you are still undecided, the next two exercises can help you further clarify which types of careers are most desirable to you, and which chapters of this book you'll probably want to turn to first.

Dream Careers Quiz

If you're not sure what you'd like to do — you just know that what you're doing now isn't it — you can find some clues to your dream career by taking this fun quiz which looks at what you prefer doing in your time off. Your answers to the following questions can help you start to identify the type of jobs you'd most likely enjoy.

1. If you had an evening off, what would you rather do?
    a) Go to a party
    b) Stay home and surf the Internet
    c) Work on a hobby such as scrapbooking or model-building
    d) Go to a movie

2. Which section of the newspaper do you turn to first? (If you don't read the newspaper, pick the section you'd be most likely to read.)
    a) Advice column or letters to the editor
    b) News
    c) Sports
    d) Entertainment

3. What would you prefer to do at a party?
    a) Greet people at the door
    b) Join in a discussion of current events
    c) Make hors d'oeuvres
    d) Entertain

4. Which book would you most like to receive as a gift?
   a) *Chicken Soup for the Soul*
   b) *A Brief History of Time*
   c) *How Things Work*
   d) An art book for your coffee table

5. What would you rather do in your spare time?
   a) Catch up with friends
   b) Organize your closets
   c) Garden or do home renovations
   d) Write poetry

6. It's your turn to choose the movie. What's your first choice?
   a) A romantic comedy such as *Sleepless in Seattle*
   b) A thought-provoking drama such as *A Beautiful Mind*
   c) An action-adventure movie such as *Star Wars* or *Indiana Jones*
   d) An independent film such as *What the Bleep Do We Know?*

7. You're at a social event. Who would you rather join?
   a) A large group that is laughing a lot
   b) A small group having a lively discussion
   c) Several people playing a game such as pool or darts
   d) An individual who looks like an interesting person

8. You have the chance to be on a reality show. You choose:
   a) A show where your interpersonal skills can help you win, such as *Survivor*, *The Apprentice*, or *The Bachelor*.
   b) None. You think reality shows are a mindless waste of time.
   c) A show that gives you the chance to work hands-on to improve something, such as *Trading Spaces*.
   d) A show where you can win on the basis of your talent, such as *American Idol*, *Last Comic Standing*, or *Project Runway*.

9. Which of the following would your friends say best describes you?
   a) A "people" person
   b) Intelligent
   c) Handy
   d) Creative

Your answers to these nine questions can give you some clues to your ideal career. While virtually all careers involve working with people, information, and things, and many allow some creativity in doing the job, most careers focus on one particular aspect and most of us have a distinct preference.

If you answered mostly As, your ideal career probably involves *working with people*. According to Human Resources Development Canada's National Occupation Classification, these careers may involve: mentoring, negotiating, instructing, consulting, supervising, persuading, speaking, serving, or assisting. Possible career choices include: clergy person, daycare owner, flight attendant, human resources professional, life coach, and public relations consultant. Check out these careers and others in chapters 8 and 10.

If you answered mostly Bs, your ideal career probably involves *working with information*. These careers may include tasks such as synthesizing, coordinating, analyzing, compiling, computing, copying, or comparing. Possible career choices include: editor, financial planner, forensic specialist, private investigator, and professional organizer. Check out these careers and others in chapter 9.

If you answered mostly Cs, your ideal career probably involves *working with things*. Tasks you might do in these careers include setting up, precision working, controlling, operating, feeding, tending, or handling. Possible career choices include: antiques dealer, auctioneer, brewer, restaurant owner, and wine merchant. Check out these careers and others in chapter 7.

If you answered mostly Ds, your ideal career is probably *creative*. Possible career choices include: actor, advertising copywriter, fashion designer, interior decorator, and musician. Check out these careers and others in chapters 5 and 6.

Choose Your Ideal Job

In this exercise, to help you narrow down your choices, imagine you have six job offers. To help you decide which one to take, compare the benefits of each job. You'll notice that some of the benefits are offered by more than one of the jobs, so choose the one you're most attracted to based on its entire "benefits package."

Job A

- Flexible hours
- Chance to be creative
- Challenge
- Variety
- Potentially high pay
- Having fun

Job B

- Job security
- Continuous learning
- Challenge
- Work with information
- Control over your work
- Sense of achievement

Job C

- Expressing yourself
- Being the center of attention
- Excitement
- Using your talent
- Getting applause
- Variety

Job D

- Being your own boss
- Making things happen
- Control over your work
- Working with people
- Chance to use your business skills
- Pride in your work

Job E

- Working with people
- Making a difference
- Meaningful work
- Teamwork
- Variety
- Job satisfaction

Job F

- Challenge
- Making things happen
- Making a difference
- Being respected
- Teamwork
- Sense of achievement

It's possible that any career could offer any of these benefits. For example, if you reach the top, chances are you will earn high pay no matter what your profession is. However, each benefits package reflects benefits that you're more likely to find in a particular career field, so it can help you choose which ones to start looking into.

- If you are most attracted to Job A, check out the creative careers in chapter 6.
- If you are most attracted to Job B, check out the analytical/critical thinker careers in chapter 9.
- If you are most attracted to Job C, check out the careers for entertainers in chapter 5.
- If you are most attracted to Job D, check out the careers for buyers, sellers and entrepreneurs in chapter 7.
- If you are most attracted to Job E, check out the people-oriented careers in chapter 8.
- If you are most attracted to Job F, check out the careers for movers and shakers in chapter 10.

And of course if you're attracted to more than one, check out the others too.

These chapters are your starting point for gathering as much information as you can about possible dream careers. But as we pointed out at the start of this book, the write-up about each career is simply an introduction to that career.

If you were hoping to get married wouldn't you need more than an introduction to someone before agreeing to tie the knot with that person? The same applies to finding your ideal career. So check out the websites and books we recommend for learning more, talk to people working in the careers that interest you, take classes related to those careers, and so on.

If gathering information isn't enough to give you a clear sense of which career is best for you to pursue at this stage of your life (remember, you can likely pursue some of your other choices later in life), then get some hands-on experience in the career. Ways to get experience include a part-time job, an internship, volunteer work, or even starting your own business – which you'll learn about later in this book.

But before you start looking into your dream career, spend a few minutes with the material in chapter 4, up next. Without the information in chapter 4, going after your dream career may feel almost as painful as trying to run a marathon without proper training.

4

What Is Holding You Back?

*How to Overcome Whatever is Keeping
You From Your Dream Career*

By the time you have finished this book, chances are you will have discovered at least one and possibly several careers that could give you everything you have been looking for.

But you won't go after your dream career. It's too risky. You might fail. Besides, you can't afford to go after it. You don't have the right education. You're the wrong age. You're not talented enough. And secretly you know you don't deserve it.

Hopefully, no one you know is going to say such terrible things to you. Unfortunately, the comments above are exactly the types of negative things many job seekers tell themselves. At some point in our lives — often as early as in childhood — many of us begin to believe that we can't be or do what we want in life.

A belief alone usually isn't enough to stop us. (You may believe that only a fool throws himself out of an airplane, and go skydiving anyway.) But when we let our beliefs influence our behavior, it most definitely can hold us back from what we want.

By "behavior" we simply mean the things that people do. There are thousands of different behaviors someone can exhibit once they decide they are unsatisfied with their work. Some will choose to complain about their job to their friends. Others will take action to get a new career by learning about the industry, checking job advertisements, networking, writing a resume and cover letter, going on interviews, and following up.

At every stage of the process there are numerous options. For example, on the day of a job interview, you decide what to wear. You either show up for the interview or you chicken out. If you do show up, you're either on time, early, or late. When you get to the employer's office, you might walk up to the reception desk to introduce yourself and shake the receptionist's hand or you might take a seat and wait until you're acknowledged.

You get the picture… there are countless different ways you can behave while you're looking for a job.

Here's a simple example of how beliefs can affect behaviors: Jo believes there is a shortage of good jobs, so that belief can affect the way she behaves when she goes on a job interview. Lacking confidence, she might shake hands less firmly, make less eye contact, keep her head down, and speak more softly. She may be so afraid of saying the wrong thing that instead of being honest, she says what she thinks the employer wants to hear.

Unfortunately, appearing too timid and agreeable is a turn-off to many employers. The result? It could cost her dream jobs that she might otherwise be perfect for.

In this case a job-hunter's belief (there's a shortage of good jobs) has a direct influence on her behavior (displaying less confident body language and saying what she thinks the employer wants to hear). Her behavior then has a direct influence on the result (not getting the job).

But it doesn't end there. When she doesn't get the job she wants, her belief is likely to be reinforced. ("I knew it. There's a shortage of good jobs. Why should they choose me when there are so many other people to choose from? I guess I'll have to figure out how to make them like me more next time.") It then becomes a cycle as shown on the facing page.

The cycle can be broken by good fortune. For example, you happen to go on a job interview with a dream employer; they see through your behavior, and you work together happily ever after. Or, you can break the cycle by becoming aware of your beliefs and changing your behaviors.

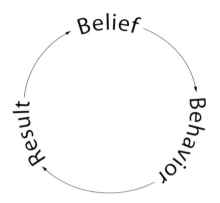

The following checklist identifies some beliefs which can interfere with getting your dream job. By honestly acknowledging the beliefs that you are aware of, you can get great insights into what might be holding you back. After that, we'll explain what to do to overcome what's holding you back.

Negative Belief Checklist

Consider which of the following beliefs are true for you — even a little.

I'm Lacking Something

- ❑ I don't have enough money to pursue my dream career.
- ❑ I don't have the right skills.
- ❑ I don't have the proper education.
- ❑ I don't know the right people.
- ❑ I'm too young.
- ❑ I'm too old.
- ❑ I'm not smart enough.
- ❑ I'm not in good enough shape.
- ❑ I'm not outgoing enough.
- ❑ I'm too lazy.
- ❑ I don't deserve it.
- ❑ Other: _____

I'm Afraid I Will Fail

- ❑ I might choose the wrong career.
- ❑ There's too much competition.
- ❑ If I get an interview I'll say or do something to mess it up.
- ❑ I usually get rejected.
- ❑ If I don't succeed I will look foolish.
- ❑ I won't be able to handle it if I don't succeed.
- ❑ It will take too long to make it.
- ❑ Other: _____

I Might Succeed

- ❑ If I get the job, someone else who needs it more than me won't get it.
- ❑ If I get the job, someone else who deserves it won't get it.
- ❑ I might not be good at it.
- ❑ Even if a job seems great at the start, it will probably turn out to be something I don't like.
- ❑ If I get the job I really want, my friends will resent me.
- ❑ If I succeed people will be jealous of me.
- ❑ If I get my dream job, people will expect more of me.
- ❑ If I get my dream job, my family will want me to give them money.
- ❑ I'll have to work longer hours.
- ❑ If I settle on one career, I won't be able to do something else I might enjoy more.
- ❑ Other: _____

These are some of the most common types of beliefs held by people who want a dream career but are having difficulty creating one. But this is not an exhaustive list. Each of us has many beliefs, both positive and negative, that affect our results in all areas of life.

You may be able to identify other attitudes that are holding you back from the career of your dreams by doing a personal inventory of your beliefs. What are some of the things you find yourself thinking or saying about work?

For example, do you repeatedly find yourself experiencing the same problems, such as feeling underpaid or overworked? How do these beliefs affect your behaviors, and what results are you experiencing? If you find it difficult to identify your own beliefs, consider asking your friends what kinds of things they have heard you say about work.

How to Get Different Results

Once you know what beliefs are holding you back you can just change them, right? Actually, if you want to have different results in your career, the easiest place to break the cycle is with new behaviors. You can try changing your beliefs, too, but that can be a slow and painful process. (You would prefer to do this the easy way, wouldn't you?)

That's because a lot of our beliefs are solidly established. Some of them have been around since childhood and some we aren't even consciously aware of. A belief we've had for 20, 30, or 40 years is not going to change easily. But no matter what we believe, we can change our results by changing our behavior.

For example, let's say you have a belief that jumping out of airplanes is foolishly dangerous. That belief will affect the way you behave. If someone asks you to go skydiving you will decline (and might even give them a lecture on the hazards of taking risks). Your results from not going skydiving (watching comfortably from the ground or spending your time elsewhere) will not be the same as if you did go skydiving (either having an exhilarating experience or being slammed into the ground).

Now let's say that for some reason (maybe someone's offering you a lot of money) you decide to go skydiving. You are going to have to change something. Will you change your belief before you go skydiving? No matter how much you try you are probably not going to be able to instantly change your belief. You will probably continue to believe skydiving is foolishly dangerous. In fact, the more you think about it, the more fearful you will probably feel at the thought of what you are going to do.

But no matter what you believe, or what you are feeling, if you decide it is worth it to you, you can change your behavior. You can go up in the plane and jump out (or be pushed out if you're still terrified once you get up there). So you've done it — you've changed your behavior. Now what happens?

By changing your behavior, you change your results.

Instead of watching comfortably from below you are now flying through the air. As long as you are not slammed into the ground (the possibility of this happening is actually very slim), your result will be a successful skydive. When that happens, you may change your belief that skydiving is foolishly dangerous — but don't bet on it. It would probably take at least a few more successful skydives before you change that belief.

The bottom line: You do not have to change your belief to get a new result. You only have to change your behavior.

You do not have to analyze where your beliefs came from. You do not have to blame Mom and Dad or your past teachers/bosses/co-workers/customers/people who didn't help you or anyone else you're upset with for the roles they played in helping you to develop your beliefs about careers. All you have to do is change your behavior and do something different.

In Parts 2 and 3 of this book you will find many things to do that can help you break into your dream career.

However, you might be wondering how what you do can lead to success, because your belief is true. "After all," you may be thinking, "there really is a shortage of good jobs, a lot of competition, a minimum height required to play professional basketball, etc."

So we'd like to tell you that your beliefs are not true. You and the people you learned them from made them up. With very few exceptions, most of the "rules" you have heard about work are flexible. Someone with talent and persistence can have the career of their dreams no matter what their age, education, past experience, the amount of money they have in the bank, or anything else people might believe can hold them back from their dream career.

Consider just a few examples of people who broke the rules about careers:

- Arnold Schwarzenegger has a dream career as Governor of California although he was born in Austria and did some embarrassing things in his youth as a professional body builder.
- J.K. Rowling has become a billionaire as a bestselling children's book author. Yet she was once a poverty-stricken single mother who couldn't afford to heat her home all day, so she handwrote her first Harry Potter book in cafes to keep herself and her daughter warm. Her manuscript was rejected several times before it was published.
- Peter Jennings was the top television anchor in the U.S. for many years even though he was a Canadian who never finished high school.
- Anna Mary Robertson Moses taught herself to paint when she was in her seventies. Known as "Grandma" Moses, she became one of the most famous folk artists of the 20th century.

- Muggsy Bogues played professional basketball in the NBA despite the fact that he is just a few inches over 5 feet tall (five-foot-three, to be exact).
- Jim Carrey became one of the highest-paid comedians in the U.S., although he was born in Canada and raised in poverty (including living homeless for part of his youth). The first time he performed as a stand-up comic, he was booed off stage.

There are many, many other examples of people who have achieved the career of their dreams. Each of these people took action in spite of whatever fears or beliefs they might have had about how "impossible" it was for them to succeed.

Changing your own behaviors won't necessarily be easy. In fact, whether you're throwing yourself out of a plane or going on a job interview, you may feel downright uncomfortable at times.

So ask yourself if it's worth experiencing a little discomfort to create the career of your dreams. If the answer is "yes," try some of the techniques we suggest in this book — especially if they're not what you would "normally" do.

Chances are you won't experience "overnight success" (unless you do). But establishing new behaviors could help you achieve the career of your dreams much more quickly.

Now turn the page to find out more about the dream careers that you can choose from.

Part Two
Choose

5

Fab Entertainers

Careers for Stars

All the world's a stage... and that suits you just fine. If you desire to be a star in front of or behind the camera, this chapter is for you.

Has anyone ever told you how fabulous you are?

Actually, it doesn't matter what you've been told, because you *know* you have what it takes to be a star. If you are bursting with natural talent that you have a burning desire to express through your work, your dream career could be in this chapter.

The careers profiled here all touch on some aspect of entertaining. While a few are behind-the-scenes, most give you an opportunity to shine in the spotlight, and all offer you a world of fun and excitement. You can read profiles of each of the following 19 careers in the pages that follow:

- Actor
- Dancer
- Film Crew Member
- Model
- Motivational Speaker
- Movie Reviewer
- Musician

- Professional Athlete
- Radio Announcer
- Recording Star
- Screenwriter
- Songwriter
- Stand-up Comic
- Stunt Person
- Talent Agent
- Talk Show Host
- Television Producer
- Television Reporter
- Voice Over Artist

THE CAREERS

Actor

Imagine talking about your latest movie as a guest on a popular talk show, or taking a bow as the star of a hot Broadway show, and then signing autographs for a crowd of admirers. Welcome to the exciting world of acting.

What They Do

Actors are people who play roles in movies, on TV and on stage, in order to entertain the audience and express ideas or tell stories. Their talent lies in making each character they play believable, and bringing them to life. They read a script, and then behave in a way that they think that character would.

Actors get work by auditioning for roles and/or through their agents. The vast majority of actors find work in Los Angeles or New York in the U.S., and Vancouver or Toronto in Canada, although there are acting opportunities all over North America. Acting assignments are usually short-term, so a lot of an actor's time is spent on the lookout for new roles.

In addition to TV shows or movies, actors may also appear in commercials, on the radio, in music videos, and in theatrical productions. Actors must spend time learning their lines, and rehearsing with the other actors he or she will perform with.

As an actor you may do some or all of the following:

- Take voice or acting classes
- Learn your lines and develop your character
- Go to auditions
- Read industry publications to see what roles are available
- Send out headshots, postcards and/or announcements
- Rehearse and perform your roles
- Meet with your agent
- Attend promotional events for your projects

Because the entertainment industry is so diverse, there are many opportunities for you to begin acting right now, even at a local level. You might find yourself signing autographs and rubbing elbows with celebrities before you know it.

Who is Likely to Succeed

Actors have a desire to perform for others, a knack for observing and imitating people, determination that can carry them through multiple auditions and rejections, and a passion for all things entertainment.

It's also a given that to be successful, you'll need a certain degree of acting talent. The actors who succeed in the industry are also comfortable networkers, and tireless self-promoters. It helps to be good-looking, or at least have a unique appearance to land "character" roles.

How to Learn It

Aspiring actors want to work on developing their voice and the way they move or carry their body. You need to train your voice, which is the key to your expression. A vocal coach will teach you how to breathe properly, and eradicate any local accent you may possess.

Your voice is only part of the picture. Your body is the extension of whatever character you play, and it must be relaxed and well trained to function at its best. Start right now on getting into better shape, and take some dance or movement classes to learn how to control your body to the best of your ability.

Acting classes are also a useful option. You can employ an acting coach to help you hone your skills, and so you can get some outside feedback. You can find both acting classes and coaches in the Yellow Pages, or in entertainment industry publications such as *Variety* (**www.variety.com**) and *Backstage* (**www.backstage.com**). And the *FabJob Guide to Become an Actor* by John Havens is an excellent and insightful resource.

When you are ready to do some hands-on learning, be prepared to start at the bottom. You should be willing to take off-stage roles as well as performing ones — don't try to be the prima donna in everything you take part in. You may also be able to find internships or apprenticeships by approaching a local theater.

If you prefer to act in film or video, pair up with other people who are interested in making independent productions, or audition for them. You may be able to get clips that you can add to your video reel that you can use to apply for bigger and better roles.

What It Pays

According to the Bureau of Labor Statistics, median hourly earnings of actors are $11.28. Of course income is related to how many days or jobs you work a year. Unionized motion picture and television actors with speaking parts earn a minimum daily rate of $716, or $2,483 for a five-day week. The minimum weekly salary for actors in Broadway productions is $1,422. Actors in off-Broadway theaters receive minimums ranging from $493 to $857 a week. And if you make it to the top, you might find yourself becoming a millionaire many times over.

Dancer

Are you sure that you could out-dance those contestants on the hit show *Dancing with the Stars*? Then let the music move you into this dynamic and dazzling career. If you love expressing yourself through movement to music, a career as a professional dancer is calling you.

What They Do

Dancers are performers who move their bodies to music or rhythms using any of the many different styles of dance, including ballet, tap dancing, jazz or modern dancing, or other cultural or traditional styles.

Professional dancers work onstage in dance productions, as well as in TV shows, movies, commercials and music videos. They also find employment with theme parks, dinner theaters, cruise ships, large nightclubs or trade shows.

Highly trained dancers may join professional dance companies like the New York City Ballet. Many dancers are also talented singers or actors, and combine these talents in musical theater productions that tour the country. Some dancers, especially those hoping to work on stage, in TV, film, or music videos, have agents who look for job opportunities for them.

Dancers audition to win dance roles, then they rehearse their role with the rest of the dancers and/or actors until they are ready to perform. Most dancers move from project to project once a production or project wraps up, although there are some opportunities for full-time employment, including teaching dance classes, or as a choreographer.

As a dancer you may do some or all of the following:

- Rehearse and learn new dance routines
- Exercise and train to stay in peak physical condition
- Attend auditions for dance roles
- Perform before audiences
- Teach or choreograph other dancers
- Travel with a touring company
- Look for or meet with an agent

Who is Likely to Succeed

Professional dancers have physical stamina, perseverance, and an ability for artistic expression. It is also important to be graceful, coordinated, and have good balance. Dancers need an extraordinary level of concentration, discipline, and a lot of patience to practice routines for hours at a time.

If you are interested in a touring dance company, you should have the personal freedom and desire to be away from home for weeks or months at a time. You should also be the kind of person who loves to be in front of an audience and perform.

How to Learn It

Start by taking several dance classes in different styles to get an overview of dance as a medium. The graceful movements and stretching routines of ballet, for example, will help you build the strength and coordination needed as a basis for all other types of dance. While some professional dancers do work towards degrees in dance, a degree isn't a necessity for most professional dance work.

When you are ready, look for a training environment designed for those who hope to move from amateur dancer to professional dancer. The National Association of Schools of Dance (**http://nasd. arts-accredit.org**) is a great source of information for those who are looking to break into a dancing career.

To learn by doing, look for audition opportunities in the "trades" — a term for the show business newspapers available to performers that list auditions for shows. Get several of these trade papers and search for paying dance gigs regularly in them. You can also look for auditions listed in your local arts and entertainment weekly.

Professional associations are also a great source of career information and advice on accredited training programs. Dance/USA (**www. danceusa.org**) advances the art form of dance by addressing the needs, concerns and interests of the professional dance community.

Fab Fact: Dancer, choreographer and singer Paula Abdul (of *American Idol* fame) started her entertainment career as a dancer/cheerleader for the NBA's Los Angeles Lakers. Paula became a highly sought-after choreographer in the 1980s, most notably for her work with singer Janet Jackson.

What It Pays

Dancers' salaries vary based on how much they work, but average salaries range from $12,000 to $60,000 annually. According to the Bureau of Labor Statistics, median hourly earnings of dancers employed by performing arts companies are $14.82. Dancers who were on tour received an additional allowance for room and board, as well as extra compensation for overtime.

Earnings of many professional dancers are governed by union contracts, and as such are entitled to some paid sick leave, paid vacations, and various health and pension benefits. Some dancers perform for part of the year and then supplement their incomes as dance teachers. Dance teachers charge from $10 a class to several hundred dollars or more a month for a series of classes.

Film Crew Member

As a film crew member, you can be part of the team that makes movie magic happen. And as the popular saying "Lights, camera, action!" implies, you may work the cameras, adjust the lights, or otherwise help to create a memorable movie.

What They Do

A film crew member is anyone who works on a film who is not one of the actors. The crew is often made up of hundreds of individuals, from the production assistant who fetches coffee, to the producer who runs the show.

Film crew members may specialize in a certain area of production, such as art or set design, makeup and hair, costumes, camera work and filming, props, editing, or lighting and sound. You'll see the long list of crew members every time the credits roll.

Since many movies are filmed on location, film crew members get to travel a fair bit, and like actors, will work long days to get the job done. The reward is being in the midst of the excitement of producing a much-awaited or brilliant movie, and rubbing elbows with the celebrities who star in them.

As a film crew member you may do some or all of the following:
- Run general errands for the producer and director
- Make sure the cast's needs are met
- Apply makeup or style hair
- Make costumes and help actors into them
- Adjust lighting and sound
- Move props on and off stage
- Move and operate cameras
- Fine-tune the film in editing and post-production
- Other tasks related to producing a film

Who is Likely to Succeed

Film crew members should be cheerful, flexible, and good problem-solvers. They don't mind taking a behind-the-scenes role, and work well as part of a team. You will do well to develop good people-reading skills, so you can respond appropriately to the capricious needs of producers, directors, and celebrities.

Although many films are shot on location around the world, you better your chances for employment if you already live in, or are willing to move to where most films are shot: Los Angeles and New York in the U.S., and Vancouver and Toronto in Canada.

How to Learn It

Many of the jobs on a film crew (although not all of them) require a certain degree of technical knowledge. Your community or local arts college should offer some classes in film production you can take to hone your skills.

The easiest way of breaking into this career as a beginner is as the "jack-of-all trades" production assistant. You can be hired as a production assistant with little or no film experience, although you may want to spend a bit of time on set as an extra or something similar to get a sense of how things work in production.

The pay is not great and the work isn't glamorous, but working in the presence of great talent is a fabulous way to break into the film production environment without spending years in a classroom.

By working as a production assistant, you will get a chance to do a little of everything, and a lot of hands-on learning. It's also a smart way to get a taste for all aspects of film production, so you can figure out what part of making a movie is best suited to you, and seek out formal training in that area.

What It Pays

Earnings of workers in the motion picture and video industries vary, depending on education and experience, type of work, union affiliation, and duration of employment. According to the Bureau of Labor Statistics, median weekly earnings of wage and salary workers in the motion picture and video industries are $592. Median annual earnings for television, video, and motion picture camera operators are $37,610, and median annual earnings for film and video editors are $43,590.

Model

Strike a pose! Models pose, either for photographs or in person, so that their image will be associated with a particular product. The most popular models (supermodels) achieve a celebrity status that goes far beyond looking good to total stardom.

What They Do

During a photo shoot, a model poses in a series of different combinations of positions, outfits, locations, lighting, and with different facial expressions, as a photographer takes a series of pictures of him or her. During a fashion show, the model brings a piece of clothing to life by showing an audience how it looks when worn.

Models work mainly with makeup artists, fashion designers, photographers, magazine editors, and other models. They may work only a few hours at a time, or only a few days a week. They take good care of their bodies and themselves so that they are attractive to the general public.

As a model your daily activities may include:
- Exercising to maintain your ideal weight
- Receiving beautification treatments
- Sending out postcards and packages to agencies and photographers

- Meeting with agencies, photographers and other employers
- Posing for photographs
- Rehearsing and modeling in fashion shows
- Promoting yourself to the media

Who is Likely to Succeed

Models should be photogenic, comfortable with their bodies, and express themselves naturally in front of a camera. Some acting ability is also a plus. They should be healthy-looking, and attractive in either a conventional or unconventional way. They will likely already have an interest in looking their best, and be motivated to maintain themselves.

Models are patient people, and don't mind redoing a shot even if they think it was fine the first time. Certain types of fashion models must have set physical characteristics regarding height and clothing sizes.

How to Learn It

Keeping on top of current trends should be a priority for anyone contemplating a career as a fashion model. Who are the top models? What designers are in the news? Study fashion magazines and professional websites to keep current with the latest. *Tear Sheet* magazine is an excellent insider's guide to the modeling and fashion industry.

Another way to learn more about modeling is to attend modeling conventions, model searches and beauty pageants. These events will allow you the opportunity to take a peek inside the industry. The *FabJob Guide to Become a Model* by Barbara Carr Phillips has resources and contact information to help you find events in your area, as well as all the information you need to break into a modeling career.

Formal training is available through modeling schools, but the industry is an unpredictable one — an agency is just as likely to select untrained models and train them in their own way, rather than trying to "unteach" undesirable traits to a schooled model.

Modeling is a career with a strong focus on physical characteristics. Knowing beauty basics and taking care of yourself is important to your career as a model. You can also build your hands-on knowledge if you seek out opportunities to pose or perform for charity fashion shows, small clothing catalogs, up-and-coming photographers or art students, and the local theater.

You can become a better model by learning more about related professions, such as photography, makeup artistry, and fashion design. You are likely to make connections with these individuals who can really advance your career. Look for courses on these topics at your local college or a specialized school.

What It Pays

Beginning runway models may earn $100 to $150 per hour. Showroom models (working in a fashion designer's showroom) will earn $35 to $150 per hour. Editorial print models earn $150 to $300 a day, while catalog models can earn the same amount per hour.

Fit models, who test the size and features of a sample garment, earn about $150 an hour. Commercial models (non-fashion work) earn anywhere from $50 to $250 an hour. Top models for their agency can earn more than $300,000 a year, or $10,000 per fashion show. Models occasionally receive clothing or clothing discounts instead of, or in addition to, regular earnings.

Motivational Speaker

If you have ever made a class presentation, spoken up at a meeting, or given a toast at a wedding reception, you have spoken in public. Since public speaking is many people's greatest fear, if you enjoyed the experience, you might have what it takes to become a motivational speaker.

What They Do

Just as the job title suggests, a *speaker* is anyone who is paid to speak in front of an audience. A *motivational speaker* aims to motivate audience members to overcome challenges, achieve their goals, and improve their life.

From the storyteller around the campfire to great spiritual and political leaders, speakers have motivated people throughout history. Today's motivational speakers inspire students to stay in school, say no to drugs and gangs, and prepare for life after graduation. Adults are motivated by speakers to follow their dreams and achieve success in business and in life.

Speakers are hired by companies, associations, and other groups to speak at conventions, seminars, meetings, dinners, and other events. Usually, a speaker is hired by an organization to do a single presentation, which may range in length from 20 minutes to one or more days. For those who prefer the security of a regular paycheck, there is the opportunity to earn a steady part-time or full-time income as a "trainer" for a seminar company.

As a speaker you may do some or all of the following:
- Develop your public speaking skills
- Choose topics to speak about
- Identify audiences you would like to speak to
- Write speeches or work with a speechwriter
- Prepare promotional materials including a video demo and information package
- Market yourself to people who can hire you
- Promote yourself in the media

Who Is Likely to Succeed

Some successful professional speakers are former Olympic athletes or leaders in fields such as politics, business, or religion. However, people from a variety of backgrounds have been able to make an impact as professional speakers. Before becoming speakers, they may have been stay-at-home moms, small business owners, or even students.

What they have in common is a desire to inspire others and a talent for speaking in front of groups. If you are dynamic, confident, and able to communicate effectively to audiences of any size, you might have what it takes to succeed in this career.

How to Learn It

The best way to develop your public speaking skills is by speaking in front of as many audiences as possible. Many speakers get practice by doing free speaking engagements for local non-profit organizations such as service clubs, networking groups, professional associations, and other organizations. Start by volunteering to speak to any groups you belong to.

There are a variety of seminars and classes that can help you to improve your speaking skills. Continuing education programs in speaking and presentation skills are offered by many universities, colleges, and other continuing education providers.

The National Speakers Association (NSA) and Canadian Association of Professional Speakers (CAPS) also offer a variety of events to help improve speaking skills. You can find out about upcoming events and search for a local chapter at their websites at **www.nsa speaker.org** or **www.canadianspeakers.org**.

You might also consider joining Toastmasters, an international non-profit organization. Toastmasters clubs usually meet for an hour per week, and provide the opportunity to practice speaking. Each member also receives written resources on how to speak. To find a club near you, check your local phone book, visit the Toastmasters website at **www.toastmasters.org**.

Another place to learn speaking skills is through Dale Carnegie Training. Check your phone book for a local office, or search for a location and courses near you at **www.dalecarnegie.com**. If you can afford personal coaching, you could hire a speech coach.

There are many excellent books and online resources to assist you with developing your speaking skills, speechwriting, and marketing yourself as a speaker. *FabJob Guide to Become a Motivational Speaker* offers step-by-step advice on how to get hired as a speaker.

What It Pays

Most speakers are paid a fee for each speech. A beginner who speaks to schools might start at $200 while a beginner who is booked to speak at conferences might start at $1,000 per keynote speech (up to 90 minutes). Most speakers increase their fees as they get more experience. A 2005 survey by the National Speakers' Association found more than 45% of respondents reported average earnings of over $3,000 per keynote speech with 3% reporting earning over $10,000 per speech.

Trainers for seminar companies typically earn several hundred dollars per day, with the greatest number of respondents in the 2005 National Speakers' Association survey reporting an annual income of $76,000 to $100,000.

Movie Reviewer

As a movie reviewer, you will watch movies for free (usually before they are released), and then tell people what you thought of them. You will use your powers of persuasion to influence people's movie selections and, like Ebert and Roeper, you may attain celebrity status and even influence the world of cinema itself.

What They Do

Movie reviewers, also called film critics, are an essential component of the entertainment industry. They exist to give the general public an unbiased opinion of a movie's quality and value. At the price of going to the movies these days, people want to know they are spending their money on something worthwhile.

Movie reviewers watch movies in advance, consider their pros and cons, and explain their interpretations to the public. They present their opinions in a concise and unbiased way, and are looked to as experts in the industry.

Movie reviewers can find work in a variety of markets, from local to national or even international audiences. And it's something nearly all of us have experience in. We all like to sit down with friends or family to debate the merits and entertainment value of the latest films — now imagine getting paid for it instead!

As a movie reviewer, you may find yourself doing some or all of the following:

- Watching nearly every new movie that comes out
- Thinking critically about the movies you watch
- Reading promotional material about movies
- Keeping up with the entertainment industry
- Writing reviews for print publications
- Writing query letters to editors and other employers
- Appearing on TV or the radio to present your reviews
- Attending entertainment industry events to network

Who is Likely to Succeed

A great movie reviewer will have a talent for critical thinking, and a keen eye for details you can bring to the reader's attention. You will benefit from a good memory, since you'll be seeing many, many films, and will need to be able to remember what came out when, and who starred in what.

You will have a genuine love of film so your passion shines through in your reviews, and a professional attitude, so you'll come across as a true expert. Essay-style writing talent will help you, as will being at ease and personable on camera or on the radio. You should be confident forming opinions and debating them with others.

How to Learn It

To start your career as a movie reviewer, you'll want to learn as much as you can about great cinema past and present. If a current film references Citizen Kane and you think that's a horror flick from last year, you're not going to come across as a reputable source of movie-going advice. Expand your horizons by viewing types of films you wouldn't normally go to see, on DVD or in independent theaters.

You might be lucky enough to have a movie reviewing course taught in your area, but if not, any kind of journalism or creative writing courses will help you develop your writing ability, and film courses will help you learn more about your subject. The *FabJob Guide to Become a Movie Reviewer* by Mark Juddery is also a wonderful source of expert information on the topic.

Talk to the editor of your local paper about whether they have any interest in publishing your weekly or monthly reviews. Maybe they aren't looking for a movie reviewer right away, but could take on an entertainment-related column or a monthly review of local restaurants instead. Either way, you'll benefit from the experience.

You can also browse movie reference guides and study weekly movie reviews in whatever format you have access to. There are movie review websites you can bookmark such as Rotten Tomatoes (**www.rottentomatoes.com**), and the Internet Movie Database is a fantastically comprehensive movie reference (**www.imdb.com**).

What It Pays

Freelance movie reviewers get paid per review or article that they sell. The best-paying magazines pay anywhere from 50 cents to $1.50 per word, although the norm is less than that — it usually works out to a few hundred dollars per piece. Newspapers pay in the range of $25 to $45 per review (about 5 cents a word), but if you syndicate you can earn that per newspaper that prints your review. Online markets don't always pay, but some will give you a small fee ($100 or so) for publication.

Musician

A cello player in an orchestra, a drummer at a recording session, a harp player at a wedding, a horn player on *The Tonight Show…* what do all of these people have in common? They are professional musicians. As these examples show, there are opportunities for professional musicians in virtually every type of music. If you play an instrument and you would like to get paid for it, you could join the ranks of these professionals.

What They Do

Professional musicians are people who get paid to play musical instruments. Musicians typically work as solo artists or as members of a band, group or orchestra. Some opportunities are for musicians playing live (before audiences), and others are for musicians who share their talents in recorded music. Some musicians are also singers or music composers and combine playing an instrument with singing or writing songs.

Musicians are usually self-employed, and some use booking agents to help them find work. Some musicians get recording contracts with major record labels and get the chance to record their music.

As a musician you will do some or all of the following:
- Practice new songs on your instrument
- Go to auditions and rehearsals
- Send demo recordings to agents and/or employers
- Meet with your agent
- Play music in a public setting
- Travel to play music to new audiences each night
- Play in studio music sessions

Who is Likely to Succeed

The most important skill you need to be a musician is a professional level of skill playing your chosen instrument. You should have the focus to practice for hours at a time. You should be comfortable in front of an audience, and work well as part of a group. You have belief in your talent, and in the value of the music you play.

Professional musicians have a unique ability to express a message with their music. Perhaps you write music of your own, either formally or by ear. They have a sense of timing, and know instinctively when to come in, how loud, and with what emphasis.

How to Learn It

If you have an instrument and have been playing at an amateur level for some time, you may want to step things up with some formal training. If you are just learning a new instrument, most community colleges have a variety of instrumental music classes you can join relatively cheaply. There are also online music courses available for musicians who want to do things at their own pace.

While musicians don't need college educations, some do get degrees in music — especially those who are considering careers as classical musicians. Occasionally musicians are self-taught, however, most spend years taking music lessons, and practice their instruments every day. You can get more information about music schools and training from the National Association of Schools of Music (**http://nasm. arts-accredit.org**).

You'll also want to learn about the business of playing music before you break into this career. Read music industry magazines like *Rolling Stone* or *Billboard Magazine*. Canadian musicians can keep informed about the Canadian music industry by reading publications such as *Canadian Musician*.

Before you get hired as a professional musician, you can get experience by playing for free every chance you get. Getting in front of an audience as much as possible will prepare you for later paying gigs.

What It Pays

According to the Bureau of Labor Statistics, median hourly earnings of musicians and singers were $17.85 in May 2004. According to the American Federation of Musicians, weekly minimum salaries in major orchestras ranged from about $700 to $2,080 during the 2004/05 performing season.

Musicians who play in their own bands are often self-employed and must work out contracts for each gig they get — usually a few hundred dollars for beginners, and several thousand a night once you draw a big crowd.

Professional Athlete

Are you the greatest? Professional athletes are the best players in any sport. They mix world-class skill and drive with near physical perfection, often resulting in astronomical salaries. Top athletes are role models and celebrities, and always in the public eye.

What They Do

Professional athletes are members of the elite league in their sport, where they compete for a win, money and/or prizes in front of an audience. They must be talented and win frequently, or else they are sent down to compete at a lower level. Top athletes often work with agents to help them cut lucrative contract deals.

Professional athletes spend most of their time training for their sport, both mentally and physically. Because of the demanding nature of professional sports, athletes usually only "work" a few hours a day (or even only a few hours a week). Many professional sports are seasonal, but athletes must still keep in shape in their off-season.

In some sports, you must renounce all amateur competitions, including the Olympic Games, in order to be considered a professional. And although your stint as a professional athlete may be relatively short, many athletes move into coaching and training when they can no longer compete.

As a professional athlete you will do some or all of the following:

- Practice your sporting skills
- Maintain peak physical condition through training
- Study videotapes of your previous performances
- Study the play of other athletes in your sport
- Meet with your coach or team
- Do mental exercises to help your focus
- Recover from physical injuries
- Travel to compete in games or competitions
- Interact with the media
- Do product endorsements

Who is Likely to Succeed

The most important skill you need is superb ability in your chosen sport. You should have a genuine love of the sport, so that you will be motivated to train and practice for hours at a time. You should have the flexibility to travel to competitions outside your state or country.

In addition to natural talent, a professional athlete must have a competitive spirit and an incredible drive to be the best. You are the kind of person who forms a natural camaraderie with your peers, and inspires loyalty and respect. You are comfortable taking direction from a coach or trainer, and have a focused approach to everything you do.

How to Learn It

Training is vital for anyone who wants to become a professional athlete. There are a variety of sports camps and clinics that amateur athletes can use to train and perfect their skills, where you can learn insider tips from professionals. Seek out the best level of trainers you can afford.

Probably the best way to get some experience is to participate in amateur sports at the high school and college level. Find out what amateur leagues are the "feeder" leagues for your sport (i.e. new participants come from these leagues) and aim to excel in those leagues.

Each sport is likely to have a variety of amateur and professional associations you can join to help you find coaches and teams to play on. Putting yourself in the position to play in competitions, games or tournaments that attract professional scouts will help you get attention.

If you are looking to find a way to finance your training, approach corporations about sponsoring you early on. In particular, companies who manufacture the equipment you use, or stores that sell your equipment are logical targets.

Whenever possible, document yourself performing in your sport with a video or photographs, so that you will have evidence of your skill for sponsors, coaches, and the media. You can also learn a lot about your performance by watching tapes of yourself.

What It Pays

In the National Basketball League and the National Football League, minimum salaries for first-year basketball players are on average $696,300, and football players start with about $225,000. The rookie salary cap in the National Hockey League is currently set at $850,000 US. At the other end of the scale, the top ten individual salaries in professional baseball are all over $12 million annually.

In other professional sports like golf, tennis, or bowling, a professional competitor makes their salary by winning tournaments and receiving a large cash prize — top prizes are in the hundreds of thousands, or even millions. Some sports also pay performance bonuses or league revenue incentives, and a good chunk of your income may come from product endorsement deals arranged by your agent.

Radio Announcer

Do you have a wonderful voice and way of speaking that people often comment on? If you like the idea of using your voice to make a living, consider a career as a radio announcer or disc jockey — the voice and personality of the airwaves.

What They Do

Radio announcers and disk jockeys are employed by radio stations. They might work as part of an on-air team who chat with each other, or they may speak directly to the listener. They work to generate ongoing interest in the radio station by being funny, informative, or simply creating an enjoyable ambiance for the listener.

Radio announcers may host talk shows; read the news, traffic and weather; or work as journalists who research, write, and report their stories. They may also do some voiceover work for radio advertisements. Disc jockeys are radio announcers who introduce upcoming music and discuss musicians and their recordings.

Some radio professionals have a specific area of expertise that they use as the theme of their radio show — like a radio psychologist, or a gardening or cooking expert. This is also true for radio sports announcers or commentators, who are experts in the sport they announce.

As a radio announcer you will do some or all of the following:

- Research, write and read news stories on air
- Interview guests on air
- Work with show producers to plan daily music, show topics and guests
- Read commercial scripts live or in prerecorded commercials
- Act as commentator for sporting events
- Speak with talk show callers about topics on air
- Make public appearances or attend events for your radio station

Who is Likely to Succeed

Your voice is your instrument in this business. It should be interesting, understandable, and pleasant to listen to, and you should be able to speak clearly and enunciate. Radio announcers are quick thinkers who can respond to guests or call-in listeners intelligently. They are able to ad-lib changes and think on their feet.

You should be curious about the world around you, and the type of person who questions the way things work, so you can bring new insights to your audience. It helps to have a broad range of interests so you can relate to a diverse audience.

How to Learn It

While it isn't necessary to go to college to become a radio announcer, many people do study communications or journalism. In addition to traditional colleges there are also private colleges that offer courses for radio announcers. College broadcasting programs offer courses, such as voice and diction, to help students improve their vocal qualities.

Future radio announcers benefit from speech and drama classes. Some find that improvisational acting classes can be helpful. Some radio announcers work with voice coaches who help them to learn to breathe and use their voice correctly.

One interesting way to break into radio and see how a radio station works first-hand is to work as an intern. For example, NPR (National Public Radio) has opportunities for interns to work in a variety of capacities. Interns working for NPR can have the chance to work for notable shows like *All Things Considered* (**www.npr.org/about/jobs/intern**). Check for other intern opportunities on the websites of radio stations that interest you.

Most successful radio announcers start at a small station — usually in a small city or town. Often they start as unpaid interns and then progress into paying jobs at the same station. If a radio announcer is talented and experienced he or she may then try to break into larger markets. General information on the broadcasting industry is available from the National Association of Broadcasters (**www.nab.org**).

What It Pays

Pay for radio announcers varies based on several factors. Smaller markets generally pay less than larger metropolitan areas, and radio announcers are compensated based on their experience, popularity, and ratings.

Beginning radio announcers in small markets average around $20,000 to $30,000 a year. Those in larger markets with excellent reputations will make $35,000 to $100,000 or more. Median hourly earnings of radio and television announcers are $10.49 in the radio and television broadcasting industry, according to the Bureau of Labor Statistics.

Fab Fact: The controversial "shock jock" radio talk show host/announcer Howard Stern set a new precedent in pay for radio personalities in October 2004, when he signed a five-year, $500 million contract with Sirius Satellite Radio.

Recording Star

As a recording star you will get paid to record and perform music for your fans to enjoy. You will have an amazing opportunity to share your music with the world.

What They Do

Recording artists have a talent for singing, and/or can play a musical instrument. They are signed to a record company for the purpose of recording music to be sold to the public. Recording artists either write or discover great music, and then record the songs for albums. The music is played on the radio, and the albums are promoted and sold to the public. Recording artists frequently perform their music live as well.

The most significant step along the road to musical stardom is getting a record contract. When you get a contract, you will become a recording artist. In order to get a contract, recording artists send demo recordings of their performances to agents or record companies in order to pique their interest.

As a recording star you may find yourself doing some or all of the following:

- Recording songs for album projects
- Performing in music videos
- Rehearsing and perfecting your music
- Doing interviews for radio, TV, and print media
- Appearing for photo shoots
- Performing live shows
- Meeting with agents and record company representatives
- Appearing for autograph signings
- Interacting with fans

Who is Likely to Succeed

Future recording artists have an ability to sing and/or perform, and so much more. You have star quality too: the ability to project an image, and a personality that (sometimes literally) leaps off the stage. You are captivating, and you are gracious. You come across as "real" in front of thousands of screaming fans, and just as real one-on-one with the media.

You are most likely to be successful if you have a clear vision of what you want, and it includes not just small-town success, but the real deal. You'll have the business sense to negotiate contracts and promotional deals that will best represent you. You have close family and friends who will support you through thick and thin, and to whom you can retreat when the pressures of being in the public eye are too much to handle.

How to Learn It

To start planning for your new career, think about your personal or musical style. What hit musicians or pop stars do you relate to?

What type of music do you like to perform or listen to? Your musical style should be a natural extension of your creative self. You should try to develop a truly unique persona that audiences will fall in love with.

If you aren't sure where you might fit in, you can learn about the recording industry by reading books, magazines and information on the Internet, attending industry events, and staying on top of what is hot and what is selling in music stores.

The best way to improve your singing voice (if that's your talent) is to take lessons from a vocal coach. You'll learn things like methods of proper breathing, hearing and pitch, how to extend your range, and how to keep from damaging your vocal cords. Look for private instructors or schools. You may also wish to take music or dance lessons to expand your skill set.

For complete instruction on how to break into the music industry, pick up the *FabJob Guide to Become a Recording Star* by Kathy Baylor, which is packed with insider tips and expert advice on shooting for the top, including how to record a demo and shop it around to agents and record companies.

Once you are ready to hit the stage, audition for performance contests like *American Idol*, *Canadian Idol*, *Rock Star*, or *Nashville Star* (depending on your genre), or book in to perform at big showcases like South-by-Southwest (SXSW), where scouting agents come to find new talent.

What It Pays

Recording artists are paid a royalty (percentage of sales) from each album of their songs sold, minus any money they were advanced to cover recording expenses. The amount of money they make therefore depends on how many albums are sold, how much they are sold for, and what percentage of royalties you and/or your agent negotiate.

According to the Bureau of Labor Statistics, median hourly earnings of musicians and singers are $17.85. Additional income may come from endorsement contracts, merchandise sales, and special appearance fees.

Screenwriter

Movies are one of North America's favorite pastimes, and you can be a part of this exciting industry. Screenwriters dream up characters and plots, and then format their ideas into scripts that they sell to producers, who make their vision a reality.

What They Do

Screenwriters come up with the stories that become the movies we watch in the theaters. They write out the dialogue and plot it into specially formatted scripts, and then sell the scripts to production companies for large amounts of money. Screenwriting is not always solo work, either — many successful movies are written by talented teams. For example, Ben Affleck and Matt Damon co-wrote the Oscar-winning screenplay for the movie *Good Will Hunting*.

The tough part is finding the right buyer for your screenplay. Screenwriters shop their scripts and ideas around to gauge interest, and seek out the best offer. Some screenwriters work with agents for this purpose. You may write your screenplay "on spec" (complete a script, then sell it), or you may pitch an idea to a studio executive and try to get an assignment.

A working screenwriter may do any of the following:
- Research and plan out script ideas
- Write (and rewrite) scripts
- Keep up with what's hot in the movie business
- Network and make contacts at movie studios
- Send out scripts for evaluation
- Meet with your agent
- Pitch new movie ideas to the studios
- Consult once the film is in production

Who is Likely to Succeed

Successful screenwriters are usually movie buffs themselves, and they know what they do and don't like about cinema. They have a knack for creating realistic dialogue and interesting plots. They can tell a story in the simplest terms, and with the fewest distractions — they leave the interpretation up to the director.

The best screenwriters will also have a touch of the salesperson in them, so they can get buyers excited about what they have written. They have a talent for networking in order to become well connected in the industry. Like all great writers, they are open to feedback, and don't mind the tedious work of revision.

How to Learn It

Many people who write movies do not have any formal training, just a knack for telling a great story. To become a better storyteller, study the best movies that were ever made. Think about why they are (or were) popular with their audience. Remember, if these movies were produced, that means somewhere a screenwriter got paid, so they are worth more than a glance.

To learn screenwriting style and format, you can read one of the many guidebooks on the subject. Even reading scripts of movies you have seen will help you see how much or little information you should include. To keep up with what's hot, read entertainment articles and websites, especially ones that talk about movies just going into production. See who is selling what, and why.

You can also collect and read screenwriting books, and refer to them as you write. There are writing courses at your local community college, and if you live in or near New York or Los Angeles, there are filmmaking schools you can attend. There are screenwriting conferences held annually in Austin, TX, as well as sporadic ones in Los Angeles.

The *FabJob Guide to Become a Screenwriter* by Angela Hynes has some great information on writing and polishing your screenplay into perfection, and insider advice (Hynes has optioned a few screenplays herself) on pitching it to prospective buyers.

Once you are writing, consider joining or starting a critiquing circle so you can get candid feedback on your work — if you like online interaction, a well-known website dedicated to this purpose is **www.zoetrope.com**.

What It Pays

Screenwriters get paid when they sell or option the rights to a script. If you are a member of the Writers Guild of America you are guaranteed a minimum of approximately $50,000 per original screenplay that you write, although you or your agent can negotiate for more. The top screenwriters for big Hollywood movies earn in excess of several million dollars per script.

Songwriter

As a songwriter, you will use your creative talents to create powerful and popular music for recording artists to perform, and you will be paid in royalties for each song you sell. Imagine the exhileration you will feel the first time you hear a song you wrote being played on the radio!

What They Do

A songwriter writes songs, usually containing both music and words (lyrics). Instead of performing it themselves, though, songwriters sell their work to others for a small percentage of what is earned when the song is recorded or performed.

Once a song is written, songwriters must market it to publishers, record companies, and recording artists or their managers, to try to find someone to buy or record it. Typically, this process begins with producing a "demo" or low-budget recording of the song, and then sending it out to gauge interest in it.

If a popular singer chooses your song to record or perform, you stand the chance of making a sizable amount of money. If you work with a publisher, you will share your royalties with that company. You can also have your songs used on TV or in films, or you might be hired as a staff writer for a publisher or record company.

Songwriters may do any or all of these activities:

- Brainstorm music ideas with a partner or alone
- Write song lyrics
- Create the basic music for a song
- Refine and edit songs, bringing music and lyrics together
- Record demos of songs
- Study what is selling in the industry
- Send out demos to publishers and record companies
- Negotiate royalty contracts

Who is Likely to Succeed

A good songwriter understands how music is structured, even if they don't know the technical terms for what they are doing. You may already write songs for your own enjoyment or to perform. While knowing how to play an instrument is not a prerequisite, it can help you communicate your ideas to others more easily.

Songwriters have broad tastes in music and an appreciation for musical diversity, so they can work across different genres. A songwriter can quickly get a grasp on the theme or mood of a song, and the audience it is intended for. They are thick-skinned and take criticism as an opportunity to make a better product.

How to Learn It

Expand your horizons by listening to a broad range of musical styles, including those that wouldn't normally appeal to you. Think about where the songs you write fit in, and what artists you might market them to.

If you have an idea of what style of music you write, you should become familiar with the greatest hits in that genre. Think about what is similar in each of these songs, and what sets them apart as a hit.

Getting feedback on your songs is a big part of developing your craft. See if there are songwriting classes or workshops that are nearby for you to attend, or join a local or online critiquing group. You should pay particular attention to any feedback you get from those who are professionals in the industry.

Joining music industry organizations and associations can help you make important connections and network with those who can advance your career. Some you should consider are ASCAP (American Society of Composers, Authors, and Publishers); Songwriters Guild of America; and the Songwriters Association of Canada. There may also be associations particular to the genre of music you write.

Trade publications you can pick up, such as *American Songwriter* (**www.americansongwriter.com**) and *The Music Connection* (**www.musicconnection.com**), contain writing tips, industry news, and other tidbits that can advance your career. You can also check out the *FabJob Guide to Become a Songwriter* by Libbie Hall, which is a fantastic source of insider advice on making a living through songwriting.

What It Pays

According to ASCAP, a songwriter makes money when a CD containing one of his or her songs is sold, when the song is played on the radio or performed, when the song is used in a movie or TV show, or even when sheet music is sold.

Although you may earn only a few cents at a time, those pennies can add up. If you wrote two songs for a popular artist at a royalty of eight cents per song, for example, if the CD sold two million copies you would earn $320,000 for that one release. Writers of commercial music are paid per piece, usually a one-time fee of $2,000 to $3,000.

Stand-up Comic

Doing stand-up comedy for a living can be so much fun you may feel guilty referring to it as your "job." In return for "working" only 2 or 3 hours a day, you can see the country or the world and earn applause, laughter, and money.

What They Do

Stand-up comics, also known as comedians, tell jokes for a living. They write humorous material, edit and rehearse it until their timing is just right, and then perform their act. They may perform locally, or travel across the country performing in comedy clubs, bars, colleges, or other venues.

There are different comic styles you might use and perfect, such as monologues, impressions, silent acts (miming), comedy duos, or sketch comedy. The best stand-up comics may get gigs on late-night talk shows, write books, or perform at televised comedy festivals. Stand-up comedians are also popular as stars of TV shows, since they already have material and their timing down pat.

As a stand-up comic, your activities may include:
- Observing the world around you for humor
- Writing comedy material
- Editing your material until it is perfect
- Rehearsing your performances
- Doing live shows in front of audiences
- Promoting yourself to land more gigs
- Meeting with an agent
- Traveling to your next performance

Who is Likely to Succeed

Successful stand-up comics have a unique way of looking at the world. They see the humor in everyday events, and can tell concise, clever stories that people can relate to. They may have a particular talent for careful observation and imitation. They are flexible when it comes to change, and are thick-skinned to deal with hecklers.

The best stand-up comics are in the business because they love to make people laugh. It helps if you like to travel and meet new people, and if you are comfortable getting up and speaking in front of a group of strangers.

How to Learn It

Since a lot of stand-up is based on observational humor, keep a note-pad handy to jot down when funny things happen to you or the people around you. Take these notes and rework them into stories you can tell. Cut out any details that don't contribute directly to the punch line, and practice telling them to friends or family. Ask them for feedback too.

Finding out which style of comedy is best suited to you is a lot like choosing a major in college: you shouldn't do it right away. Your comedic voice should grow naturally out of your stage experiences. And sometimes the kind of comedy you like watching is not the kind you like to perform.

If you are just getting started, it's possible to buy a few jokes for your routine. When you are developing as a comic, you might even hire a comedy coach or take a few classes or workshops to guide your material and performance. Also, the *FabJob Guide to Become a Stand-up Comic* by Stephen Kruiser is an excellent and insightful look at what it takes to make it in stand-up.

Most medium-sized cities will have at least one comedy club to their name, and there is almost always an amateur night. You can build your confidence and develop your routine in this more forgiving atmosphere. See if you can get a friend to record your performance for you to analyze later, so you can see what's working and what's not. Make sure to talk to the other comics there too and build your network of contacts.

Fab Fun:

The list of stand-up comics who have gone on to fame and fortune (many becoming multi-millionaires) by starring in their own television show or in movies is impressive! Here is a sampling of some of these comedians. How many of the following have you seen on TV or in the movies?

Roseanne Barr	Steve Martin
Jim Carrey	Bill Murray
Dave Chappelle	Eddie Murphy
Billy Crystal	Rosie O'Donnell
Ellen DeGeneres	Chris Rock
Will Ferrell	Ray Romano
Jamie Foxx	Adam Sandler
Whoopi Goldberg	Jerry Seinfeld
Lotta Laffs	Jon Stewart
Jay Leno	Chris Tucker
Bernie Mac	Robin Williams

What It Pays

Stand-up comics are usually self-employed and are paid per performance or per week. Clubs generally give a local comic between $100 to $150 for a week of MC work (where you warm up the audience and introduce the speakers). Feature acts can usually make between $400 and $600 for a week.

Road headliners (traveling comics with a bit more clout) can earn anywhere from $800 to $1,800 on average for a week's work, depending on the number of nights they'll perform. Corporate comics and big-name acts earn fees ranging from $1,500 to $15,000 per gig or more.

Stunt Person

Stunt people experience action and adventure every day as they do the stunts that make movies, television, and even live action shows exciting to watch.

What They Do

Stunt people are the adventurers who perform dangerous or challenging scenes in movies and television shows. Despite how easy it might look on film, it takes a highly trained professional to run through a burning house or film an underwater escape from a sinking ship.

Some stunt people are "stunt doubles" for famous actors. This means that while an actor plays the main part, their stunt double stands in and performs the "action sequences" in place of the actor. While some actors who are athletic and adventurous might attempt some of their own stunts, most rely on stunt people for these scenes.

Stunt people usually specialize in specific areas of the industry like driving cars, stage combat or fighting, firearms, or scuba and underwater stunts. Some stunt people are professional pilots or accomplished martial artists. Some come to the career after successful careers as professional athletes or members of the military.

As a stunt person you will do some or all of the following:
- Maintain a high level of physical fitness
- Practice your stunt skills regularly
- Go to auditions for stunt roles
- Meet with your agent
- Read scripts
- Rehearse scenes with other actors and stunt people

- Perform and repeat stunts as many times as needed
- Travel to film on location

Who is Likely to Succeed

Those who are likely to succeed in this business are smart problem-solvers who can figure out ways to make stunts look dangerous but still be safe. You should be in top physical shape to prevent injury and perform stunts successfully. You will have developed a wide range of hard-to-master skills from horseback riding to juggling to increase your versatility and appeal.

Successful stunt people are committed to the work they do, and take each job seriously. They understand the risk involved for stunts and only attempt those that they feel completely qualified to perform. Successful stunt people also take direction well.

How to Learn It

To begin with, you will need to assess your own physical shape and those areas of talent and expertise that you already have that you may be able to translate into stunts. Gymnastics or related classes that improve your flexibility are always a good route for basic training, plus you should choose an area of specialization, and focus your training on that. Get certification or licensing where necessary, and make copies for your portfolio.

Next you will need to meet other entertainment industry professionals, and network to find out about jobs. (Most successful stunt people say that this is a vital part of their industry.) By networking, stunt people become aware of job opportunities and chances to train with other stunt people. Consider being an extra or stand-in on productions to get a chance to meet others in the industry.

Stunt people may also take classes to perfect their skills. There are a number of stunt schools in North America that focus on various aspects of stunt work. For example, the United Stuntmen's Association runs an International Stunt School (**www.stuntschool. com**), which gives stunt hopefuls a practical overview of the industry and the basics of many stunts including high falls and precision driving.

Besides what is called "union work" there is also non-union work available for stunt people — and this is where many stunt people start their careers. Many of the actors' trade publications have listings for auditions for stunt people for non-union work. *Backstage West* (**www.backstage.com**) is one such publication, and it is a good place to begin to find places to audition for work.

What It Pays

The average salary for a stunt person varies depending upon how often a stunt person works, and whether or not that work is union work. The average salary for a stunt person who works regularly is about $60,000 a year. A typical "shoot" may average around $2,000 for a week's work. Stuntmen and women are paid additional compensation called "adjustments" for difficult or dangerous stunts, varying from several hundred to several thousand dollars extra, based on the stunt.

Talent Agent

A talent agent acts as a "matchmaker" between writers, entertainers, celebrities, and rising stars, and their employment opportunities. By choosing only the best offers and negotiating top dollar, an agent can turn a fledgling talent into a star.

What They Do

Talent agents are hired by professionals in the entertainment and literary industries (as well as a few others) to help these individuals grow their careers in the right direction. Agents find their clients work, investigate and approve promotional opportunities, and negotiate and arrange for payment.

Agents spend much of their day putting out feelers for good opportunities for their clients, and keeping in touch with industry buzz. They have to be at the heart of what's going on in their clients' industry to be effective. Agents may also have a more personal relationship with their clients, giving career advice and sometime moral support when it's needed.

Agents can work independently or in affiliation with an agency. Independent agents are paid a commission of their clients' earnings, usually in the range of 10 to 20 percent. (So basically, you don't get paid until your client does.) Agents new to the business may pool their commissions into the agency, and draw a regular salary instead.

Talent agents spend their time:
- Searching out fresh talent
- Meeting with potential new clients
- Networking to solicit existing talent
- Investigating possible opportunities for clients
- Meeting with clients and their managers to present offers
- Negotiating contract terms

- Arranging for payment
- Staying in touch with their industry

Who is Likely to Succeed

The best agents are the ones with previous experience in the industry their client works in. This gives them credibility with the client, as well as the confidence to negotiate what they know is possible from employers. You are comfortable handling confrontation (in fact, you may even enjoy it) and are able to resolve conflict amicably. You'll be helped if you are fluent in legalese (that confusing language of contracts) as well.

Agents hoping to "catch a rising star" should have a knack for what talent looks like in its early stages. Every agent in the biz will be clamoring to sign the next phenom, but if you can spot the diamond in the rough, you can shoot your way to big bucks along with your talented client.

How to Learn It

Most agents specialize in a certain type of profession, so think about what industry interests you the most, and then immerse yourself in learning as much about it as possible. Most industries have at least one professional association and several trade publications that can be valuable sources of information.

If there is a talent agency where you live, you should apply for an entry-level job with them, or even offer your services for free as an intern. Any related work you can do first, such as public relations, marketing, or legal assistance will make you a more attractive hire.

Express your willingness to do whatever anyone else finds tedious, such as washing the company car or sorting the mail. Once you are in, work on building relationships with the people you assist — help them look good to their supervisor and clients, and you will find you are kept close at hand. You may find an agent who is willing to mentor you or take you on as a personal assistant. Then you've got it made, as long as your work performance is good.

If you don't have an agency where you live, you can approach potential clients directly and see if they are willing to work with you. Attend music showcases, local auditions for film or TV productions, or wherever you think up-and-coming talent might be lurking. Explain to them that they have nothing to lose — you don't make any money until they do. Then get a contract in place and work your butt off to show them they made the right choice.

What It Pays

Self-employed agents earn anywhere from 10 to 20 percent of what their client earns. So if your client is paid $5,000 for a club appearance or endorsement contract, your cut is anywhere from $500 to $1,000. According to Salary.com, the median expected salary in the United States for an agent who scouts for new talent is $51,316.

Talk Show Host

Talk show hosts get paid to voice their opinions, chat with celebrities and other guests, and debate issues of current interest for a radio or TV program. Famous talk show hosts like Oprah Winfrey influence public opinion as much, or even more than, the most powerful politicians.

What They Do

A talk show host is the moderator of a TV or radio program that features interviews with experts, celebrities, or everyday people with a story to tell. The host and guests may debate an issue, chat with each other, or take questions from the audience.

Talk show hosts are employed by radio stations, TV stations, or production companies. They may work independently, or as a team of hosts on one or more themed or general shows.

Some talk shows have a focus topic like politics or gardening, while others are devoted to life challenges or anything of general interest. Most parts of talk shows are unscripted, so the host must be able to go with the flow, but also direct conversation if it gets off topic.

Some talk show hosts are experts in their field (e.g., Dr. Phil), but expert or not, all talk show hosts spend a great deal of time preparing questions and researching topics that are scheduled to come up in the show. Hosts for smaller shows may also book the guests for each show.

As a talk show host, your daily duties will include some or all of the following:

- Brainstorming new show ideas
- Researching your show's topic
- Preparing interview questions
- Booking or meeting with future guests
- Writing monologue material for your show
- Working with your production team

- Moderating your show
- Responding to queries from viewers or listeners
- Promoting your show to increase its popularity

Who is Likely to Succeed

As a talk show host, you are quite comfortable performing in front of an audience of hundreds or millions of listeners or viewers. You have a habit of forming opinions, and the ability to defend them with logical explanations. The most respected talk show hosts are intelligent and informed about a broad range of topics, and/or an expert on their pet topic.

Talk show hosts should be good conversationalists who can get their interviewees talking candidly. This skill may be a natural talent, or it can be developed with training.

How to Learn It

Most talk show hosts will say they learned from watching the greats: Johnny Carson, Phil Donohue, Oprah Winfrey, David Letterman, and the like. Any time of day you turn on the TV there are talk shows of all kinds on, and all-talk radio will fill in any gaps if you want to listen to "talk" day and night.

Pay attention to how the host moderates the conversation, and the techniques they use to create an entertaining product. If you get the chance, attend a talk show taping in person so you get a sense of what goes on behind the scenes.

If you are intrigued by radio and TV broadcasting and have the time and money, an educational background will prepare you to break into these media, and then move your way up the ladder to "host." Some colleges and universities are affiliated with stations that are staffed by volunteers.

You can also volunteer or intern at the local radio or TV station in your market. Do the menial jobs in exchange for the chance to see how broadcasts are prepared. Bigger shows may also hire research assistants and writers, which are logical transitions to hosting a show yourself.

If you are an expert on any topic, one way to break into talk shows is to appear on them. Call the producer of the radio or TV show, and pitch your show idea to them. If that doesn't work, you can go solo — put on your own show on your local public access station, or broadcast it on the Internet.

What It Pays

A career as a talk show host pays at the high end of the broadcasting scale. According to the Bureau of Labor Statistics, median hourly earnings of radio and TV announcers in 2004 were $10.64 in the radio and television broadcasting industry, but the highest 10 percent (hosts or other positions of responsibility) earned more than $27.61 an hour.

Salaries in broadcasting are largely dependent on the market (that is, how many viewers or listeners your broadcast reaches). The radio and TV talk show hosts who are household names earn more than $1 million annually.

Television Producer

A TV producer coordinates, organizes and oversees all aspects of a TV production. They are the ultimate decision-maker for everything from money to script to crew to distribution. As a TV producer, the buck stops with you.

What They Do

Every TV production from game shows, to dramas, to sitcoms requires at least one, and sometimes several producers to make the magic happen every day or week. Executive producers are at the top of the seniority list, and are typically the "money people" behind a program. Producers are assisted by associate producers, and several field producers (who supervise on-location shooting) may report to them as well.

Typically, a TV producer needs to know a little about everything that goes into creating a TV program. While the producer doesn't actually perform the different tasks, he or she needs to be familiar with the duties of each crew person in order to make intelligent decisions about the creative process.

TV producers can work on staff for a TV station or production house. Once you have built a reputation for yourself, you can strike out on your own as a freelance producer, and be hired on a per-project basis.

As a TV producer you will do some or all of the following:
- Come up with ideas for new TV shows
- Write the program's script or outline the plot
- Determine the budget of the project
- Set a production schedule

- Hire the director, cast and crew
- Supervise production on the set
- Supervise editing and approve a final version
- Arrange for distribution and promotion of your shows

Who is Likely to Succeed

TV producers should be creative, since the whole look, feel and sound of a project depend on the producer. Hand in hand with creativity goes organization. A producer will juggle hundreds of details at a time, each of them important in moving a project from concept to finished product.

A TV producer must be a good communicator and a motivator who is not only able to communicate the project's message to the audience, but is able to communicate his or her vision to the crew. You make decisions easily, and take responsibility for them.

How to Learn It

Almost all TV producers begin their career as members of TV crews: usually as a production assistant, a writer, a videographer, or an editor. If you can get hired into one of these roles and work your way up as you learn the job, you may not need to acquire a formal education to be a success. Production assistants in particular can be hired with little or no specialized training.

Your local public access cable TV station gives the people who live in a community the chance to produce their own programming and present it to the public. Pitch a unique show idea or volunteer, and after just a few technical training lessons, you could be shooting and editing your own programs. This is a great chance to learn the technical side of things and build material for your demo reel.

It's also useful to go out and observe any professional production work that is being shot in your area. Your state film bureau can tell you if there are any motion pictures being shot locally to you. Even being a member of the audience at a TV show taped near you can let you observe TV production at work.

Although it's not a necessity, if you have the time and money an associate's or bachelor's degree in TV/Radio Production, Communications, Media or Broadcasting will give you an attractive edge in this competitive market. Select as many hands-on courses as possible to give you a chance to put your learning into practice, and be sure to inquire about internship placements.

Fab Fact: Mark Burnett, mega-successful producer of *Survivor, The Apprentice*, and many other reality TV programs, was a member of the British Army and a Beverly Hills live-in nanny before starting his career as a TV producer.

What It Pays

A producer can typically expect to earn $30,000 to $60,000 annually in their first five or ten years in the business. According to the Bureau of Labor Statistics, median annual earnings of salaried producers and directors are $52,840. Successful network television producers make the big money — annual salaries of $100,000 or more.

Television Reporter

TV reporters are an essential part of the way we learn about and understand the world around us. They gather information, prepare stories, and make broadcasts that keep the public informed about local, national, and international events.

What They Do

TV reporters are journalists who use television as their information medium. They spend time gathering information on stories of interest, using research techniques and interviews. They will sometimes deliver a broadcast live from the scene of an event. They may also tape additional commentary or an introduction to their stories back at the studio, matching the words to what viewers will see on their screens.

Some TV reporters specialize in a particular kind of news, such as crime, health issues, or politics. Depending on the employer, some TV reporters may also occasionally or consistently anchor a broadcast.

In a larger TV station an assignment editor will tell you what you are covering that day, but in a smaller station you may be expected to come up with the stories yourself based on leads you dig up. You might travel to cover assignments in other parts of the country or around the world.

As a TV reporter you will do some or all of the following:

- Keep up with events related to your "beat" or area
- Call around to inquire for leads on stories
- Do research to decide what approach to take with a story
- Help camera people set up for a shot

- Interview people on camera
- Write and record introductions and transitional material
- Help edit your segment

Who is Likely to Succeed

Successful TV reporters, like all journalists, have what's called a "nose for news." They have the ability to identify issues that are likely to be of interest to the general public. The best in the business can find an interesting angle for even unremarkable events. You should also have a certain degree of writing ability, so you can communicate your ideas effectively.

A knack for interviewing comes in handy — usually it goes hand in hand with the kind of disarming nature that causes people to open up to you naturally. You should also develop and maintain a pleasant voice and appearance, so they don't distract from the information you are trying to present.

How to Learn It

The first step to learning TV reporting is to become a true news junkie. Watch as many local and national newscasts in your viewing area as you can. With satellite television, it's possible to watch broadcasts from all over North America, and when the news isn't on, you can turn to stations like CNN and MSNBC. Listen closely to how the stories are written and presented.

Since most entry-level jobs are for general reporters, getting a broad base of general knowledge is important. Read as much as you can about the area you'll be reporting on. You might be covering a city hall meeting one night and a crime case the next day, so you'll need to be prepared for whatever comes your way.

If it's available to you, consider an education in journalism or broadcast news. Look for schools that have stand-out internship programs, such as the University of Missouri, where students actually staff the local NBC affiliate. In general, internships at small stations will give you more hands-on experience than at the larger ones.

If you want to build your skills, you can get valuable related experience working as a radio journalist, where the work will be very similar to TV reporting. You'll learn to talk on air, ad-lib, and control your voice. Try to get involved with the news portion of the station, if possible. Acting or public speaking classes will also help you with your on-camera skills.

Fab Fact: Oprah Winfrey began her media career while still in high school, when she was hired as a radio newscaster. At 19, Oprah become the youngest person and first African-American woman to anchor the news at Nashville's WTVF-TV.

What It Pays

Salaries vary widely with market size (how many people you reach with your broadcast) and whether you are a general or specialty reporter. Median annual earnings of reporters and correspondents are $31,320. A general reporter salary ranges from approximately $18,000 annually in the smallest markets to more than $65,000 in the largest markets. Anchors earn a median of $36,980 annually, and triple that (and sometimes even more) in the largest TV markets.

Voice Over Artist

A voice over artist is someone with a great voice and a talent for using it to communicate. They are hired to contribute speaking commentary to a variety of entertainment or educational projects.

What They Do

Voice over artists are talented individuals who are hired for their ability to speak in a unique and appealing manner. Their talents are used in radio commercials, movie trailers, documentaries, cartoons, or any medium where the speaker is heard but not seen.

Voice over comes in a variety of styles — think of the quiet, matter-of-fact documentary narrator who sounds like he is literally hiding in the bushes near the action, or the typical squeaky cartoon character kids love. The key to success in voice over is to have a broad range of sounds you can use to suit the style and the audience.

Voice over artists work in much the same way an actor does. They look for work, go to auditions, rehearse with or without other actors, and perform their voice work. They will usually work off a script, reading into a microphone in a sound studio. Many voice over artists will still use movements and expression as they record, even though they won't be seen, since they find it makes them sound more realistic.

As a voice over artist, you will:

• Spend time observing and listening to other people talk

- Practice new voices to add to your repertoire
- Send out your demo package to agents or casting directors
- Audition for roles
- Study scripts to develop a character
- Rehearse and perform your voice work
- Network in the entertainment industry

Who is Likely to Succeed

If people have always told you that you have a great "radio voice," or you have a habit of making up accents and outrageous voices to amuse your friends, you have the basics that most voice over hopefuls start with. You should be persistent and determined, since gigs can be as short as ten minutes and a lot of your time will be spent looking for work.

The best voice over actors are truly great listeners, and they learn from everyone they hear. They recognize that there is much more to communication than words, and can make their voice speak its own message. It helps if you enjoy the challenge of meeting on-the-spot requests, and take direction well.

How to Learn It

Voice over artists learn best with non-stop practice. You can order voice over scripts to practice with, or just try reading the text on anything from mayonnaise jars to shampoo bottles out loud. Pretend you are reading for young children, then mix it up and read it with an accent. You should also practice reading at different speeds. Get a stop watch and read something in ten seconds, then see if you could cut it down to eight if you had to. You'll use these exact skills on the job.

There are a number of voice over training programs you can attend, and even some that can be done through distance learning. You should graduate the program with a professionally recorded demo tape (or several tapes showing different specialties) that you can use to market yourself.

You can also learn a lot by listening to and studying different genres of voice over. Take notes you can refer to later. Notice the style and pace of the speaker, and then think about who the intended audience is. You will discover the different styles and techniques that match best to different kinds of voice over work, from commercials to on-hold messages.

What It Pays

How much you earn in voice over work depends largely on how many jobs you book a year. You can usually expect a few hundred dollars for a short commercial that runs on local TV or radio, or several thousand dollars per gig if you are working on something that will run nationally. Some movie and TV show work will pay residuals (ongoing payment) instead of a flat fee. Members of the entertainment unions (SAG and AFTRA) are guaranteed minimum pay rates that are at the high end of the ranges quoted here.

HOW TO BREAK IN

Competition is fierce for the top spots in entertainment, but the playing field is wide, with lots of opportunity. You can entertain at a variety of levels, from local celebrity to international superstar. Many big talk show hosts started with their city's morning show, famous models started with department store catalogs, and star musicians played little clubs long before the stadium shows.

So stand up and take a bow! It's time to find out the steps to breaking into an entertainer career: first putting together a professional representation of your talent, and second, shopping it around to the people who can hire you.

Professional Photos

Professional quality photos of yourself are the way you will most likely land jobs as an actor or model, and may also be part of your presentation package for other entertainer careers, because you are the "product" you are selling. Before you arrive and after you leave an audition or interview, your photos serve as a statement and reminder of who you are.

There are different kinds of photos you might need, depending on what career you are pursuing. Just make sure that you are submitting the right kind of photo, as industry standards are fairly specific. Some photo types are:

Headshot: This is a close-up photo of you from the shoulders up. In the entertainment industry, the standard for headshots is 8" x 10," and black and white, although some industries will accept or prefer color if the headshot is for promotional purposes (as opposed to landing you a job).

3/4 Shot:	A picture of your head, your upper torso, and a bit lower — what you would imagine to be 3/4 of your body. If your physique is going to be a selling feature, as it sometimes is in entertainer careers, your photo can help you show that you have the look they want.
Full-body Shot:	A picture of your whole body, perhaps posing in the latest fashions, or just looking your best. These photos are more common in modeling, where your entire body will be scrutinized.
Composite:	This is where you have a variety of pictures of you laid out together on one page, to show the range of looks you are capable of. You can have your composite made into a postcard that you use to send to agents, photographers, directors, or whoever hires in your industry.

The most important thing about your photos is that they are professionally shot and duplicated. If you want to be taken seriously, this is not the place to cut corners. You will need to find and work with a professional photographer, which you can find online, in your Yellow Pages, or through referrals from others in the industry. The photographer should be experienced in producing the type of photo you require.

Your photos should also be up to date. Even if you have some great photos taken a number of years ago, you will not impress producers, directors, scouts or agents if they call you in for a meeting and you look nothing like your photo. It should look like the most attractive "you" possible.

TIP: There are unscrupulous photographers out there who are not professionals. They may disappear with your money, or may even be dangerous. Always meet first in a public place to review their portfolio and get a sense of their skill, and check references as well.

Getting your photos done is not cheap, but it's the only way in many industries to get work or attract an agent's attention. Expect to spend between $100 and $400 to get a single headshot, and $500 to $2,500 if you are looking for a number of shots for a composite or portfolio. Find out from the photographer in advance how many shots they will take for you to choose from.

While a model can continue to use fashion photos in a portfolio to show the breadth of his or her talent, headshots need to be re-taken once a year, so don't blow the budget. If and when you sign with an agent, they will probably want to redo your photos anyway. In some cases you may be able to land an agent without photos, depending on how the agency searches for talent.

Video/DVD Demos

In certain entertainer careers you will need to prepare a "demo reel" or recording of you performing what you do best. In some industries you'll definitely need a demo before you get hired. In others you won't absolutely need a demo until you are further along in your career, or only if you are applying to certain kinds of employers, but having a demo can give you a competitive edge at any point in your career.

So how do you get material for your demo? Either by recording a variety of your paid performances, recording anything you work on while you assist or intern, doing free performances in order to be able to record them, or staging "fake" performances where you part-ner with other people looking to build their portfolio of demo mate-rial as well.

For example, an up-and-coming TV reporter, TV producer, actor, and film crew member could partner together to produce a short pre-tend "interview" for all of them to use on their demo, and share the production costs.

Note that if you are a performer who relies on an audience's reac-tion (e.g. stand-up comic or motivational speaker) you will need to have an audience present in any performance you record. And if you want to show audience members reacting, you'll need to get written releases from them in advance.

Again, professionalism is a key component of your demo. It should have a good quality picture and sound recording, and be professionally edited. Demos in any industry tend to be short — up to three min-utes for a single clip, or up to 15 minutes for a selection of three or four clips. For this reason, your demo must contain only your best material. Follow this rule: if in doubt, leave it out.

Decision-makers in the entertainment industry receive many, many demos, and may only watch the first 30 seconds of your demo before making a decision about your talent. If you don't capture their atten-tion in that span of time, you may not get another chance to change their mind. Make sure your most powerful material goes right up front.

To ensure that your video can be viewed by as many people as possible, you should make it available on CD-ROM or DVD in addition to VHS. You should label your demo with your name and the length in minutes of the content, in the following format:

J. Smith Demo
Phone: (123) 555-1212
Title: Soup Kitchen Exposé
Length: 2:12

You can also ask the video editor to put a name and address slate (a graphic that appears for about 10 seconds) at the beginning and end of your demo. And make sure your tape is cued up to the right place when you submit it, or it may not get watched at all.

Audio Demos

The advice about video demos generally applies to audio demos, although there are some differences. Firstly, in audio you certainly want to send a CD, not a cassette. Inferior sound quality issues aside, many people no longer own cassette players, so your muffled recording won't even be listened to.

You will need to find a small studio to record your demo, or a friend or acquaintance with quality recording equipment. How many tracks you include depends on the type of career you are pursuing — for music demos, anywhere from four to seven tracks is best. Put some thought into the sequence of your material so it showcases your most attractive material.

Once you have the master disc, you can burn your own copies of the disc or have them professionally duplicated, label them (label making software looks better than handwriting), and put them in a jewel case. You'll send these CDs out with your bio and copies of any press you have received.

Other Ways to Present Your Talent

The entertainer careers span a wide variety of specialties, some of which may require you to present your talent in other ways than a demo. Here are some other typical requirements in the industry.

Bio/Resume

Entertainment agents may want to know what your "story" is, so they know how to sell you to the public. For some entertainer careers, you will submit a short professional biography in addition to or in place of your resume. While not exactly the story of your life, it details the highlights of your progress towards success in your chosen career. The rest of your resume lists your experience in the industry, but the format is slightly different because your "jobs" don't tend to last as long as typical ones would. You can see a sample entertainer bio/resume on the facing page.

Written Material

Screenwriters and movie reviewers will need to submit a query based on material already written, or some sample reviews in order to catch the decision-maker's attention. As with any written submission, check these carefully for typos, and have a friend proofread them as well before you submit them. Screenwriting in particular has a very specific format for you to follow, so make sure you research the submission requirements before you send anything in.

In-person Presentation

In addition to your materials, entertainer professions like actor, dancer, model, stand-up comic and, sometimes, professional athlete require you to make an in-person appearance to show off your talent, in the form of an audition or tryout. Be physically and mentally prepared — you may even want to work with a coach in advance to prepare you for the actual tryout or audition, so you have a professional opinion on what the decision-maker will be looking for.

Standard Resume

Entertainer careers like TV reporter, TV producer, talent agent, and film crew member will require you to submit a resume along with your materials, to show that you have the technical skills to back up your natural ability. In addition to what you already learned in Chapter 2, Chapter 12 has more details about how to prepare a fabulous resume.

How to Get an Agent

In certain careers, it's not enough to be talented and want to share it with the world — there's a process. You need to have someone with clout put in a good word for you, make a few phone calls, and then things start to happen. These "people with clout" are called agents, and signing with an agent is what you'll want to do to take your dreams to the next level.

C. J. Goulet

Chris James (C. J.) Goulet is a one-man music show that must be seen to be believed. His raw vocals and simple tunes reveal the 27-year-old talent as a poet and a true musician's musician. Since 2004 he has filled bar rooms and outdoor festivals with his unique blend of reggae-inspired pop. A self-taught musician, his songs are unaffected and clear. Following in the steps of famed indie rocker Les Gibbard, C. J. is on a fast-track to success, so catch him at the small venues while you still can.

Live Appearances since 2004 at:

- Overtures – Orlando, FL
- Red Dog Pub – Jacksonville, FL
- Molly's – Daytona Beach, FL
- Culture Club – Port Orange, FL
- McGillicuddy's, Florida State University

Special Appearances at:

- 2006: Showcase, South by Southwest Music and Media Conference, Austin, TX
- 2006: *Good Morning Orlando*, WBXY-TV
- 2006: Opening act for The Wishbones, Folgers Theater
- 2005: Summer Music Festival – Daytona Beach, FL
- 2005: Audition for *American Idol* – made top 40

Press:

"The most entertainment possible from one human being." — Daytona Daily

"Goulet has talent beyond his years. Look for him to release some great material, hopefully sometime soon." — Muse Magazine, Orlando

See more at: www.cjmusic.com

Contact:

C. J. Goulet
(123) 555-1212; cell (123) 555-1313
Box 234, Port Orange, FL 12345
cjgoulet@cjmusic.com

Be careful though, because you don't necessarily want to sign with the first agent who'll take you. Like any other business, there are agents who are great at what they do, and those who are mediocre. You want to ask your agent pointed questions about what they will do for you. Also, you need to find the right agent for you. Some agents have niches or represent the same type of talent time and time again. They have the advantage of experience and connections in your industry to take your career where it needs to go.

You can expect an agent to find you work, help you prepare your promotional materials, bill and collect for your services, and negotiate payment for you. However, an agent is not exactly a career manager. They are there to help you get work, and have a vested interest in your career, but are not as intimately involved with directing your career as a manager would be.

An agent may discover you when you are performing at an amateur level, or you may be recommended to an agent by another professional in your industry who recognizes your talent. There may also be industry events where agents gather to see the latest talent perform. These are the easy ways to find an agent.

The more challenging (but usual) way to find an agent is by preparing packages of your demo, your materials, or some other manifestation of your talent, and mailing it to the agent's office. If he or she is interested, you'll get called in for a meeting.

To find agents to send your materials to, see if your industry has trade publications that publish agency names and contact information. If you are unsure, contact a professional association for the industry and ask. Some agencies are more open to newcomers than others, and the ones listed in trade publications are usually interested in discovering new talent. You can also search the Internet for "talent," "agency," and variations of your dream career's name.

When you send your materials to an agent, enclose a letter that states that you are looking for representation, what recent related education or experience you have had, any highlights in your career history, and if possible, where the agent can come to see you perform.

If you don't hear back from an agent after sending your materials, it might be tempting to contact them, but be aware that in the entertainment business, it's strictly "Don't call me; I'll call you." What you can do is send an email, hand-delivered note, or even one of your promotional postcards to remind them of your package, as well as any updates on your recent successes. Don't take rejection personally — you may not be a fit with that particular agency, but you'll find one that will want to work with you.

When you do hear back from an agent, it's time to go meet them and see what they can do for you. They'll be feeling you out as well, and will ask questions about where you see yourself heading, what your career goals are, and how your career has been going to date.

If the agency asks you to sign on with them, you are going to have a number of questions for them as well. Signing with an agent most often means that you are agreeing to let them represent you exclusively, so you want to be sure that the deal meets your needs. Here are some questions to consider:

- How is their communication? Are your phone calls returned promptly? Will you have your agent's cell phone number?
- What other entertainers do they represent? Are those individuals close enough in type that the agent will know how to promote you, but different enough that they won't be directly competing with you for work?
- Does the agency and agent have a good reputation in the industry? If you speak to other entertainers they represent, what is their perception of the agent?
- Is the agency asking you to sign exclusively? Some agents will offer you a "honeymoon period" where either of you can go in a different direction if the relationship doesn't suit you.
- How does the agency make money? Agents generally take a percentage of all your earnings as commission. Each industry sets its own standards, but a common percentage is 10 to 20 percent. Although it's not unusual for agents to get reimbursed for expenses, be cautious of any agency that wants to charge a fee to represent you.
- What's in the contract the agency sends you? It's a good idea to have a lawyer review the contract before you sign.

If you decide that the agent is right for you, congratulations! With talent, persistence, and professional representation, you could go far in your dream career.

6

Fab Creatives

Careers for Creative People

What are you doing reading a book? Shouldn't you be creating something?

If thoughts like that are going through your head… if there's a nagging feeling of restlessness when you're not actively involved in creating something new… then you have come to the right place.

We're going to give you tools to turn your talents into a career that will satisfy those creative urges. The careers in this chapter allow you to come up with new ideas, solve problems, and create things of beauty. When you succeed in any of these careers, you get to do something you love, make your mark on the world, and secretly be envied by everyone who is not expressing their own creativity. The work you do will bring joy to people's lives, including your own.

The downside to all this is that there are many more people who want to do these jobs than there are jobs available. That's why this chapter includes a section packed with useful tips to help you prove to employers and clients that you are the creative genius they're looking for. Here is the list of creative careers, followed by a more detailed description of each:

- Advertising Copywriter
- Animator
- Art Curator
- Cartoonist
- Caterer
- Chef/Personal Chef
- Children's Book Author
- Event Planner
- Fashion Designer
- Fashion Stylist
- Fiction Writer
- Fine Artist
- Graphic Designer
- Home Stager
- Illustrator
- Interior Decorator
- Inventor
- Jewelry Designer
- Landscape Designer
- Makeup Artist
- Photographer
- Video Game Designer
- Wedding Planner
- Window Display Designer

THE CAREERS

Advertising Copywriter

Advertising copywriters use their persuasive communication skills to write the influential language for print, radio and television advertisements.

What They Do

Ad copywriters develop information provided by clients into scripts for television or radio commercials, or produce the text that appears in print advertisements. They write in a clear, concise, and persuasive manner that attracts the reader's attention.

They may write short messages to appear on billboards and posters, or long documents that promote the many benefits of a product or business. When they work at agencies, they may develop entire advertising campaigns, which promote a product or business across various media. In a smaller agency, the copywriter may even sell a few ads.

Advertising copywriters are hired by advertising agencies and large media outlets (newspapers, radio and TV stations, etc.) on a staff, contract or freelance basis to develop and write ad campaigns for in-house use, and for advertisers who do not use agencies.

In a typical day as an advertising copywriter you might:

- Spend time researching new ideas and trends
- Meet with the client's in-house representative to discuss their needs
- Write fabulous, persuasive copy for a new campaign
- Think of a great new slogan while in the shower
- Brainstorm ideas with the art department
- Revise copy based on client feedback
- Consult on production of the ad to make sure it stays true to the idea
- Work on "jingles"— short, catchy songs that accompany radio and TV ads
- Proofread a prospective ad for typos

Who is Likely to Succeed

The best copywriters are excellent communicators who can listen as well as they can speak and write. If you're a clear and concise writer who can work quickly to convey a complicated message in a few words, you'll be a good advertising copywriter.

You probably have a sense of humor and a quick wit, and are full of creative, clever ideas. Your understanding of people's needs and desires will help you determine the best ways to sell products to particular markets. If you've got an ear for dialogue and music, and a good ability to rhyme words, you might find work as a jingle writer or a commercial script writer — particularly if you've ever written plays or skits.

How to Learn It

You don't need to go to school to learn to be a copywriter, though if you've taken any creative writing, technical writing or journalism courses, you'll have a good background to apply to this job. Courses in business and marketing are also useful, but not essential.

Some employers will offer to train you on the job, based on your present talent and portfolio. And the *FabJob Guide to Become an Advertising Copywriter* is an excellent resource for those looking to train themselves in the essentials.

Read as many advertisements and listen to and watch as many commercials as you can. Pay attention to the type of language they use, and the way they use it. Notice the words and sentence structures used for different types of ads. Keep a journal of your favorites and your least favorites. Study the difference between them — what makes one successful, and another unsuccessful.

You can also practice writing new ad copy for products or services you use frequently. What appeals to you about them? How would you convince others that they, too, should choose these products or services? Listen to radio scripts that use dialog and sound effects to promote a product. Practice using these techniques to heighten humor or suspense. Consider the various visual images you could add to your script to transform it into a television commercial.

What It Pays

An entry-level copywriter in the United States can expect a salary of about $35,000 per year. Senior copywriters can earn as much as $75,000 or more per year. Special skills like layout program experience, advanced editing skills, and additional languages can increase the amount they are paid. A freelance copywriter's rates generally range from about $35 to $100 per hour. Per-project fees often fall in the range of $200 to $3,000 dollars.

Animator

As an animator, you will develop and create moving drawings, cartoons, or computer graphics that communicate a message or tell a story. Animators work on feature films, TV programs and commercials, the Internet, and CD-ROM production.

What They Do

Animators work in a variety of styles, from painting cartoon "cells" (still frames that are shown in sequence to appear to be moving) to creating animation with a computer program. Since animation is a big project, animators usually work in teams, with each member handling various duties.

A 2-D animator works in the traditional way by using art skills such as drawing and composition. A 3-D animator combines the skills of a 2-D animator with computer software to render more realistic characters.

As an animator you may find yourself doing some or all of the following tasks:

- Meeting with clients to discuss their needs
- Brainstorming with team members to plan an animation project
- Developing characters and story ideas
- Drawing or painting characters or scenes
- Using computers to create 3-D computer animation
- Filming puppets and sets

Who is Likely to Succeed

An eye for color, form, and motion is very important to an animator. Computer skills are desired, as most animation is digitally created or enhanced. Also important is the ability to draw. This doesn't mean you need to be an accomplished artist to succeed as an animator, but it helps if you can use pictures to communicate your ideas effectively, and draw the same thing consistently.

You may be destined for a career as an animator if you already enjoy creating characters and scenes, or telling stories using pictures. You may have the ability to visualize gestures, movements, and actions of animated characters, or maybe you just grew up drawing, doodling, or creating.

How to Learn It

The best way to learn animation is by doing it. Drawing the world around you gives you insight into scale, perspective, and form. Use your artistic renderings to create comic strips, animated frames, promotional ads or characters for games or films. Study animated films for insight into successful animation.

Take advantage of any opportunity to learn about art, color, light, and motion. No matter what your preferred method of art is, try your hand at different forms such as sculpture, painting, computer graphics, and photography to expand your knowledge base.

While you can teach yourself animation, you may want to consider an internship to increase your knowledge of the industry and develop your portfolio. Many major film and TV studios use interns in the animation departments. This offers a great opportunity to learn the business of animation and develop contacts in the industry.

If you have the time and money, there are animation programs available from four-year degree programs to certificate programs. You can also find classes and courses in animation at some continuing education schools.

Many animators get started by working for small companies doing the small jobs. Look for these opportunities with an independent film or production company. You could also consider volunteering your services to create animated ads for a non-profit or other worthy organization.

What It Pays

A typical starting salary for an entry-level animator is $13 to $20 per hour, depending on the part of the country you work in. More seasoned animators earn in the $28 to $40 per hour range, and the lead animators in the business can earn more than $100,000 per year. According to the Bureau of Labor Statistics, median annual earnings of salaried multi-media artists and animators are $50,360. Median annual earnings are $67,390 in motion picture and video industries, and $46,810 in advertising and related services.

Art Curator

As an art curator, you will gather, display and sell paintings, sculptures, photographs, and other artwork for a public or private gallery.

What They Do

Art curators maintain the art gallery on a daily basis, running it like a business. They survey new artwork for potential use in the gallery, purchase and install artwork for the gallery's collection, and prepare thematic or single-artist shows on an individual or ongoing basis.

Art curators can also be self-employed and operate their own commercial galleries, where they earn their living by selling artwork to clients.

As an art curator, your day may include any or all of the following:

- Networking with artists to discover new talent and new pieces for a collection
- Keeping in touch with art collectors and benefactors about your collection
- Arranging and installing artwork within the gallery
- Hosting opening galas to celebrate new shows or collections

- Writing and preparing catalogs of the artwork in shows you put on
- Promoting your art shows to the media to encourage reviews and public attention
- Keeping track of sales in order to ensure the artist and the gallery are paid
- Being available to the public at the gallery for questions about artists' work

Who is Likely to Succeed

You probably admire beautiful things, and enjoy collecting original artwork for display in your home. You have insight and can recognize good craftsmanship and artistic abilities when you see them. You may have an entrepreneurial streak, which will prepare you for running your own gallery.

You'll use your communication and negotiating skills when you meet with artists and plan shows or choose to represent their work in your gallery, and when you explain the artwork to the public. You'll use your interpersonal skills to network with art collectors, benefactors, and critics in order to draw attention to the work on display in your gallery.

How to Learn It

A degree or diploma in art or art history is helpful for this job, but not at all a requirement. You can learn this job by volunteering at a local gallery or museum, by cultivating your own art collection, and by reading all the art magazines and books you can. You can also consult the *FabJob Guide to Become an Art Curator* by Elizabeth Schlatter for great ideas on how to jumpstart your career.

Apply your knowledge to your own art collection. Arrange it in the most meaningful, attractive manner. Create labels for the artwork, and prepare a statement about the collection — what does it mean? How are the works chosen?

Make a "fantasy gallery" by collecting images or postcards of artworks (almost all galleries sell these, or even give them away on invitations). Spend time figuring out how you would arrange them: by theme, by artist, by time period, or in some other way that enhances their meaning as a whole. Write an essay explaining why you put those particular works together. These exercises can be part of your portfolio once you're looking for a gallery to employ you.

You can volunteer to collect the artwork of art students, and prepare a show of their work for the local art school or college gallery. You can also volunteer at local galleries and museums. These organizations are often in need of help with installing shows, showing the public around, and other tasks which will allow you to experience this job hands-on.

What It Pays

Art curators working for public galleries make anywhere from $20,000 to $50,000 per year or more. A curator operating their own gallery makes typically 40 to 50 percent of the retail price for each work of art sold. So for example, if a piece sells for $1,000, they would make $500. But that portion must also cover gallery costs like rent, electricity, staff, and promotions. A successful self-employed curator may make $40,000 to $50,000 or more each year.

Cartoonist

Cartoonists use their sense of humor and artistic abilities to produce drawings that tell stories and amuse their audience. Cartoonists are usually self-employed individuals who create their cartoons and sell them to various markets on a freelance basis.

What They Do

Cartoonists create black-and-white line drawings, colored drawings or computer-generated images, or sometimes work with modified photos. They may draw in pencil first, then "ink" using black ink on white paper, or they may use a computer.

Cartoonists produce single-panel cartoons (sometimes called gags), or strips, which are three- or four-panel cartoons that tell a quick story, usually with a humorous punch line at the end. They may write six- to ten-panel color strips for use in newspaper comic sections, or may also illustrate the story and text written by a cartoon writer for use in a comic book or graphic novel.

As a cartoonist, your day might include:
- Sending samples of recent cartoons to potential buyers
- Reading about a topic you specialize in (politics, children, etc.) for ideas
- Sketching out ideas in a notebook
- Using a computer to draw your art
- Promoting your work through public appearances
- Finding additional markets to print your cartoons

Successful cartoonists use the same sets of characters over and over to create a series, such as *Peanuts* or *Andy Capp*. They may sell individual cartoons on a one-time-only basis, or they may "syndicate" their work (sell the rights for each cartoon or comic strip to more than one publication) for more exposure and more money.

Who is Likely to Succeed

If you spend every spare moment doodling amusing characters and pictures on scraps of paper, you're probably well suited to this job. You should be able to draw consistently — that is, create the same character numerous times, in various poses and outfits — and create amusing or humorous situations for your characters. Creative drawing abilities in a variety of media such as pen and ink, computer and charcoal will all help.

Cartoonists see the world in a unique way, and reflect on their unique observations with their art. You should have a talent for observing life from different perspectives, and communicating your views clearly with pictures. Writing and storytelling abilities will also assist you in putting together cartoons that amuse your audience (not just yourself).

Fab Fact: Scott Adams, creator of the *Dilbert* comic strip, says he held numerous "humiliating and low-paying jobs" in his career, including one as a bank teller in which he was robbed at gun point — twice! These experiences gave Scott ammunition to create the extremely successful *Dilbert*, which is syndicated to more than 1,200 newspapers worldwide.

How to Learn It

You don't need any special training or certificate to be a cartoonist — you'll learn best by actually doing it. You become a professional cartoonist the moment you're paid for your first piece. You can consult the *FabJob Guide to Become a Cartoonist* by T Campbell for a wealth of insider tips and expert advice on breaking into the cartooning market.

Practice your drawing style, experimenting with shapes and characters and different types of lines and colors until you have a specialized style that you find easy to replicate. Work to develop a distinct character or set of characters.

Keep a notebook with you for ideas and jokes. Pay attention to the conversations and amusing moments going on around you, and jot down funny things people say whenever you hear them. These will become fuel for your future cartoons.

If you have funny ideas but can't draw, you can trace templates or use collage (pasting together existing images) to get the effect you want, or you can partner with someone who can put your great ideas onto paper.

Once you've got at least 25 to 50 finished cartoons, you can begin to submit them to publications or syndicates (companies that publish cartoons, such as United Feature Syndicate, Inc.). Browse different newspapers and magazines to determine which ones will be most interested in seeing your type of work, and then follow their submission guidelines. You can use their feedback to polish your work.

What It Pays

The median salary for a syndicated freelance cartoonist is about $50,000 per year. If you self-syndicate, you can expect to earn between $5 and $100 per published cartoon from each market that publishes it. A cartoonist working full time for one employer can expect a salary of about $32,000. Your type of work affects the payment as well: a topical political cartoon done to deadline would earn a higher amount than a stand-alone gag.

Caterer

When you work as a caterer, you are hired to use your culinary knowledge and food preparation/presentation talent to supply the food and beverages for people's gatherings and special events. Sometimes hands-on food service is part of the package as well.

What They Do

Caterers are called upon to provide breakfasts, business lunches, brunches, dinners, finger food, and cocktails in a variety of styles, including formal sit-down service and buffets. Events may encompass intimate dinner parties, backyard barbecues, weddings, political rallies, conferences, cocktail receptions, even children's parties —any occasion that brings a group of people together.

As a caterer, your tasks may include the following:
- Developing menus and prices for your services
- Finding recipes for unique, tasty dishes or developing your own

- Meeting with clients to determine their needs and to specify what you can provide
- Negotiating with suppliers
- Advertising and promoting your business
- Shopping for food and supplies
- Hiring cooking and/or serving staff
- Transporting and delivering food, and presenting it attractively
- Remaining on site for the function
- Keeping current with food trends and local tastes

Caterers need to master the split-second timing that makes the main course arrive at the table piping hot, the vegetables crisp and colorful, and the salad cold and fresh. Caterers are therefore organized, and adept at doing several things at once.

Who is Likely to Succeed

Most caterers love every aspect of working with food — shopping for it, preparing it, cooking it, serving it, and eating it. If you love the look of food, the feel of it, the taste and texture of it, and the compliments that come your way when you serve a great meal, you've probably got what it takes to be a caterer.

Successful caterers enjoy researching new foods, cooking methods and techniques, have the physical stamina to withstand long working hours mainly spent standing, and have good interpersonal skills.

How to Learn It

To turn your talent for cooking into a profitable business, become an expert on food and its preparation. Read everything you can find about ingredients, cooking methods, and innovative serving styles. Find a new way to use a familiar ingredient, significantly cut prep time, adapt a calorie-rich recipe into a calorie-wise sensation, or grow herbs to develop your own spice blends.

Many excellent publications are available for cooks of all skill levels, beginner to expert. Bookstores, magazine stands, libraries, and the Internet are packed with information about food and cooking, and TV has channels devoted to the topic 24 hours a day.

Taking part-time cooking classes is a great way to hone your skills or develop new ones. Cooking classes offer instruction in everything from basic cooking skills, to advanced knife techniques, preparing sushi, and making pastry. Check with your local college, high school, community center, or library for upcoming classes.

Many colleges offer food service programs, although formal schooling is not a pre-requisite. You can teach yourself what you need to know to break into catering (or becoming a personal chef, covered in a subsequent profile) with a great guidebook like the *FabJob Guide to Become a Caterer or Personal Chef* by Lex Thomas.

Begin offering your services to family and friends for a cost that includes ingredients, supplies, and a reduced hourly fee for your time. Make a note of things that work at these events, and things that need some work.

Another option is to earn while you learn by going to work for an established caterer whose operation and techniques you can observe. Be prepared to work in every aspect of the business, from serving to dishwashing, and post-event clean up. After an event, spend a few minutes with the business owner or chef to ask questions.

What It Pays

Your fee for most catering events will fall in the range of a few hundred to a few thousand dollars, and full-time self-employed caterers can earn anywhere from $30,000 to $100,000 or more per year. Caterers in the U.S. who work for employers have an average starting salary of about $22,000, and will likely earn between $30,000 and $40,000 after a few years in the business.

Chef/Personal Chef

As a chef or personal chef, you will use your culinary talents to develop menu items, prepare dishes and oversee preparation at a dining facility or private household.

What They Do

Chefs are responsible for the smooth functioning of a kitchen, from developing menus and new recipes to supervising staff, to inventory and cost control, and ordering supplies. They are responsible for creating the best dishes possible within the budget of their employer. They need to be aware of their kitchen's inventory at all times, and choose and order supplies.

Some chefs may own their own restaurant, or report to the manager or owner of the restaurant that employs them. They may also work for a hotel, catering company, private club, or independently for private clients as a personal chef.

The executive chef is the top chef in a restaurant. He or she supervises the other staff, which might include a sous-chef who is responsible for the daily operations of the kitchen, and a pastry chef who prepares desserts and baked goods. In a small kitchen, there may be only one or two chefs to perform all of the above roles. In each case, chefs are likely to:

- Design menu items using seasonally available or specialty ingredients
- Prepare food for diners
- Prepare soups, stocks, sauces and other food items needed regularly
- Educate and advise servers about the foods being served
- Hire and supervise kitchen staff
- Keep track of all meals ordered and ensure they are made quickly and properly
- Meet with the restaurant manager or owner to discuss inventory and cost

Who is Likely to Succeed

You probably love giving dinner parties, preparing huge family meals, or painstakingly preparing and decorating baked goods for special occasions.

You have a keen sense of taste, and an appreciation for subtleties of flavor and varieties of food — in fact, you're probably passionate about food in general. You're probably already known to friends and family as a good cook, you have a creative flair with food preparation and presentation, and love to invent new ways of serving foods.

How to Learn It

There are numerous culinary courses you can take, from cooking lessons offered through kitchen stores and community centers to extended culinary training programs offered by colleges and cooking schools. If you have access to any of these, they will put you in good standing for future employment, but they are by no means a requirement.

You can work as a chef with no formal credentials whatsoever, as long as you have a solid background of experience in cooking. You can teach yourself to be a chef by reading cookbooks, watching cooking shows and videos, and, above all, hands-on practice and experimentation in your own kitchen.

Make every interesting recipe you come across. Experiment with ingredients, and try new methods of preparation and presentation.

Study the photographs in illustrated cookbooks, and subscribe to magazines like *Cook's Illustrated*. Stock your kitchen with the right equipment and supplies to do your job well.

Taste everything critically. Record your successes, and your failures. Keep track of the recipes you make, and the ones you master. Plan ways to improve even your successful recipes.

Certain volunteer work is another excellent way to gain experience that may land you a higher position in a kitchen. Offer to help prepare meals at a local soup kitchen, community center or seniors' center — this will give you a sense of what it's like to work in a kitchen, and an ability to feel confident cooking large quantities of food.

What It Pays

The median income for an executive chef in the United States is about $70,000, though they can earn as much as $85,000 or more. According to the Bureau of Labor Statistics, median hourly earnings of chefs and head cooks are $14.75. Median hourly earnings of cooks in a private household are $9.42.

Fab Fact: Chef Rachael Ray is the enthusiastic, entertaining, and down-to-earth star of four shows on TV's Food Network, including her breakout show *30-Minute Meals*. She started her career in New York City working at Macy's, first at the candy counter, then later as the manager of fresh foods. She worked in many different food industry environments, including pubs, restaurants and gourmet markets. Although she is now a celebrity chef, Rachael has never had formal training as a cook.

Children's Book Author

As a children's book author, you will use your imagination to write stories and/or explain interesting aspects of the real world for a young audience.

What They Do

Children's book authors may write fiction (picture books, storybooks and chapter books) or non-fiction (reference books, how-to books, and even textbooks) for kids to read and understand. They may also write articles, poems and stories for children's magazines. A few work as illustrators on their own books.

They may focus on a specific age group or a specific type of book, such as joke books, books with science experiments, or books that have pop-up pages. Some successful children's book authors develop a series based on a single character or set of characters, such as *Paddington Bear* or *The Rugrats*.

Authors may write independently, or be hired on a staff or freelance basis by a publisher, book packager, magazine or website.

In an average day as a children's book author, you might:

- Research trends and recent publications in kids' books
- Work on storylines or character development
- Brainstorm new story ideas
- Contact potential publishers with book proposals
- Meet with your agent or work on self-promotion
- Spend an hour critiquing a colleague's manuscript
- Give direction or feedback to an illustrator

Who is Likely to Succeed

Maybe you've been making up stories for your own or other people's children, and they thoroughly enjoy them. Perhaps you have vivid childhood memories you think would make good stories, or you have expertise in a certain area of interest to kids. If you have entertaining stories to tell, and can tell them in a lively manner, you are likely to succeed in writing for children.

To succeed in getting your children's book published, you must be determined to find the right market, and keep sending your work to potential publishers until it has found a home in print. Even for established authors, this can be an ongoing challenge.

How to Learn It

There are many courses in writing children's books, but you can become a successful children's book author without ever taking a course. You do, however, need to devote almost as much time to understanding the genre as you do to writing in it.

Become familiar with the stories that are out there. Know the popular characters, stories and topics. Meet with librarians to ask what kinds of stories children are currently passionate about. You should also spend time with children, and ask them about the kinds of stories they like.

Visit the children's 'section of local bookstores to find out what kinds of books are currently being published, and read these as well. Learn more about the kinds of stories and books being printed by subscribing to a magazine like *Horn Book*, which is devoted to children's literature. The *FabJob Guide to Become a Children's Book Author* is also an excellent resource on this topic.

You can join a writing group devoted to writing for children, or create one of your own by advertising for like-minded writers in your community newspaper. Meet with the goal of improving each participant's work through constructive criticism. Then hone your writing abilities by editing and re-writing your work to make it as simple, beautiful and active as possible.

What It Pays

You may be paid a lump sum of anywhere from $100 to $5,000 or more for a manuscript, or be paid a royalty from 10 to 15 percent of sales. Picture book royalties are split between author and illustrator. Articles in magazines usually pay from 10 cents to $1 per word. *Harry Potter* author J.K. Rowling makes millions, so remember, just as in the world of children's stories, anything is possible.

Event Planner

Event planners have an exciting job that lets them use their creativity to organize fun and fabulous events including parties, corporate events, and public events. Some get to plan spectacular events such as the Academy Awards, Mardi Gras, Presidential Inauguration, and New Year's festivities in Times Square.

What They Do

Event planners are the people responsible for choosing elements and bringing them together to organize gatherings such as birthdays, corporate meetings, conventions, and reunions. They ensure that all the participants' needs are met, and that the event is a success. They often work behind the scenes, but the events they coordinate stand out as memorable.

They may work in one city, coordinating conferences, parties and other events in a geographic area, or they may be hired to travel to organize specific types of events in different locations. Event planners might be hired by a company to plan events in-house, but the majority of event planners are self-employed.

Some of your key responsibilities as an event planner include:
- Scouting possible locations for events
- Negotiating contracts with caterers, equipment suppliers and other vendors
- Coordinating the guest list
- Planning menus
- Booking hotel or transportation for event participants
- Booking entertainers and performers for the event
- Arranging for the set-up of audio-visual equipment, decorations and props
- Keeping track of timelines to ensure the event goes off without a hitch
- Paying attention to detail so that needs are anticipated and met in advance
- Attending the events to ensure they run smoothly

Who is Likely to Succeed

If you're a "people person" who enjoys big parties, group activities and other gatherings, you're ideally suited to becoming an event planner. You love helping people have fun, enjoy organizing and coordinating, and are skilled at making sure everyone's needs are met. You probably throw great birthday parties for your kids, or you're always enlisted to get the annual office party off the ground.

You've got an eye for detail, and a flair for bringing unique touches to special occasions. And above all, you're an excellent communicator who is organized, detail-oriented, and able to make clear decisions and delegate tasks in an efficient way.

How to Learn It

To begin, find out what convention centers, hotels and banquet facilities are available in your area. Keep track of their fees, seating capacity, special amenities and other features in a notebook, or better yet, a computer database. Build a similar base of information about caterers, entertainers, equipment suppliers, transportation and decoration vendors. When you contact them, ask lots of questions, and record the answers.

To get some practice, think of an imaginary event, and make lists of all the elements that will need to be covered, from location to food to participants to activities and entertainment. What is the purpose of the gathering? What is the budget for it? You'll find detailed checklists to help you figure these things out in both the *FabJob Guide to Become an Event Planner* and the *FabJob Guide to Become a Party Planner*.

Turn to your list of resources in your community and identify the ones that could go towards making your imaginary event a real-life success. You can also purchase software packages, such as The Ultimate Event Planner, and learn as it walks you through planning an event.

When you're ready, practice by volunteering to coordinate an event, such as a school outing, an office gathering or family re-union. Record what works, and pay attention to what doesn't work about the event so you can plan differently next time. Some colleges and universities offer courses in "leisure studies" or in the hospitality field for event planning as well.

What It Pays

According to the Bureau of Labor Statistics, median annual earnings of meeting and convention planners are $39,620. Independent event planners charge on a contract, per-event basis, either by the hour (starting at about $20 to $40 per hour) or several thousand dollars for the complete event package, depending on the work involved.

Fashion Designer

Working as a fashion designer, you will use your sense of style and flair for the original to design clothing and accessories for production and sale.

What They Do

Fashion designers may work for a large company, designing clothing for sale through large retailers or boutiques, or a small, exclusive company, or even for themselves.

You may choose to focus on one type of clothing — for example, children's wear, women's sportswear, or men's formalwear, or accessories like purses or shoes. You can also specialize in only one of the steps in fashion design, such as patternmaking, sewing samples, or "trend-spotting."

As a fashion designer, you might spend your day:
- Browsing fashion magazines and websites for inspiration
- Shopping for new fabrics and accessories
- Meeting with clients to measure and discuss one-off projects
- Sketching ideas in a journal

- Creating patterns for various sizes by hand or with computer-aided design (CAD)
- Creating samples of your designs by sewing or having them assembled
- Meeting with sales or production people to discuss your product
- Making theme or presentation boards to show off new ideas
- Attending and/or participating in fashion shows
- Promoting yourself and your designs to potential clients

Fashion designers will work flexible, but often long hours, in a creative and dynamic industry. They may find motivation in striving towards being the next Versace or Donna Karan, or simply working at something they love.

Who is Likely to Succeed

Successful designers need to be able to tap into what people want, and understand how human beings see themselves, to create designs that make people feel a certain way. Sketching or some artistic ability will help you communicate your ideas, and independent designers can translate entrepreneurial and sales skills into running their own business.

Trendsetters, who like to stand out in a crowd, make great fashion designers. You should love fashion and be familiar with the latest trends in fashion design. And if you're one who loves shopping for new clothes, or remaking old clothes into something new and exciting, fashion design is definitely for you.

How to Learn It

There are many schools for fashion design out there, although many top designers (such as Tommy Hilfiger) are self-taught. To become a fashion designer, you just need to start doing it. Say you have an old outfit that needs freshening up with a new hemline or a different collar. The moment you've created those new details, you're on your way.

You should study the way clothing is made — take apart old clothing by ripping out the seams, then make notes about the different parts. Collect patterns and assemble them. Make modifications as you go, experimenting with materials and colors.

Draw constantly, using a sketchbook to keep your drawings in one place. Experiment with color and texture, and collect samples of fabrics you like. Translate those sketches into real outfits by draping fabrics on yourself or a friend until you've got the shape. Cut and stitch the outfit together, or hire someone to make a sample for you.

Read all the fashion magazines you can, and follow the industry. You could also volunteer to help dress and accessorize models at local fashion shows to build a network and learn the ropes. Also, the *FabJob Guide to Become a Fashion Designer* by Peter J. Gallanis and Jennifer James is a thorough guidebook to help you learn all you need to know to break into this industry.

What It Pays

According to the Bureau of Labor Statistics, median annual earnings for fashion designers are $55,840. Entry-level clothing designers in the United States make anywhere from $20,000 to $25,000 per year, while designers for large companies, or with their own popular line of clothing, can expect to make up to $100,000 per year or much more, depending on their following.

Fashion Stylist

As a fashion stylist, you'll use your impeccable taste to choose clothing, props and accessories that create a distinct image in photo and film shoots or fashion shows.

What They Do

Fashion stylists are responsible for gathering together the many items needed to create a successful photograph or video image, or to pull off a fashion show. In addition to shopping for the items, they advise how they should be used or worn, maintain them and return them to their source if required.

Fashion stylists work with photographers, fashion magazine editors, designers and movie directors. They may work for a print publication, a movie company, an advertising agency, a photographer or a fashion house, or run their own independent business. Fashion stylists work in a fast-paced environment, and get to work with the latest and greatest in clothing, accessories, furniture, etc.

As a fashion stylist, you might do any of the following in a day:
- Shop for items for upcoming projects
- Choose the clothing and accessories that will be worn by stars/ models
- Advise on hairstyles and makeup that complement the look
- Scout locations for possible shoots

- Negotiate with suppliers and retailers to "borrow" their merchandise
- Assist stars/models with dressing, makeup and hair
- Monitor the items as they are used
- Keep current on styles, trends and fashions

Who is Likely to Succeed

If you love shopping then this is your dream job, because much of its responsibility lies in finding the perfect outfits, items or products for a fashion shoot or other event. You need to have a creative flair and an understanding of what is fashionable.

You will be resourceful and determined when it comes to tracking down the things you need. People skills will help you negotiate with suppliers, and when you are explaining how an item should be used or worn.

You'll succeed at this job if you have an eye for detail, color and texture, and can pull together a distinct "look" with a variety of items. You're also organized and responsible, able to work with your hands, and find solutions for creative challenges.

How to Learn It

You can start to learn this job by paying close attention to fashion photographs in newspapers and magazines. Consider how each was made — someone chose all those clothes and accessories. Imagine how you would showcase a specific item or set of items. Keep on top of current trends and styles, and yes, shop as often as possible so that you are familiar with the resources available in your area.

You might want to work in a retail fashion store, or as a clerk in an accessories store, to learn about the different types of items available. If you can take a job working as a photographer's assistant, you will gather important information about the lighting, set organization and other specific needs of photography. There are often photographers looking for help online, and they may offer portfolio photographs in exchange for your help.

You may also want to volunteer as a set dresser at a local amateur theatre, to better understand what would be required on fashion shoots and movie sets. Better yet, apprentice with or volunteer with an experienced stylist, watching them as they go about their job.

Often, local newspapers will be glad for assistance in this area. Contact the editor and offer your services as a stylist on a volunteer basis. You can also volunteer to help with local fashion shows, and give your business cards to industry people who attend.

What It Pays

Beginning freelance stylists can expect to earn $25 to $60 per hour, or $150 to $300 per day. Top stylists can earn thousands of dollars a day (called their "day rate"). The annual salary for sought-after stylists can be more than $100,000, and this may translate to only 30 to 50 days of work. Some fashion stylists prefer to charge a flat fee for certain services they provide frequently. Many fashion stylists work as photographer's assistants or stylist's assistants for little or no pay in order to get connections and experience in the industry.

Fiction Writer

As a fiction writer, you will use your imagination and writing skills to create stories for popular or literary audiences to be published in magazines and as novels.

What They Do

Fiction writers develop believable characters, realistic settings and compelling plotlines for their stories. They write short stories (up to 20,000 words long), novellas (30,000 to 50,000 words), and novels (50,000 words and up). They may specialize in genres such as romance, mystery, action, suspense, or western stories.

Fiction writers are usually self-employed, and sell their manuscripts individually to magazines and publishing houses. They may occasionally be commissioned to write a piece for a particular client.

On a typical day as a fiction writer, you might:
- Browse new titles in your chosen genre to keep up with trends
- Meet with a critique group or editor to get feedback on a chapter
- Plot out the events of a new book
- Develop characters by writing detailed descriptions of them
- Write short articles that will promote a larger piece of work
- Promote your latest work with a reading, book signing or interview
- Write several pages of a new novel

Who is Likely to Succeed

Perhaps you have always wanted to write a book about your life, or a certain experience you had. And of course, you're talented at putting words together into interesting and dramatic stories. You're likely to be on the road to success if you are able to see a writing project through from the beginning idea to the end goal of publication.

You'll do well if you can match your style of writing to markets willing to pay you to print it. And ultimately, the difference between a successful and an unsuccessful fiction writer is simple: the successful one is persistent and tireless in their quest for publication.

How to Learn It

There are numerous courses, workshops and even degree programs you can take to become a fiction writer, but there is no need for formal education in this career if you practice your writing skills by working at them daily. You will learn more about writing by sitting at your computer and writing every day than you will in many courses.

To excel as a writer, you must read a lot, especially in the genre in which you write. When you read, think about how each piece of fiction tells a story, and consider how you can use the techniques and language in your own work. Copy the styles of your favorites, and then adapt them to your own style. You'll also benefit from reading the *FabJob Guide to Become a Published Writer* by Sheila Seifert, which is full of great tips and insider advice.

To improve your writing, spend time talking to other writers about your craft. It can be helpful to "workshop" (meet to read and critique each other's work) with other writers in your area, or on-line at one of the many message boards devoted to the craft of writing.

Determine which publishers print the kind of writing you do, and contact them for submission guidelines, which you should follow exactly. Some places will have you "query" the editor first with a letter about your work that will pique their interest. Learn how to write an engaging query letter that is a lot like a great cover letter for your resume: it will make the editor want to read your whole story.

You can find lists of publishers online or in books like *Writer's Market*. You increase your chances of success by being familiar with works the publisher has printed in the past, so you don't have to convince them to publish your genre, just your written work.

What It Pays

A publisher's advance payment for a novel is typically $5,000 to $10,000 or more, with royalties of up to 10 to 15 percent only after the advance has been earned back through sales. Some genre novel publishers pay a flat fee of $1,000 to $5,000 or more per book.

To earn additional wages, some writers teach writing courses, earning between $100 and $5,000 per course. Others collect admission fees from audiences at readings, or sell fiction to magazines at anywhere from 5 cents to $2 per word.

Fine Artist

As a fine artist, you will use your hands and ideas to create original works of art to sell for display in private and public spaces.

What They Do

Fine artists work independently to create two-dimensional (paintings, drawings, etc.) and/or three-dimensional work (sculptures, displays, computer designs, etc.) using a variety of materials. They display this work for sale in galleries, retail stores or online. They may make custom pieces for clients, or create their own work.

A fine artist might work with "media" such as paint, charcoal, crayons, pencils, ink, paper, glass, wood, metal, stone, wax, plaster, clay, or they may use computers. Some common specializations include painting, sculpting, illustrating, printmaking, computer design, woodworking, glassblowing, and metalworking — but you are only limited by your imagination.

The exact day-to-day tasks of this job vary, but commonly you can expect to spend time:

- consulting with clients on commissioned pieces
- spending time researching ideas and getting inspired
- choosing and purchasing materials
- physically creating your art
- solving design problems of size, media, concept
- arranging for displays/showings of your work
- promoting yourself as an artist

As a fine artist you will have a creative means of expressing your ideas. You will usually set your own hours, and you will have the satisfaction of frequently completing a project and seeing the results of your work.

Who is Likely to Succeed

Successful fine artists must cultivate a talent for what they do, and develop a thorough knowledge of their chosen medium. They tend to be self-motivated, meaning they can produce art even when they have not yet found a buyer. They have good problem-solving skills to help them when they hit an impasse in their work.

Artists use their interpersonal skills to convince clients or collectors to buy their work. An artist who spends as much time promoting their art as they do making it (by showing it at galleries and selling it online or in retail stores) will be most successful.

How to Learn It

Many successful artists are self-taught, and you, too, can take this kind of hands-on approach. Experiment with the media and styles that appeal to you. This allows you to develop your own "look" based on your natural abilities and inclinations, and provides you with work to sell.

For more focused learning, turn to the masters, a time-honored method of learning art.

If you want to make art that resembles the work of a famous artist, you can study their artwork in books or photographs. Learn to replicate their style, which you can then apply to your own original images.

Some established artists also take apprentices. To become an apprentice, find an artist in your area whose work you admire, and contact them through the gallery representing their work, or directly by phone or letter. In exchange for lessons or the opportunity to watch the artist at work, apprentices may help the artist by performing art-related tasks such as cleaning brushes, preparing canvases, or even installing shows at galleries. You can then request they give you some feedback on improving your work.

What It Pays

According to the Bureau of Labor Statistics, the median salary for fine artists in the United States is $38,060 per year. However, artists are usually paid per piece, not per hour. They set their own prices, and sell as many works as possible.

Artwork is priced according to size, materials used, and complexity. For example, an oil painting by a particular artist may sell for $200 to $500, while the same size watercolor may be $75 to $200, and a sculpture of comparable size may sell for $1,000 and up. Of course these amounts can be much more (in the thousands), depending on the following of the artist. If an artist is represented by a gallery, the gallery will take a commission of 40 to 50 percent on each sale.

Graphic Designer

Working as a graphic designer, you will use your artistic abilities and computer design skills to create original and appealing artwork and layout for communications material.

What They Do

Graphic designers create and design print advertisements and editorial pages for newspapers and magazines, as well as things like corporate logos, outdoor advertisements, books, and other printed material. They work on computers, using software like Illustrator, InDesign, QuarkXpress and Photoshop to create and manipulate the look of each advertisement or printed page.

Graphic designers create the layout of newspaper pages, and design many of the advertisements that appear on them. At a magazine, they may design the cover as well as editorial pages. For a book publisher, they may design covers, do the layout, and place illustrations or photographs.

At an ad agency, graphic designers create advertisements tailored to appear in a variety of media, including print publications, on billboards, and even on T-shirts and clothing. They may also design logos, or do complete image makeovers for a corporate client.

As a graphic designer you might spend your day:

- Meeting with clients to discuss their needs
- Preparing preliminary sketches for client feedback
- Trying different colors together to see what works in a design
- Revising art according to the client's wishes
- "Pre-flighting" material to make sure there are no glitches from computer to print
- Exchanging ideas with copywriters and other designers on the team
- Sending a portfolio to potential new clients
- Marketing your freelance services

Who is Likely to Succeed

To be a successful graphic designer, you should have an excellent sense of design and proportion, and an appreciation of the techniques used to make print ads successful. An inclination for trying new things or seeing the potential in ideas are helpful traits. You enjoy immersing yourself in your work, and are quick to pick up new design programs you have dabbled in.

You'll have the drive to convince your clients of their need for your skills, and the determination to sell new looks and images that are totally cutting edge. You'll also take direction well — part of your job is turning other people's visions into reality—and must be able to work well as a member of a creative team.

How to Learn It

You don't need a professional certification or degree to do this job, but it helps if you have some background in art, web design or electronic layout.

You'll need to know at least one or two graphic design programs to swiftly create a design on demand. Buy at least one layout and one photo manipulation package, or obtain a free demo version, until you know what you like. Use it until it is completely familiar. Practice creating ads for imaginary products or services, or see if you can recreate ads you see in magazines, to determine how they have been put together.

Make yourself familiar with the entire printing process by visiting a print shop or press. Find out the specific technical needs of different types of presses, so that you'll be able to accommodate those in your area.

You can also learn by volunteering for a community newspaper, where you will be able to get hands-on experience with ad design and electronic layout. You can also take a job as a layout designer at a newspaper or magazine — these positions will give you a firm grasp of the skills you'll need as a graphic designer. Or you can make newsletters for a club or community group you are part of, experimenting and honing your skills as you go along.

What It Pays

An entry-level graphic designer working in the United States can make anywhere from $15,000 to $30,000 per year, or freelance for $25 to $50 an hour. According to the Bureau of Labor Statistics, median annual earnings for graphic designers are $38,030. Experienced designers can make $50,000 to $80,000 per year, and charge up to $100 per hour or more on a freelance basis.

Home Stager

Do you know instinctively what little touches a home needs to look better? As a home stager, you'll help clients make living spaces more attractive by recommending and/or implementing alterations to the décor for a stunning before-and-after effect.

What They Do

Home stagers (also known as interior redesigners) are hired by real estate agents and private clients to make living spaces more attractive. They analyze what is/is not appealing in the space as is; then they rearrange existing furniture, clear out and/or store excess clutter and personal items, and may add a few props such as artwork, plants, and/or accessories in order to complete a harmonious look.

When stagers work with home sellers or real estate agents, the purpose is to help the home sell quickly and for a higher price. When homes are vacant, home stagers may even move in a complete set of new furniture and artwork to make the place seem more desirable.

Home stagers can also apply their skills as an interior redesigner, helping clients modernize, beautify, and make better use of the living space for their own enjoyment. Rather than redecorating like an interior decorator might, redesigners usually work with what clients already have in their home.

Home stagers may make recommendations only, or they may choose to do hands-on work to implement the changes. As a home stager or interior redesigner, your day may include some or all of the following:

- Speaking with potential clients about what you do
- Booking and traveling to appointments
- Viewing a living space and making notes about the décor
- Preparing a list of recommendations for clients
- Keeping up with modern decorating trends
- Sourcing or renting furniture and props
- Doing hands-on organizing, rearranging and removal
- Marketing your services to new clients
- Networking with professionals who do related work

Who Is Likely to Succeed

Chances are your own living space is well arranged, and that people often comment to you about how nice it looks. You are organized and on time for appointments. You are a stickler for efficiency, and are always looking for better and faster ways to get things done. You think and work quickly, and are energetic.

Home stagers have to be critical of something most people are very proud of: their homes. Therefore the best home stagers are diplomatic, tactful, and friendly. They present their recommendations in a way that is not condemning of the existing décor. Since they are "artists" of a sort, home stagers should have a sense of what looks good; what makes a space more open, attractive, or homey; and what is currently in style.

How to Learn It

Home staging is a skill you can develop on your own. There are a number of books on the topic that cover tips and tricks of the trade, and offer room-by-room advice for staging. You'll also benefit from learning about interior decorating concepts such as color, lighting, patterns, texture, etc. from books and decorating magazines.

Study other staged homes for ideas, too: show homes for new neighborhoods are an obvious place to start, and many home stagers post before-and-after photos on their websites that you can compare.

A wide variety of home staging and interior redesign courses are offered across the U.S. and Canada by companies/associations such as StagedHomes.com (**www.stagedhomes.com**) or Interior Redesign Industry Specialists (**www.weredesign.com**). Also look for the *FabJob Guide to Become a Home Stager*.

Learning as much as you can about related fields such as real estate and professional organizing will help you build your skills, and training in them will increase your network of contacts. In fact, many home stagers and redesigners combine their work with one of these two related fields.

You can get great experience staging a variety of homes, learning how to run your business, and working with clients if you volunteer to assist another stager or redesigner with the hands-on work. You offer them the benefit of free labor they would otherwise pay a helper for, and you will benefit yourself from on-the-job learning.

What It Pays

Home stagers and redesigners may charge by the project or by the hour, although a per-project fee is more common. Rates will vary depending on whether you are offering consultation only, or if you are doing hands-on staging, and the scope of the work involved.

Inspection and putting together a list of recommendations is usually billed out at a flat rate of $100 to $300, and a one-day redesign or staging project ranges from $500 to $2,500. If more extensive repairs, redecorating, or furniture rental is involved, the fees go up from there. By the hour, an average rate for beginner stagers/interior redesigners is $50 to $75, while the more experienced professionals charge $100 to $400.

Illustrator

Illustrators create images for books and magazines, gift cards and giftware, stationery, software and clipart, children's toys, game boards, company logos, packages, advertisements, and websites.

What They Do

As an illustrator, you will use your artistic skills to bring stories and ideas to life through images. Not only children's books, but also books on topics from biology to technology have a need for attractive sketches.

Illustrators might be employed by giftware companies, publishers, software companies, toy makers, or advertising departments. Others work as freelancers for a variety of companies and individuals.

As an illustrator, you may work with a variety of media, from paints to charcoal to pastels. But you're not limited to the typical art supply inventory — you can use fabric dyes, food coloring or collage techniques to create your art. You may also create using graphic software programs like Illustrator, Adobe Dimensions, Streamline, and Photoshop.

Your typical day's work might include:
- Creating art to practice, experiment, and add to your portfolio
- Sending out samples of your work to art directors
- Making cold calls and meeting with potential clients
- Brainstorming with clients about what they need
- Creating preliminary sketches for client direction and approval
- Working with a team of design professionals on a large project
- Communicating back and forth with clients
- Sending hard copies of the completed work to your client

Who is Likely to Succeed

An illustrator's main key to success is to love to draw, paint, or create in whatever medium you work in. Your illustrations can be simple or complex, but should have a consistent style. You should have a gift for communicating messages and stories in images, and the ability to see beyond obvious interpretations.

An illustrator should be self-motivated and disciplined enough to keep sending work out in the face of criticism or rejection. You need to have the self-confidence to believe in your art, but at the same time, remain flexible enough to incorporate the visions of your clients.

How to Learn It

The best way to learn illustration is to draw and create your art every day. You can use illustration software tutorials and experiment, and work through how-to art books. Study the market that you want to enter, whether that means reviewing hundreds of picture books or studying the illustrations on greeting cards and other products.

To hone your work, join an illustrator critique group, or become a member of a professional association, like the Graphic Artists Guild (**www.gag.org**) or the Society of Children's Book Writers and Illustrators (**www.scbwi.org**) to take advantage of workshops and online forums. Attending conferences may allow you to meet one on one with art directors, and give you a chance to share your portfolio in person.

If you take art and business classes through a community college, university, or private art school, the connections you will make can be very helpful. You might also find and enter art contests — you'll learn how to meet deadlines, submit your work properly, and conform to a theme while maintaining your unique style.

Get an internship or apprenticeship with any of the employers listed above, as internships can lead to paying work. Seek out companies or publishers that use a similar style to yours so you can focus on selling them yourself, not your style.

What It Pays

Book illustrations pay anywhere from $50 per page up to $150 or more per page, or are royalty-based. The royalties for a picture book are split between the author and the illustrator, with 10 to 15% being the typical royalty rate. Typical salaries for a full-time illustrator range from $20,000 up to $50,000, and six-figure salaries are possible for the most successful in the field. Small businesses may pay $80 per illustration on a per-project basis, while larger companies will pay up to $800 for the same work.

Interior Decorator

Most interior decorators are hired to decorate home interiors, but they are also hired to decorate interiors of a wide variety of businesses such as boutiques, restaurants, and offices. You will use your creativity to make homes and businesses more beautiful, comfortable, and functional.

What They Do

Decorators may decorate the entire interior of a building, or a single room such as the living room, kitchen, bathroom or bedroom. They recommend what should be involved in decorating the room including color, furniture, paint, window coverings, fabrics, flooring, lighting, art objects, hardware fixtures, and accessories such as vases, cushions and plants. A decorating job may be as simple as rearranging furniture, or it may involve hiring and supervising contractors.

You should not confuse interior decorating with interior design — an interior design career requires certification, and can be considerably more difficult to break into, whereas you can start calling yourself an interior decorator as soon as you start decorating.

If you'd rather not spend years studying or have to worry about things like building codes and writing an exam to be certified, then interior decorating is a better career choice for you. Your tasks may include some or all of the following:

- Meeting with clients to determine their needs
- Reviewing and taking measurements of the space
- Preparing proposed room layouts
- Obtaining cost estimates
- Showing samples (e.g. colors, fabrics, tiles) to clients
- Scheduling the work to be done
- Arranging and overseeing painting, wallpapering, flooring, etc.
- Shopping for items and materials
- Coordinating deliveries
- Hands-on decorating of the space
- Ensuring the decorating project runs smoothly and on time

An interior decorator will have the satisfaction of making their vision a reality. You will meet interesting people, and because many people who hire interior decorators are wealthy, you will likely spend time in many beautiful homes.

Who is Likely to Succeed

The most important trait for a decorator to have is a strong aesthetic sense — also known as a "good eye." This comes naturally to some people, while others have to work to develop it. You appreciate beauty in art, in people, in nature, or in things, and you have a strong sense of the best placement for things within a particular space.

You probably love to redecorate your own home and rearrange the furniture. When you visit someone's house for the first time you notice ways they could make their home more attractive, functional, or comfortable.

How to Learn It

The best way to train your eye is to study what people consider to be good design. Seek out beautifully decorated interiors to look at. You can find numerous examples of beautiful interiors in decorating magazines, books, television shows, and websites.

Also take advantage of opportunities to view interiors in person. Check out show homes in new residential developments and open houses of homes for sale in upscale neighborhoods. Visit furniture showrooms, historic homes, museums, art galleries, and offices of businesses that attract upscale clients, including architectural, law, and interior design firms. Attend home shows and design trade shows. To learn more about specific products, talk to retailers and manufacturers.

While teaching yourself can be an inexpensive and fun way to learn interior decorating, you will probably be able to learn decorating more quickly from experts by taking an educational program. Your local college or university may offer interior decorating courses through a continuing education department. Many programs are also available by distance learning. In addition, the *FabJob Guide to Become an Interior Decorator* is an excellent resource for those who prefer to learn at their own pace.

You can earn while you learn by getting a job with a retailer that sells related products, such as home furnishings, lighting, fabrics, house paint, house wares, hardware, art and antiques. Look for a position where you can work with and learn about a broad range of decorating styles.

Fab Fact: Nate Berkus (Oprah's favorite decorating expert) has been passionate about and experimenting with decorating since his childhood. Nate started his home design career working in the antiques field, and he is a seft-taught interior decorator.

What It Pays

A typical starting salary for entry-level interior decorators is $10 per hour, with commissions beginning at 6% (for those working with retailers that pay commission). Decorators working for retailers, wholesalers or manufacturers may also receive discounts on merchandise.

Most self-employed interior decorators charge fees ranging from $25 to $150 per hour, although a few top decorators command hundreds of dollars per hour. Many interior decorators earn additional income by charging clients a mark-up on furniture and materials.

Inventor

Inventors see a need and meet it. They look for ways to make products better or more efficient. You will use your inspiration and technical skills to create new products or improve existing ones.

What They Do

Inventors research ideas, test these ideas, and keep making changes and adjustments until they hit on just the right mixture that will take the idea from paper to the marketplace.

Inventors with ideas search for funding, write patent applications (to register their ideas as original), and market their inventions. Inventors might be self-employed, or they may work for one company that sells a number of products.

As an inventor you may find yourself engaged in any of these activities:

- Brainstorming new design ideas with colleagues or friends
- Studying objects to determine if they can be improved
- Determining if your latest idea has a market and any competition
- Deciding if the invention can be manufactured for a reasonable cost
- Keeping an inventor's journal to record ideas and their progress
- Building a prototype (or model) of your invention to show to buyers
- Applying for a patent to protect your idea
- Presenting the invention to manufacturers or investors
- Marketing and selling the invention yourself

Who is Likely to Succeed

An inventor is always looking for a way to make things around their house more useful. Inventors are often interested in research and enjoy spending quiet time studying a design idea, but inventors should also enjoy marketing their products and pitching their exciting new ideas to manufacturers.

Successful inventors are curious, creative, and persistent people. They not only come up with ideas for exciting new products, but they can also sell these ideas to investors and the buying public. Many successful inventors have a background in product design and development.

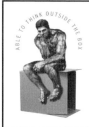

Did You Know? Thomas Alva Edison did not invent the lightbulb on his own. In 1879, Al (as his friends called him) spent considerable time improving on the then-50-year-old concept, which was put forward by other inventors.

How to Learn It

You can become an inventor by inventing — it's that simple. Train yourself to think like an inventor by studying other inventors. Study the major inventions of the past and find out how the inventors made their decisions. Look at recent successful inventions and follow the path from idea to market.

Take advantage of any nearby museums that focus on inventing, such as the Smithsonian Institute and science centers. Check out science and technology conventions and shows. Subscribe to magazines about inventing, and join inventors networking groups to keep up with what type of inventions are selling.

While you can begin your career as an inventor without additional education, you may shorten the time from idea to invention if you take a few courses. Some universities, colleges, and technical schools offer courses that focus on design, building, and testing products. There are also seminars, forums, and distance-learning opportunities. The Internet has many inventing-based forums that are filled with information, insight, and suggestions for the budding inventor.

If you want to gather understanding about product invention, consider working with a design company that specializes in developing new products. Toy companies or engineering firms are constantly creating new products for the market and this can be a good place to learn about inventing new products.

What It Pays

Entry-level design engineers (inventors who work for a particular company) working in the U.S. can expect a salary of about $53,000, although salaries fluctuate with the industry you are designing products for.

For private inventors, earnings depend on what you do with your invention. You can sell your patent to a company for a flat price, or you can license your inventions, which means you receive a royalty fee for every unit sold, or a flat fee while your product is being sold. If you have the entrepreneurial spirit, you can market your product yourself and keep all your earnings, minus production costs.

Jewelry Designer

Jewelry designers create "wearable art." They use a range of materials to create attractive body adornments that complement the wearer's style and personality.

What They Do

Jewelry designers create necklaces, bracelets, anklets, rings, brooches, and earrings, as well as new-era body jewelry like tongue and navel rings. They may work with or combine a variety of materials such as metal, stones, glass, wire, leather, and beads.

You can sell your jewelry to individuals or boutiques, or work for a jewelry design company. You might make the jewelry by hand, or if you don't have the equipment or the know-how, design only and sell your ideas to manufacturers.

As a jewelry designer, your tasks will likely include some or all of the following:

- Sketching jewelry designs
- Displaying items at art shows and craft fairs, or at your own boutique
- Shopping for and selecting materials
- Preparing samples for retailers and prospective buyers
- Meeting with clients or buyers to determine their specific needs
- Manufacturing your pieces or arranging for production

Who is Likely to Succeed

The most important trait for a jewelry designer is a keen sense of design and color. While some people have a natural eye for combining colors and creating pleasing designs, others have to develop it.

Successful jewelry designers enjoy working with their hands and have patience with intricate tasks that require dexterity. If you love jewelry — wearing it, looking at it, and combining it in interesting and unexpected ways — and if you have a good sense of style, chances are you've got what it takes to succeed.

How to Learn It

While you need no formal education to become a jewelry designer, making certain metal jewelry involves heating metal and using tools you probably don't yet own. You can learn metalworking techniques more quickly if you take a jewelry design course taught by experts at craft shops, design schools, and community centers.

Design books are full of patterns you can adapt to the styles you prefer, technical advice, and techniques, such as stringing beads, setting stones, and creating intricate designs using wire.

Even part-time work in a jewelry retail store or supply shop will give you access to materials and ideas. Train your eye to recognize good design. Study what people wear, especially those whose style you admire. Browse other jewelry shops and attend art shows and craft fairs that feature handmade jewelry. Talk to other jewelry designers about their craft, and inquire about good resources.

The best way to learn about jewelry design is to start designing and making jewelry. Visit a craft store or a bead specialty shop and select materials that are easy to work with, and some inexpensive tools. Purchase a magazine or beginner book that offers patterns and advice. You can earn while you learn by selling at art shows and craft fairs.

Once you have created a good collection of original pieces, you can host a "trunk show" to let your circle of friends and/or business acquaintances have the first chance to buy your pieces before they see them in a fancy boutique at double the price.

What It Pays

Most jewelry designers are self-employed, so income is determined by the price they charge and the volume they sell. If you sell on a circuit of art shows and craft fairs, you can make anywhere from $5,000 to $30,000 or more a year. Jewelry designers with retail outlets, or who sell through established retailers and on the Internet may earn anywhere from $25,000 to $50,000 or more a year.

Landscape Designer

As a landscape designer, you will use your eye for natural beauty to come up with ideas to make outdoor spaces visually stunning, functional, and an oasis of relaxation and enjoyment for home owners.

What They Do

Landscape designers create a plan for the outdoor space surrounding a residence. But you're doing much more than deciding where a tree should go — you're planning spaces where people can feel a sense of serenity, creating an environment that looks like nature and functions as a refuge.

A designer advises on topography, water's role in the space, number and kinds of plants (trees, bushes, flowers, etc.), and appearance of walkways, driveways, fences, etc. Landscape designers may be self-employed or may work with architects and interior designers as part of a full-service residential design company.

There is work in the landscaping field in almost any area you live. A landscape artist enjoys working outdoors some of the time, and many times can work a non-standard work week. This profession also lends itself well to starting your own business.

A typical day as a landscape designer might include any of the following:

- Reading home design and landscaping magazines to keep up with trends
- Brainstorming ideas with clients and architects
- Walking around the space you will design to take a look at the environment
- Evaluating site surveys and related environmental information
- Choosing the natural components and layout for the space
- Presenting a proposal to the client
- Selecting and meeting with suppliers and contractors
- Supervising installation of vegetation, ponds, etc.
- Attending a "housewarming" for a space you worked on

In most states landscape designers are limited to working on residential projects, and cannot call themselves landscape architects or work for public clients unless they pursue education and licensing

115

in landscape architecture. A landscape architect might be expected to have more advanced skills such as CAD (computer-aided design) knowledge and land or topography surveying ability.

Who is Likely to Succeed

A background or interest in artistic endeavors, interior decorating or design, plants, or architectural design will help the aspiring landscape designer be successful. The more skilled you are at scheduling and organizing, the better you'll communicate well with your contractors for an on-time and successful installation.

If you are an avid gardener who looks forward to spring every year with a gleam in your eye, chances are you have the passion to pursue this career. You may already have designed backyards for yourself or friends, and appreciate nature and park space. You have a knack for envisioning what goes where, and will plan before you plant. Strong interpersonal and persuasion skills will help you find a balance between your ideas and the client's needs and budget.

How to Learn It

Adult-education extension courses, especially those that include field trips, are an option. Visit every park and botanical garden in your area, and put gardens and parks on your itinerary when you travel. The idea is to learn how nature embraces a human-imposed landscape, hence how you can work with nature.

Learn as much as you can about different plants and soils, especially those native to where you're working, as well as irrigation methods. You must understand the local growing season and how any plant grows locally. You can also practice drawing versions of trees and shrubs that look like... well, trees and shrubs. This will help you communicate your ideas to clients.

Working as a gardener or for an established designer, architect, or landscape architect can provide on-the-job training; and designing green spaces for family and friends is a time-honored way of generating word-of-mouth buzz. Also consider working at a nursery, or on a landscaping installation crew before you apply for work.

Bachelor's and master's degrees are available in landscape architecture, but are not necessary for landscape designers working in the residential market. That said, if you choose to pursue formal education and licensing to complement your experience, you can expand your work to bigger projects like regional planning or golf course design, the corporate market and municipalities.

What It Pays

If you decide to first work under another landscape designer, a landscape-crew job in a good-sized city pays about $15 an hour. Once you are designing on your own or as a design supervisor, expect to earn from $50 to $150 an hour, depending on your reputation and experience.

Makeup Artist

Makeup artists use their eye for color and creativity to choose and apply makeup (and other cosmetics) to a wide variety of clients such as celebrities, music video dancers, TV reporters, and/or brides-to-be. They may also consult with clients on choosing a new makeup style.

What They Do

Makeup artists advise clients on facial makeup choices, then apply and retouch their makeup as needed. Make-up artists may be hired full time by retail businesses or salons to do makeovers for clients, promote makeup lines, and do special occasion makeup. They may also help clients with unusual skin needs or facial conditions find flattering looks.

Many makeup artists are self-employed, and complete work on a contract basis. They might work on theatre productions, designing and applying the makeup for actors, as well as creating any necessary special effects. They do similar work on films and in television, making sure the actors' makeup is flawless for each shot, and studying scripts to determine special looks before the shoot. Some makeup artists work with fashion designers and models on runway shows, or for magazine photo shoots.

As a makeup artist, your day might include any of the following:
- Preparing clients' skin for makeup application
- Applying and retouching makeup as needed
- Re-doing makeup from scratch if the look is not working
- Brainstorming ideas with costume designers, fashion stylists, etc.
- Consulting with clients for weddings, proms and other special events
- Shopping for and maintaining an inventory of cosmetics and supplies
- Networking within the industry to promote your services

117

Who is Likely to Succeed

If you're always thinking about new makeup combinations to get a desired effect, and notice when others have used makeup well or poorly, you're probably already skilled at the attention to fine detail that a good makeup artist requires. You're probably a trendsetter, with a sharp eye for color and design and some artistic talent.

Maybe you've done makeovers on yourself or your friends, or enjoyed getting everyone made up for a special occasion. Your manual dexterity allows you to draw straight lines and apply color with consistency. You pay attention to people's needs, and don't mind working directly in contact with other people's bodies. You're also a good listener, as you'll need to take direction from clients, directors, producers and others.

How to Learn It

To get good at this job, you need to practice regularly. Apply makeup to yourself or willing family members, and make outlines of faces on paper to use for documenting your work (just use the same colors and cosmetics on the paper face as you do on the real ones). Experiment with different types of cosmetics, and try to create different looks and different effects.

You can also apprentice with an established makeup artist, watching how they do their work. Or you can take a retail job selling cosmetics, and learn different tricks for application, or visit cosmetics counters at retail stores and watch how they do makeovers.

Study the makeup used in fashion magazine photographs and in other media, especially films. Notice what colors are current, and what looks are popular. Try to replicate these looks on your own. Read about cosmetics in books and magazines, and subscribe to fashion magazines in order to keep current with new products. You can also attend esthetician training schools and courses to learn this job. The *FabJob Guide to Become a Makeup Artist* by Jennifer James has a detailed list of training courses available in North America, as well as great information on how to break into this desirable career.

Increase your product knowledge by putting together a collection of makeup to use on your clients — you will be dealing with a variety of skin tones and colors, and you will need to have the tools to do the job. Find supplies on sale, or ask for bulk discounts. Remember that many people will have sensitive skin, so look for cosmetics that are hypo-allergenic.

What It Pays

An independent makeup artist doing bridal or prom makeup may charge $30 to $75 per application (or sometimes more). A freelance makeup artist working for film or television may earn up to $500 per day, and a highly experienced makeup artist working in these industries can make as much as $2,000 per day. A retail store makeup consultant can expect an annual salary of $25,000 to $35,000. You can also anticipate tips for a job well done.

Photographer

Photographers identify and record images digitally or on film for a variety of industries. Your work might be used to record history, tell stories, capture life's special moments or sell products. You can make time stand still, and earn a living doing it.

What They Do

As a photographer you will use your camera to capture remarkable still images for one employer or a variety of clients. Talented photographers may work as freelancers for a variety of companies in many different industries, since almost every business sector from entertainment to aerospace employs photographers. Many photographers choose one area such as sports, weddings, or nature and specialize, depending on their interests and talents.

In some cases you will take photos and submit them for sale; in others you will be hired in advance to take specific photos for the client's purposes. The majority of your work will be done "on site" getting the photos you need of your subjects.

As a photographer, you will do some or all of the following:
- Locate markets for your photos
- Promote your work to current and potential clients
- Plan and practice your technique
- Determine the correct equipment for certain subjects, conditions, or effects
- Meet with clients to discuss assignments or jobs
- Work onsite to take a variety of photos for the client to choose from
- Develop or process and "re-touch" (fix blemishes on) photos
- Select the best photos and deliver finished products

Who is Likely to Succeed

Successful photographers have the ability to see a potential shot in their minds and to visualize it in a way that will translate to a powerful message on film. They can be both immersed in their work and objective about it.

Successful photographers aren't afraid to market themselves and their work. If you can build your self-marketing skills to go along with your natural ability to create art through your camera lens, your career as a photographer will flourish.

How to Learn It

Begin to learn about your craft by analyzing the work of other photographers you admire. Be constantly on the lookout for examples of work in magazines, books, billboards — anywhere you see a photographer's work. Read books for a foundation in the history of photography, and learn about the most influential photographers in the marketplace today.

You can teach yourself to take photos, or you can take courses at your local community college or junior college, or you can even pursue undergraduate or graduate degrees in photography at major universities or art colleges. No formal training is required for this profession, though — just ability and talent.

Work for an established photographer in your community, or at the counter of a photo-developing booth. Working hands-on in your industry will help you begin to develop your talent, and might help you pick up some work.

You can learn even more by connecting with others in your profession. Doing so will make you aware of what is happening in your industry, where the hot markets are for your work, and what other photographers are charging.

Consider donating your services as a photographer to non-profit organizations who will often publish your work because you are offering it for free. This is an excellent way to begin to build a portfolio of your published photographs.

What It Pays

According to the Bureau of Labor Statistics, median annual earnings of salaried photographers are $26,080. Photographers who work in corporate settings usually make more money than those who work for smaller clients. A freelance photographer's clients will pay wildly different amounts, from $1 to more than $1,500 for a single photo.

Video Game Designer

Video game designers combine both creativity and logic to create interesting worlds that players can explore, supported by the necessary logic to take the player from start to finish — and win!

What They Do

Video game designers invent new electronic games, including the story, the rules, the procedures for players, how a player wins and the logic of the game. As a video game designer you will use your broad knowledge of video games and computer know-how to conceptualize and write games for electronic entertainment companies.

Contrary to what many people believe, not all video game designers know how to build a robot or program a computer. Although you should understand as much as possible about computers and what they are capable of, designers are "ideas people" who know gaming and can predict what video game users will appreciate, so the programmers and artists can make it happen on screen.

As a game designer, you will do some or all of the following:
- Develop written proposals for new games
- Pitch game companies on their latest concepts
- Develop games in conjunction with programmers and artists
- Tweak original concepts to work better as the game is developed
- Play video games avidly to determine what is cutting edge in the market
- Stay aware of trends in computer technology and video game design
- Attend launch parties and network in the gaming industry

Who is Likely to Succeed

Video game designers are passionate about gaming. You are likely the kind of person who plays a variety of games on a variety of platforms, and are willing to get into an argument to defend the ones you like best. When you play games you think critically and compare them to similar ones, considering areas the game is strong in, and ways it could have been more fun or user-friendly.

Video game designers who have the best success are multidimensional thinkers and learners. In very few other careers are you called upon to take logic, math, and computer skills and blend these with language, art, and communication skills. People with professional-level computer skills and experience, and artistic, storytelling, and project management abilities will have a jump-start in this field.

How to Learn It

Many of the most successful designers in the industry have been players since early childhood. Besides your hands-on knowledge of video games, there are a variety of ways to learn the skills you need.

Learn the history of the video game industry. Even if you haven't been interested in video games since the 1970s, you should still know what people mean when they talk about Atari games or Commodore 64s. Learn the short history of the industry by using the Internet or reading a book on the subject.

Go to retail stores where games are sold and take a look at what's new. Write down the names of the manufacturers of products that interest you and research them. You can volunteer to "beta test" (i.e. try out and evaluate games before they are released to the public) new video games for companies and get valuable experience and contacts.

Consider any one of a number of colleges and trade schools that offer programs for video game designers. Make sure you ask the institution about job placement opportunities and support for graduates as well. The *FabJob Guide to Become a Video Game Designer* by Phil Marley is an excellent resource written by an experienced game designer to assist you with breaking into this career.

Some existing computer and online games allow the possibility of creating new areas or bonus levels to add onto their games. Taking part in building bonus levels will give you experience in conceptualizing games without needing the know-how to program each step. Some online communities will also give you feedback on the levels you develop to improve your design skills.

What It Pays

According to the industry source *Game Developer's Marketplace*, annual salaries in the video game industry range anywhere from $30,000 to $75,000, and still more than that is possible. You will make more money as you become more experienced and work with bigger companies on more complex development projects.

Wedding Planner

Wedding planners are hired by busy couples who want to have someone handle the details of their wedding. You will use your organizational abilities to help couples choose the right elements to make their wedding day special and memorable.

What They Do

The wedding planner is responsible for overseeing the big day, and the days and weeks leading up to it, to ensure that the event runs smoothly and is enjoyable. Wedding planners are usually self-employed. They may organize weddings in their own area, or specialize in organizing weddings in exotic or unusual locations.

A wedding planner will meet with engaged couples to assess what they need, want and can afford. Then they shop around for the right elements including the officiant, florist, DJ, band or other entertainment, caterer, baker, and location. They will organize and attend rehearsals, and attend the wedding itself to ensure that it runs smoothly and to handle any unexpected challenges.

As a wedding planner your typical day may include any of the following:

- Meeting with new and current client couples
- Visiting possible wedding sites and booking them in advance
- Arranging for marriage licenses, site use agreements, and liquor licenses
- Negotiating with and choosing suppliers
- Arranging for the rental of stemware, accessories and decorative items, if needed
- Planning the reception, including the timeline, menu, seating and speeches
- Arranging for and installing the decor
- Scheduling and attending the rehearsal and rehearsal dinner
- Being on hand at the ceremony and reception to take care of special needs

Who is Likely to Succeed

You're probably a natural wedding planner if you are a "people person" and an excellent communicator. Perhaps you enjoyed planning your own wedding, or that of a friend, and want to do more. Above all, you love making people happy.

You're extremely organized, and you're also detail-oriented, so nothing is left to chance. You have creative ideas for making weddings special, and an extensive knowledge of not only a variety of wedding traditions, but local venues and suppliers. And of course, you're great at negotiating, because you'll need to work with these venues and suppliers to get good deals on behalf of your clients.

How to Learn It

Develop your organizational skills, which are crucial for this job, by building lists, databases and files in which to organize the information you gather about wedding venues and services. Learn a software package like WeddingSoft (**www.weddingsoft.com**), which can make you more efficient and able to take on more clients.

You should also learn about the many and varied wedding customs and traditions. You can find out about these on the Internet, through books and magazines like *Modern Bride,* and by joining on-line discussion groups for wedding planners. Also, the *FabJob Guide to Become a Wedding Planner* is a well-respected resource among industry professionals.

You can also take a job at a business that provides services for weddings such as a caterer or event venue, to participate in (or just see how they handle) the big business of weddings. Or you can meet with an established wedding planner to ask questions about how he or she does the job (one who works in a different area may be more willing to help than one who might see you as a potential competitor).

You can learn hands-on skills by helping a willing friend or family member organize their wedding. Photos of these events can become part of a portfolio to show others your skills. Develop your network of potential clients and suppliers before you officially start up your business by attending wedding shows, visiting wedding service providers like florists, dress shops and caterers, and attending business mixers.

Fab Fact: Colin Cowie, event planner extraordinaire, who is well known for planning lavish parties for Oprah, has planned the weddings of many celebrities such as Lisa Kudrow, Jerry Seinfeld, Kelsey Grammer, Kenny G, and many others. After planning a wedding for Hugh Hefner, Colin was officially labeled "Mr. Wedding."

What It Pays

Wedding planners typically earn between $40,000 and $80,000 per year, depending on how many weddings they plan. A typical per-hour rate is about $50, although they may also offer a package rate/ all-inclusive service for $3,000 to $5,000 or more. As a wedding planner, you can also charge your clients a percentage of what their wedding budget is.

Window Display Designer

As a window display designer, you will create attractive arrangements of products and accessories in store windows and display areas to catch the attention of potential customers.

What They Do

Window display designers work mainly with retail or chain stores, but other clients may include restaurants, hotels, shopping centers — basically anywhere the public will visit. They might also install and decorate sets for catalog and magazine photographs.

You will showcase your client's merchandise in a window or display area in a way that demonstrates how it can be used, or you'll create a mood or theme (such as for a holiday) that encourages customers to shop. Other job titles include window dresser and visual merchandiser.

Some window display designers work as staff members, occasionally with other retail duties as well. Others operate their own businesses, providing display services for clients on a per-window or hourly basis.

During a day on the job, you might find yourself:
- Meeting with clients to evaluate their needs
- Sketching preliminary drawings for client approval
- Assembling and dressing mannequins
- Installing lighting, props, and accessories
- Building props and signs for use in displays
- Photographing your latest creation for your portfolio and/or for future reference
- Researching current trends in display and marketing
- Approaching new clients about working for them

Window display designers are working on new projects all the time, and get to express their creativity on a daily basis. They usually don't spend time in a traditional office setting, since much of the work is done offsite.

Who is Likely to Succeed

Successful window display designers use fresh, innovative ideas to create eye-catching displays. You'll need to be a good listener who can translate the client's ideas into their display space, and someone who accepts input with appreciation, not defensiveness.

People who are suited to this career love making things look special, even when setting the table or wrapping a gift. You would be the type who looks for any excuse to decorate. You have an eye for color, texture and shape, and are good at working with your hands.

Having a knack for simple building and craft projects or interior design are also advantages. Outgoing people who are comfortable soliciting work from strangers are more likely to succeed independently.

How to Learn It

Anyone with the desire can create window displays, photograph them, and begin to market their work. Practice window display in an area in your own home. Purchase inexpensive track lighting or spotlighting at your hardware store, and collect lengths of material for backdrops. Create displays of your own possessions, focusing on themes or color schemes.

Arrange the items to create a pleasing display, or imitate displays you've seen in other places. Collect props, like lightweight furniture, stands and other accessories, at thrift stores or store closure sales. Build props with cardboard or foam-core, and paint them to suit your ideas.

Study window displays in retail stores. Examine the types of merchandise being displayed, and how it is presented. Watch for trends and tricks (such as the use of accessories or lighting). You can clip ideas from decorating and design magazines and keep them for future inspiration.

If you're already working in a retail business and you're not part of the display staff, volunteer to help create or install the store's displays, on your own time if necessary. Larger retailers have window display teams you could apply to as well.

What It Pays

In the United States, a window display designer who works for an employer earns a median salary of $48,443 per year, or $15 to $20 an hour. If you create your own job by marketing your work to independent businesses on a contract or per-window basis, you would charge between $25 to $50 per hour, plus props and materials. Some stores may also reward you with free merchandise as a tip for good work.

HOW TO BREAK IN

Knowing you are a creative genius who is ideally suited to a particular career is a great start. The challenge is to prove it to the people who will sign your paycheck. Whether you want to be a self-employed "creative" or get hired for a traditional job (at least in the sense of working hours), you'll need to convince clients or corporations that you are the "creative" they should choose. So how can you stand out from the crowd?

You could try convincing them by telling them how creative you are, but you'd probably be wasting your time. Most people will need proof that you have what they're looking for. So don't just tell them how creative and productive you are, SHOW them by creating a portfolio.

How to Create a Portfolio

A portfolio is a collection of samples of your work, plus any other documents that can show people why they should hire you or invest in your career. A portfolio helps you stand out from other applicants, and can prove that you have the skills to do the job. As you'll read throughout this book, we recommend that you get plenty of volunteer experience in your chosen career. Those volunteer experiences can provide the materials you need to create a portfolio. Your portfolio might include:

- Samples of work you have done
- Samples created for your portfolio
- Paperwork that gives evidence of your creative genius

To prepare your portfolio, begin by gathering items you have created that show your skill in the career.

Samples

With some careers, you can include actual samples in your portfolio. For example, advertising copywriters, illustrators, and photographers may be able to include actual works they have created. If you are a writer, you might include clippings of your work that have been published in print. If you're a jewelry designer, you might include some pieces of jewelry. But don't include originals of any items that you only have a single copy of! A portfolio can get lost, and you don't want your best works lost with it.

If you have multiple copies, you can include an original in your portfolio. Otherwise, make additional copies on your home computer, or at a copy shop or other place that can make a reproduction for you. Make sure the reproduction looks professional and the colors are true.

Photographs

What if actual samples of your work can't be brought to an interview? For example, if you are applying for work as an interior decorator, you can't bring a "sample" of a room you have decorated. For any career where it's impossible or simply impractical to include actual samples in a portfolio, the solution is to show your work through photographs.

For example, a chef can include photographs of meals, a fashion designer can include shots of clothing, and a floral designer can include pictures of flower arrangements. Think about what types of photographs would work best for you. If you're an inventor you could include a photo of someone demonstrating the prototype of your product. If you're a caterer, event planner, or wedding planner, get permission to take photographs of events so you can select the ones that best showcase your work.

It's particularly impressive if you can include "before and after" photographs. If you are applying for a job in a field such as landscape design or makeup artistry, before and after photos show employers and clients the magic you worked in creating the finished product.

Try to arrange to have photographs taken of everything you create. While you won't include every photograph in your portfolio, it's smart to have as many photos as possible to choose from. You do not need to hire a professional photographer (it could cost hundreds of dollars to hire a professional photographer for a few hours). A much less expensive alternative is to take photos yourself if you're handy with a camera, or get a friend or family member to take them for you. If you have someone else take photos for you, make sure they know the photos should be in color!

You may be able to get some ideas for your own photos by looking at portfolios of professionals in your field. You might be able to meet some pros who are willing to show you their portfolios, but you don't need to make this happen right away. Instead, take advantage of the world's best source of portfolios: the Internet! Chances are there are many professionals in your field who have posted web pages with photos showing samples of their creations. Take some time to explore their sites and see how they have showcased their best work.

Creations

Your portfolio doesn't have to be limited to work you have already done. In fact, some of the most impressive items you can show employers and clients will be items created especially for your portfolio.

This is your chance to truly showcase your creative genius. There are no hard and fast rules about what to include in your portfolio — you are the one who is making it all up. So think about what is likely to impress someone who could hire you. An advertising copywriter could include a sample ad, a caterer could create a sample menu, an event planner could make a sample invitation.

Make your samples look as impressive as possible with professional materials such as high-quality paper. You might even create more complex pieces. For example, an animator might include a CD with a sample animation or a video game designer could include several proposals for new games.

To give a more detailed example, if you were applying for interior decorating work you could create a "design board" containing samples to show what you would recommend for an imaginary decorating project. On this board you could paste samples of materials (e.g. fabrics, paint chips, carpet, flooring, wallpaper), and pictures from magazines and catalogs of items such as furniture, lights, and accessories. Your samples could be mounted onto picture matting or heavy poster board from an art supply store. Your board could be white, black, or any color you feel looks best with your samples. The size could be 14" x 17", 15" x 20", or any size that allows you to effectively display the materials. If the materials need any explanation, you could include captions.

You'll notice all the "coulds" in the last paragraph. That's because there are many ways to create items for your portfolio. Remember, whatever you create is a reflection of you and your talent. If you are a creative genius, you are probably feeling excited as you read this. You may have numerous ideas popping into your head and can hardly wait to start creating items for your own portfolio, knowing that whatever you make will show your unique genius. After all, you can ask people for feedback and change anything that's not working for you.

On the other hand, if you are struggling with this section, and think you need step-by-step instructions as to exactly what to include in your portfolio, then you should seriously consider whether you need to find a creative partner to work with! If your strengths are analytical, rather than creative, you'll find some fabulous careers you may be more suited to in other chapters of this book.

Paperwork

In addition to your samples, certain types of "paperwork" can provide evidence of your expertise. Along with your resume (see a sample resume for a creative career on the next page), you can include any official documents such as certificates, awards, or diplomas. You can also include any clippings from newspapers or magazines of items you have written or that have been written about you. As with the samples of your work, include reproductions unless you have a number of originals.

It can also be impressive to include thank-you notes and letters of recommendation. The best letters of recommendation are those written by people you have done work for (whether paid or volunteer) in the field that you want to work in. Every time you do relevant work for someone, even a friend or family member (with a different last name from yours), ask for a letter of recommendation. Recommendation letters look particularly impressive if they are on letterhead, so ask for several copies on letterhead if possible.

When you ask for a letter, keep in mind that many people are busy so they are more likely to do what you ask if you can make it as easy as possible. To help get the kind of recommendation letter you want, and make the job easier on the person writing the letter, you could supply a list of points they might mention, for example:

- What you did (write it out for them — chances are you remember exactly what you did more clearly than they might)
- You got it done ahead of schedule
- You saved them money by finding the best suppliers
- You got along well with everyone you worked with
- You came up with many creative ideas
- You listened and delivered exactly what they wanted

Of course, you don't have to include all these things. The specifics will depend on the particular job, but even a few glowing sentences can help you look good to employers and clients.

TIP: A recommendation letter should not mention that you worked for free. You want to show that your work has value, and an employer may assume the reason you received a glowing recommendation is because you didn't charge anything. Remember, good work is good work no matter how much you were paid for it.

Sample Creative Resume

C. J. GOULET
123 My Street
Mytown, USA 11111
(111) 555-1212
cjgoulet@cjdesigns.com

TARGET POSITION

An entry-level position in the women's fashion industry, where I will get the chance to apply my hands-on talent on group projects, as well as contribute fresh new ideas of my own to assist a company with their creative growth.

EDUCATION

IRT Fashion Institute
May 2005

Continuing education courses included fashion drawing, flat pattern drafting, fashion history, and fashion merchandising

PROFESSIONAL EXPERIENCE

ABC FashionWear, Sales Associate
2005-Present

- Assist clients in choosing fashionable garments
- Handle all in-store alterations for clients
- Attend fashion shows with owner to assist in trend-watching
- Maintain inventory and assist in purchasing
- Put together attractive window displays with in-store merchandise

CJ Designs, Owner, Designer
2004-Present

- Run a home-based business selling my designs to private clients
- Take designs from sketches to patterns, outsource the assembly
- Recently hosted a trunk show with $2,000 of sales in one night
- Current customer base of 60 ongoing clients

RELATED VOLUNTEER WORK

- Assistant costume designer, Mytown Players Theater Group
- Model Dresser, Anytown Charity Fashion Show (annual)

Putting It Together

Find a table or some other spot where you can spread out all your samples and paperwork. Don't worry about weeding out anything right away. For now, just focus on tracking down everything you can (and remember to keep copies of everything you create in future).

Then decide which items to include in your portfolio. Remember that your portfolio should be a collection of your best work. Most employers and clients do not have time to look through dozens of pages, so it is better to have a few outstanding examples than many average examples. A video game designer might choose as few as four game proposals, while an illustrator might choose 15 to 20 works they're really proud of (if they have that many).

If you have photos, you can arrange them in a photo album, or get them blown up to 8" x 10" (check with your local one-hour photo outlet) and put them into a portfolio case or binder. Printed portfolio items could be put into a professional-looking three-ring binder with plastic sheet covers to protect the pages. If you wish, you can mount your photographs and other portfolio materials onto thin cardboard. You can find supplies at any office supply store.

If your portfolio includes items that won't fit into a binder, consider using a portfolio case, which you can buy at an art supply store. Portfolio cases come in a variety of sizes (e.g. 11" x 14", 14" x 17", 17" x 22") and cost from about $15 to over $150, depending on the size, material, and how fancy you want it to be. However, employers are interested in what is inside of the case, so you don't need to spend a lot of money on the case itself (e.g. you could get vinyl instead of leather).

In addition to preparing a portfolio to take with you to interviews, it's also a good idea to create an online portfolio (also known as a web portfolio). This is a selection of photos posted on a personal web page which employers can access at any time. You can design a simple site yourself using software such as Microsoft FrontPage, or you can hire a web designer to build one for you.

Once you show people what you can do, it's only a matter of time before you start getting paid for your creative genius.

 **TIP:** Writers and artists can also get work by impressing an agent. See chapter 5 to learn more about working with agents.

7

Fab Merchants

Careers Running Your Own Business

Have you ever visited a local business and thought, "I could do better than this"? People have thoughts like these every day... but only the gutsy, determined ones act on them. They say, "I *will* do better than this!" and put the wheels in motion.

A merchant is anyone who is business-savvy and enjoys buying or selling products. (In this chapter, our definition of "fab merchant" also includes people who sell services.) They have the vision and courage to make unconventional decisions, and they naturally lead and inspire the people around them. They meet daily challenges with creative and thoughtful solutions.

If being your own boss has always been your dream, you can make it happen by starting your own business. Just imagine yourself in a career you love because it is one you invented, and where your earning potential is only limited by your vision and desire.

You've no doubt heard the statistics about how many businesses fail in their first year, but did you ever consider that businesses might fail because they don't plan to succeed? Don't let the odds discourage you. The profitable businesses are ones whose owners have taken the time to plan out a roadmap to success, as we'll explain in this chapter.

Here are some of the dream careers you can consider as a fab merchant, with detailed descriptions to follow.

- Antiques/Collectibles Dealer
- Auctioneer
- Bed and Breakfast Owner
- Bookstore Owner
- Brewer
- Coffee House Owner
- Florist
- Importer/Exporter
- Restaurant Owner
- Secondhand Store Owner
- Spa Owner
- Wine Merchant

THE CAREERS

Antiques or Collectibles Dealer

As an antiques or collectibles dealer you will search for and snap up valuable or rare items. Your investment will pay off when you sell these items to other collectors for a profit right away, or some time down the road.

What They Do

Antiques and collectibles dealers are people who see the value in old furniture, art, jewelry and other collectibles, and enjoy buying and selling them to other collectors. They travel to garage or estate sales, flea markets and antiques shows in order to find and purchase their treasures.

They pay what they hope is a price below the actual value of the item, and then turn these collectibles over for a profit. Sometimes an item may be less valuable on its own, but when a dealer adds it to his or her collection, it becomes part of a valuable set. Dealers are usually very knowledgeable about a certain type of collectible item, or may have a broad knowledge of all things rare and valuable.

Some antiques dealers sell antiques as their primary source of income and have their own shop. Others begin their businesses by selling antiques at local flea markets, others rent space in antiques malls or shops that sell space to a variety of antiques vendors, and still others sell antiques online — both through their own websites and through eBay.

As an antiques dealer you will do some or all of the following:
- Acquire and add to your collection of antiques or rare items
- Read and learn constantly about the value of items you own or hope to acquire
- Explain the value of your collectibles to potential buyers
- Keep an inventory of what you own and its worth
- Advertise your collectibles to find potential buyers
- Set up and maintain your antiques store, booth and/or website
- Negotiate for the best price on items you sell and buy

Who is Likely to Succeed

Antiques and collectibles dealers are passionate about the items they collect, down to the most minute details of where they were made, and how many are in existence. Because of this passion, they spend their time becoming increasingly knowledgeable about antiques — just for the joy of it.

You should enjoy haggling for the best deal possible, and enjoy meeting other people who appreciate what you buy or sell. You should have a curious mind and a keen eye for detail, so you can separate imitations from the truly valuable. Good antiques dealers can make quick decisions about buying and selling, so they don't miss out on opportunities.

How to Learn It

Start exploring your local antique and collectibles shops. Don't just browse silently — talk to the proprietors and ask about their items for sale. Subscribe to antique magazines to find out when antique shows are being held in your area, and attend these. If you or your family own anything you suspect might be rare or valuable, try to track down information to confirm your suspicions.

Another important part of becoming a dealer is learning to appraise. You can learn the basics by watching TV shows like *Antiques Roadshow* (**www.pbs.org/wgbh/pages/roadshow**) and by visiting the many appraisal websites online. Once you build a community of contacts, you can turn to other experts if you ever need help appraising an item you are not familiar with.

Ask an antiques dealer in your area if you can donate your services working for them one or two days a week. Or look for a job in an auction house or collectibles store — you need to see what items sell for to get a real sense of their value.

Many first time antiques dealers break into the business by selling on eBay (**www.ebay.com**), or other online sites. You can test the waters this way without leaping into the investment of leasing a physical space.

What It Pays

Antiques dealers' salaries vary based on whether they deal full time or start off with just a few items. Beginning antiques dealers may make around $20,000 annually. More experienced dealers can make as much as $50,000 each year, or more when they are dealing in very valuable items. Many dealers put a great deal of their incomes back into buying more items to sell.

Auctioneer

Auctions are fast-paced and exciting public sales, and the star of the show is the auctioneer who sells each item with a lightning-quick chant and a "Once, twice, sold to the highest bidder!"

What They Do

As an auctioneer you will use your smooth speaking and salesmanship skills to market items at a public sale. Auctioneers sell cars, fine art, jewelry, coins, antiques, collectibles, farm equipment, livestock and real estate — and just about anything else the public will buy. As an auctioneer you may have one or several types of auctions that you consider a specialty.

At an auction you will act as emcee and spokesperson. You will describe each item's best features, and then open the floor to bids. You'll keep an eye out for anyone indicating that they wish to bid, and acknowledge their bid verbally, keeping things moving at a quick pace. When you determine that the bidding has reached a peak, you will close the sale and award the item to the highest bidder.

Some auctioneers work for auction houses, and many run their own auction businesses. To put on your own auctions you will plan, organize and market your sale. You must be knowledgeable about appraising items too, so you know where to start the bidding.

As an auctioneer you will do some or all of the following:

- Accept and inventory items for sale
- Learn about the items you sell so you are able to describe them knowledgeably

- Promote your auctions to potential bidders
- Help sellers set their reserve prices
- Coordinate the bidding process
- Entertain the bidders and keep them in a "buying mood"
- Ensure sellers get paid and buyers receive their items

Who is Likely to Succeed

Auctioneers have or develop a way of speaking that is engaging, lively, clear, and fast. They enjoy being the center of attention, and may even have a bit of the comedian in them. Successful auctioneers may have a background working with what they sell, or a keen willingness to learn.

An auctioneer is a salesperson at heart — you like to take risks and reap rewards. Maybe you already get a thrill out of bargaining for a great deal. You are good at thinking on your feet, and don't mind an environment that is fast-paced and even sometimes unpredictable.

How to Learn It

If you are lucky enough to have an auctioneer as a friend or in your family, see if they are willing to take you on as an apprentice and teach you the tricks of the trade. If not, there are auctioneer schools where you can receive training from experienced auctioneers. The National Auctioneers Association maintains a list of auction schools on their website — you can search to find a course near you (**www. auctioneers.org**).

Of course, attending auctions is a great way to see how things work, and learn the nuances of the auctioneer's chant. You'll have to develop a voice all your own, but it never hurts to study other's techniques when you are first starting out. Taking a course in public speaking, acting, or even improvisation will help you as an auctioneer as you learn to be quick on your feet.

Auctioneers must be licensed in 27 states. Licensing requirements vary by state, but the general requirements include a high school diploma, a certain number of training hours, a written test, and a criminal background check. Some states require that novice auctioneers attend accredited auctioneer training schools or train as apprentices under experienced auctioneers. Check with your local or state auctioneers association for details specific to your region.

Some auctioneers start out working for auction houses as "ringmen" who assist the auctioneer in spotting bids and managing each sale. Even if you are not working as an auctioneer right away, working in the auction environment will give you a chance to immerse yourself and learn by observation.

What It Pays

Many auctioneers are independent contractors and take a percentage of the sales at an auction — the number of sales and price for each item determines their income. Beginning auctioneers might make low and inconsistent wages while building their business. Experienced auctioneers with excellent reputations and substantial client bases can make $100,000 or more annually.

Bed and Breakfast Owner

Bed and breakfast owners are proprietors of their own inns. But you don't leave the house to go to work every day — you live and work in your home. Having a bed and breakfast can be enjoyable and interesting work for anyone who loves to socialize.

What They Do

As a bed and breakfast owner you will use your natural hospitality, your friendly personality, and your homemaking skills to make your home into a pleasant inn for paying guests. You will offer a cozy alternative to the impersonal chain hotels.

Although your bed and breakfast can be whatever you want to make it, they are commonly found in historical or rural homes, or places that are otherwise unique. Each guest room in your inn should be special in some way. You will greet and host out-of-town guests, providing meals, conversation, and sometimes planned activities.

Bed and breakfasts with fewer than five rooms can generally be expected to provide income for one owner, or supplement retirement income for a couple. Those with more than five rooms can provide a full-time income for two, but may require hiring additional staff.

As a bed and breakfast owner you will do some or all of the following:

- Take guest reservations
- Greet your guests and check them in
- Offer guests meals, refreshments and snacks
- Clean, decorate and maintain your inn daily
- Chat with guests about their travels
- Recommend local activities or tourist attractions

- Advertise and market your bed and breakfast
- Business-related tasks such as bookkeeping and banking
- Stay at other bed and breakfasts to develop ideas for your own

Who is Likely to Succeed

With your natural sense of hospitality you will enjoy helping your guests, and enjoy having them in your home. You are friendly and like meeting people from all walks of life. You know your region well and what the interesting and fun things to do are, and have an idea of how best to market specialized services like a bed and breakfast.

You don't mind clearing the table, vacuuming or making beds — since you'll be doing these tasks daily. It helps if you are a good cook, a good home manager, and are at least somewhat handy around the house.

How to Learn It

Most bed and breakfasts have a web presence these days, so you can start learning about running a bed and breakfast by looking at these websites. Take a look at how they are run, what they look like, their services, accommodations and rates. As part of your research, spend the night at several bed and breakfasts that you have determined are most like what you envision for yours. Think about how your inn will be similar, and what you will do to stand out.

Seminars are offered on a frequent basis across North America about how to be an innkeeper or start your own bed and breakfast. Some even offer hands-on apprenticeships. You can search for courses and consultants at Bed and Breakfast Inns Online (**www. bbonline.com**), or read a good guidebook like the *FabJob Guide to Become a Bed and Breakfast Owner* by Angela Hynes.

To get some hands-on experience, look for (or create) opportunities to be an "inn-sitter" for bed and breakfast owners who need some time off but would prefer not to shut their doors. Contact bed and breakfast owners and let them know you are available, or look for opportunities in B&B-related publications and websites.

The Professional Association of Innkeepers International (**www. paii.org**) and the National Bed and Breakfast Association (**www.nbba. com**) are organizations devoted to serving owners of bed and breakfasts and country inns. PAII hosts an annual convention and tradeshow with educational opportunities, and the chance to connect with others in your industry. There are also regional B&B associations across North America.

What it Pays

As with a number of merchant careers where you will be running your own business, what you will earn will be linked to the financial success of your venture. If you are the only owner of your business, your pay can be drawn (i.e. taken out) from your business after paying all expenses. If your business has more than one owner, your salary will need to be determined in advance as an ongoing expense, and you will also earn a percentage of the profits as your business grows. Many merchants choose to put most of the profits they earn in the first few years back into growing their business.

Bookstore Owner

As a bookstore owner you will put together a collection of new and used books and magazines as well as other reading materials and related items, and sell them to an eager public.

What They Do

A bookstore is any retail establishment that sells books and related items (called "sidelines") to the public. Booksellers might sell only new books, only used books, both used and new books, or antiquarian (old and rare) books. Today's bookstore might have a physical location, or may be Internet-based instead.

As a bookstore owner you will own what is called an independent bookstore — that is, independently owned and operated by you, or you and several others. Booksellers often pick a niche for their bookstore. Some people sell only mystery books, or only books for children, for example.

Bookstore owners manage all aspects of their business, including purchasing inventory, greeting and assisting customers, setting prices, and marketing the business to book lovers. In a small bookstore you might work alone or with a partner, while in a bigger bookstore you will have a staff to assist you with day-to-day operations.

A day in the life of a bookstore owner may include some or all of the following:
- Meeting with publishers' sales representatives to see what books you can buy
- Placing orders for new inventory
- Merchandizing your books so they sell better
- Assisting customers with their purchase
- Hosting special events like book signings or book clubs

- Attending tradeshows to learn about new books
- Hiring and training your staff
- Banking and deposits of daily sales
- Shipping out-of-town orders

Who is Likely to Succeed

To be a bookstore owner it isn't enough to simply love books — successful booksellers have business sense. They make smart ordering decisions, and keep a careful eye on their profit margins. They are constantly looking for ways to promote their bookstore to new and existing customers.

You should enjoy reading across a broad spectrum of topics, so you can help a range of customers with their needs. You are a good conversationalist, and when you read something great, you just can't wait to share your discovery with others.

How to Learn It

Before you open your own bookstore, you may want to work in a bookstore part time. You'll get to know the major publishers, meet the sales reps., and get a sense of the pace of the work day. You can also visit any bookstore you see as a "mystery shopper" and investigate the service, the selection and the style of the competition. In particular, independent bookstores (i.e., not Borders, Barnes and Noble, or Chapters/Indigo) will give you a good idea of what you can expect.

Take advantage of online learning opportunities as well. The American Booksellers Association (**www.bookweb.org**) is the foremost professional association for booksellers in the world, and the Canadian Booksellers Association (**www.cbabook.org**) also has a number of resources for the new bookseller.

The bookselling industry has national and regional conventions and trade shows every year, just packed full of information for new booksellers. Network with other booksellers and express your interest in joining their ranks. Many booksellers will be happy to help you, provided your bookstore will not be in direct competition. You may even find a bookseller who will agree to mentor you in your start-up phase.

There are educational programs and consultants available to help you prepare for and plan your bookstore, if you are willing to spend hundreds of dollars. If you want to investigate the career and learn the basics for considerably less initial investment, you can pick up a great guidebook like the *FabJob Guide to Become a Bookstore Owner* by Grace Jasmine.

To do some hands-on learning, consider opening an Internet bookstore, or selling books on eBay to get yourself immersed in the business. While having a web presence is something you will want to do eventually when you open your physical location, you may even find that "virtual selling" is your preferred way to sell books.

What it Pays

As with a number of merchant careers where you will be running your own business, what you will earn will be linked to the financial success of your venture. If you are the only owner of your business, your pay can be drawn (i.e. taken out) from your business after paying all expenses. If your business has more than one owner, your salary amount will need to be determined in advance as an ongoing expense, and you will also earn a percentage of the profits as your business grows. Many merchants choose to put most of the profits they earn in the first few years back into growing their business.

Brewer

Brewers are professional beer-makers who own their own breweries. They get to combine their love of the malted beverage with their entrepreneurial skills to produce a product for adults to enjoy.

What They Do

Brewers come up with one or several types of beer, and then brew batches of it to sell to the public and licensed establishments, in bottles, cans, and kegs. If a brewer has a technical background as a brewmaster they can invent their own beer recipes, or else they will hire or partner with one to oversee taste and production.

Brewers usually run smaller local breweries called microbreweries, which don't produce as much beer as the big brewing companies, but take pride in brewing small batches with a distinctive flavor. Beer is created and matured in large vats in the brewery, and then bottled, canned, or put into kegs. The brewer and his or her brewmaster are there tasting the beer every step of the way to make sure that the beer is near-perfect.

In addition to overseeing beer production, the brewer is also responsible for promoting its brand to the buyers: alcohol vendors, licensed establishments, and of course the general public. The brewer will constantly be looking for innovative ways to market his beer, from sponsorships to product placement to billboard ads. Some micro-breweries have their own brewpub as well — a restaurant or bar that makes and sells beer as part of the menu.

As a brewer you may do some or all of the following:
- Develop and test new beer recipes and packaging
- Oversee production and shipping of your beer
- Hire sales reps. to promote your beer to vendors
- Hire and supervise your brewery staff
- Develop marketing strategies for your beer
- Network with other microbrewers
- Monitor overall sales of your beer
- Give tours of your brewery to the public

Who is Likely to Succeed

A good brewer should have a well-developed sense of taste. Perhaps you notice small nuances of flavor in your food and beverages, such as a hint of chocolate or a slight fruitiness. This will help you fine-tune your palate to create a truly delicious beer. You should love beer, or at least be able to enjoy an occasional brew.

To break into the competitive beer-making industry, you should have a clear vision of how you will market your beer, and good managerial skills to help you supervise and motivate staff. Previous experience in home-brewing is a definite asset, but not a necessity.

How to Learn It

Start your journey with some local brewery tours. Stick close to the front of the group so you can hear every word from the tour guide, and ask questions about anything you don't understand. Make mental notes of each piece of equipment involved in the process, since you will need to purchase these for your own use.

If you are still developing an interest in beer, make a habit at least once a week of bringing home a new or unique beer to try. As you sip and sample, keep a journal of your impressions of each, including packaging. If you hit on a flavor you like, you can work with your brewmaster to recreate something similar as one of your brands.

Next, start making your own home-brewed beer. It's not that complicated, and the equipment should cost you $75 or less. Start with simple kits, and work your way up to ones that require you boil up a mixture and add your own hops, so you can experiment with flavor. If you want help, contact your local homebrewers association — most regions have one. Search on the Internet to see if there is one in your area.

The U.S. Brewers Association (**www.beertown.org**) hosts the annual Craft Brewers Conference for you to see the best breweries all in one place at one time. In Canada the national brewers association is called Brewers of Canada (**www.brewers.ca**).

It is also helpful to get some brewing training before you launch your business, whether through a short seminar, an apprenticeship, or a longer educational program. Otherwise, you'll want to hire a brewmaster consultant to help you fill in the blanks when it comes to purchasing equipment and developing your brands.

What it Pays

As with a number of merchant careers where you will be running your own business, what you will earn will be linked to the financial success of your venture. If you are the only owner of your business, your pay can be drawn (i.e. taken out) from your business after paying all expenses. If your business has more than one owner, your salary amount will need to be determined in advance as an ongoing expense, and you will also earn a percentage of the profits as your business grows. Many merchants choose to put most of the profits they earn in the first few years back into growing their business.

Coffee House Owner

Coffee house owners create unique, enjoyable ambiances in their shops where friends reunite, and people come to chat, work on laptops, or read the paper. Patrons can stay and soak up the glorious smell of fresh-brewed coffee, or simply grab a cup of hot java on the run.

What They Do

Coffee houses sell a variety of specialty coffees, teas and other hot beverages, as well as treats like bakery goods. As a coffee house owner, you have the choice of opening a franchised location of a well-known coffee place, or you can start your own independent shop. You will determine the menu, set the prices, decorate your shop, and will probably serve your share of customers as well.

Some coffee houses serve up entertainment along with java, becoming local hang-outs for college crowds or jazz enthusiasts. Others offer cyberstations, allowing coffee drinkers to hook up to the Internet and surf while they are sipping a hot beverage. Some owners even operate drive-through businesses or coffee kiosks.

As a coffee house owner you will do some or all of the following:
- Meet with suppliers to purchase food and beverages
- Hire and manage a staff of servers
- Clean and maintain your coffee-making equipment
- Monitor daily and monthly sales
- Create your menu and update it as needed
- Balance the books and make bank deposits
- Market your coffee house in creative ways

Who is Likely to Succeed

If you have sales or restaurant experience you'll step into the role of coffee house owner quite easily. You love meeting and chatting with people, and have an interest in coffee as well as the culture it creates. You don't mind doing much of the same thing every day — so long as you can do it in a hip, funky atmosphere like a coffee house of your own creation.

Successful coffee house owners are smart business owners. They stay on top of the financial numbers that can make or break a business, and are constantly dreaming up new ways to draw customers through the doors.

Fab Fact: Howard Schultz, chairman of the popular Starbucks coffee chain, was hired by the company in 1982 as director of marketing and operations. Back then Starbucks simply sold high-quality coffee beans and equipment, and, after taking an inspirational trip to Italy, Howard was convinced they should also sell fresh cups of coffee, espresso and cappuccino. The original owners of Starbucks rejected this idea, so Howard left to start his own coffee house in 1985. It was a success, and a year later he bought out the Starbucks chain. There are now more than 6,000 company-operated Starbucks located in more than 30 countries around the world.

How to Learn It

Visit as many coffee houses as you can get to. Sample the menu, check out the ambiance, and count how many cups of joe they serve in an hour. Take notes about what you see, to jog your menu when you are writing a business plan for your shop.

You should also develop an interest in your main product. Learn what it means to make a cappuccino "skinny," and what goes into the perfect café au lait. The trade magazine *Fresh Cup* (**www.freshcup. com**) is dedicated to the specialty coffee and tea trade, and Virtual Coffee is an online coffee magazine you can check out as well (**www. virtualcoffee.com**).

The Specialty Coffee Association of America (**www.scaa.org**) provides a variety of resources for coffee house owners, including a widely attended annual conference boasting hundreds of hours of educational opportunities. Also, the *FabJob Guide to Become a Coffee House Owner* by Tom Hennessy contains a wealth of advice from an experienced coffee shop and restaurant owner.

If you have the time and money, you can take courses in the restaurant or hospitality industry. Most community colleges offer restaurant industry courses, and many offer certificate programs. If you have limited education or experience in retail selling, you might also consider working with a consultant with a background in the industry as you set up your business.

Don't underestimate how much you can learn from your coffee and equipment suppliers, who spend a lot of time talking to other coffee shop owners. Contact them early on in your planning — they may be able to answer questions like how much coffee you'll sell in a month, what equipment you'll need, and what trends are affecting the industry.

What it Pays

As with a number of merchant careers where you will be running your own business, what you will earn will be linked to the financial success of your venture. If you are the only owner of your business, your pay can be drawn (i.e. taken out) from your business after paying all expenses. If your business has more than one owner, your salary amount will need to be determined in advance as an ongoing expense, and you will also earn a percentage of the profits as your business grows. Many merchants choose to put most of the profits they earn in the first few years back into growing their business.

Florist

As a florist you will use your superior knowledge of flowers and plants and your talent for creating eye-catching designs to prepare and sell floral arrangements to companies, organizations, and the general public.

What They Do

Florists are artists who use fresh flowers to create lovely arrangements for gifts, special occasions and everyday enjoyment. Flower bouquets and arrangements are sent as birthday gifts, for holidays, to celebrate anniversaries, to declare love or an apology, or to show sympathy. Some people don't need a reason to send or buy flowers; they simple enjoy them for their beauty.

Some florists are employed by large floral shops, while others are entrepreneurs who own their own businesses. Some florists sell in storefront locations, others in stands or carts. As a freelance floral designer, you could work from home creating arrangements using dried or artificial flowers. You may specialize in selling to corporate accounts like hotels and restaurants, or in a particular niche such as funeral wreaths or bridal bouquets.

As a florist or flower shop owner, you will do some or all of the following:

- Help customers select floral arrangements and plants
- Receive orders in person, by phone, or online
- Buy fresh flowers, equipment, and other supplies
- Receive, prepare and arrange fresh flowers
- Care for the plants in your shop
- Display flowers and other merchandise in your store
- Hire and train staff and delivery people
- Prepare daily deposits and bookkeeping
- Market and advertise your flower shop

Who is Likely to Succeed

A florist should have a love for, or at least a keen interest in plants and flowers, and a knack for putting together colors and textures in interesting ways. It helps if you have the manual dexterity to tie bows, write message cards, and handle delicate pieces of greenery, and if you are comfortable being on your feet for much of the day.

You enjoy meeting new people and helping them through the emotional highs and lows of life. You are a natural salesperson who can help people meet their needs without feeling pressured, and will be able to make savvy business and marketing decisions to stand out from the competition.

How to Learn It

There is no substitute for being on the job preparing and arranging flowers (or learning by watching others), as well as working with customers, and being a part of the back-of-the-store routines. You can get experience by volunteering or working part time at a local flower shop, especially at their busy times such as Valentine's Day and Mother's Day.

You can also experiment with arrangements at home. Take some books about floral arrangement out of the library, and purchase some inexpensive real or artificial flowers that you can experiment with. Try to recreate the arrangements you see, and then create your own variations of them. Take digital pictures of your nicest arrangements — you can use these photos to show employers or clients when you are ready to look for work in this career.

You can join a local gardening or floral enthusiasts club in your area, and for more inspiration, read the FTD newsletter (**www.ftdi. com**), which comes out monthly and is available free online. You can get design advice as well as advice on breaking into a career as a florist in the *FabJob Guide to Become a Florist* by Alisa Gordaneer.

If you are interested in a formal education, the Society of American Florists (**www.safnow.org**) has on their website a list of schools in North America that offer degrees in floristry, horticulture, and related fields.

You can also seek out accreditation and educational opportunities with the American Institute of Floral Designers (**www.aifd.org**) in the U.S., and Flowers Canada north of the border (**www.flowers canada.ca**). Many regions also have a local association open to you as well.

What It Pays

Entry-level florists and floral designers make from $7 to $12 dollars an hour. Those with several years of experience make from $15 to $20 an hour.

If you decide to go into business for yourself, what you will earn will be linked to the financial success of your venture. If you are the only owner of your business, your pay can be drawn (i.e. taken out) from your business after paying all expenses. If your business has more than one owner, your salary amount will need to be determined in advance as an ongoing expense, and you will also earn a percentage of the profits as your business grows. Many merchants choose to put most of the profits they earn in the first few years back into growing their business.

Importer/Exporter

As an importer/exporter you will use your network of international connections and your knowledge of trade regulations to connect with buyers and suppliers around the world.

What They Do

Importers/exporters are people who trade goods (and even some services) internationally. Importers purchase hard-to-find or inexpensive or unique international products and resell them in their own country, either from their own stores, or wholesale to another retailer. Some importers just facilitate purchases between a local buyer and international seller for a fee, without actually buying the items themselves.

Exporters help local manufacturers find markets for their products overseas, and negotiate the tricky world of shipping and trade regulations. You may be finding a buyer overseas for a third party's goods, or buying products first which you then sell, pack, and ship to overseas buyers.

Importers/exporters (sometimes called international traders) can be employed by others, or may work independently. They can travel the globe looking for the products they import and/or for potential buyers for products — or they may do much of their work over the phone and the Internet.

As an importer/exporter you will do some or all of the following:
- Travel to international locations to meet with buyers and suppliers
- Respond to queries by phone or email
- Draft contracts that protect the interests of all parties
- Stay aware of changes in the global economy
- Negotiate for the best price on items you buy or sell
- Research existing trade laws and regulations in each country you work
- Purchase and/or sell products internationally
- Deal with customs regulations, duty issues, and monetary conversion

Who is Likely to Succeed

If you are happy to travel to new countries and are adept at fitting in with local cultures, you have the beginnings of a career in import/export. Speaking a foreign language is a definite advantage, and even more important is becoming familiar with cultural business styles, so you can prevent misunderstandings and create goodwill between buyers and sellers.

You don't need to know everything there is to know about international trade, but you should learn how to find answers quickly when you need them. You are a smart business person and a natural salesperson. You are confident a risky investment can pay you back well, if handled correctly.

How to Learn It

Trying to learn the regulations for all industries could be too overwhelming to start with. Consider what areas of expertise you already have that could translate into an import/export niche for you. If you've already worked in a certain industry for a number of years, or have a type of product that interests you (e.g., wine or apparel), you can start researching the companies that are already importing or exporting this product.

You can start getting a sense of the language and pace of international trade by browsing a website like the Federation of International Trade Associations (**http://fita.worldbid.com**). It is an international marketplace and forum where buyers and suppliers can connect internationally to do business. Once you are ready to start doing business, you can sign up for a full membership and make offers or bids here.

While not required to be an importer/exporter, there are useful certification and college degree programs available to those with an interest in international trade, including distance-learning courses online. Building a network of importers and exporters may also help you find job opportunities when you are ready.

Working for an import/export company is a great way to learn the ropes before going into business for yourself, so look for some opportunities to cut your teeth on. Even as a receptionist or assistant, you are going to absorb much of the details of the business.

The American Association of Exporters and Importers are experts in international trade and customs matters, and are advocates for the industry. You can visit their website at **www.aaei.org**.

What it Pays

As with a number of merchant careers where you will be running your own business, what you will earn will be linked to the financial success of your venture. If you are the only owner of your business, your pay can be drawn (i.e. taken out) from your business after paying all expenses. If your business has more than one owner, your salary amount will need to be determined in advance as an ongoing expense, and you will also earn a percentage of the profits as your business grows. Many merchants choose to put most of the profits they earn in the first few years back into growing their business.

Restaurant Owner

Restaurant owners are the people who create, plan, and run their own eating establishments. As a restaurant owner you will serve up delicious food and drink to people in a unique ambiance that is truly your own creation.

What They Do

Restaurant owners dream up and build their restaurants according to their unique inspiration. They hire chefs, managers and wait staff, design a mouth-watering menu, and then throw open their doors to a hungry public. Some restaurant owners take on all the management tasks on their own, while others hire a manager in order to delegate some of the hands-on work.

Most restaurants have some kind of theme, such as ethnic cuisine, family-oriented, fine dining, buffet-style, diner, or fast food. Restaurant owners must offer something that is needed in their area to succeed, so they carefully study the other local restaurants before they open to determine what is lacking.

Some eateries are franchises, which means that you pay a fee to open a restaurant that already has systems, an overall design, and a client base in place. Entrepreneurs with less experience running a small business may find this a faster, easier and less risky route to take.

Your primary job as owner will be to oversee all aspects of the business from start-up through operation. You will ensure your restaurant's financial success by making key decisions and hiring outstanding staff members to make your vision a reality.

When running your restaurant, you may do some or all of the following:
- Draft weekly staff schedules
- Work with your chef to select menu items
- Order fresh ingredients and supplies regularly
- Oversee food preparation and service each day
- Chat with customers to see if they are satisfied

- Respond to complaints and compliments
- Monitor daily, weekly and monthly sales
- Set and adjust menu prices
- Plan marketing and promotional campaigns
- Meet with other owners, managers and/or staff

Who is Likely to Succeed

Restaurant owners with past experience working in a food-service setting have a head start. Perhaps you waited tables in college, or are working as a chef or maitre d' right now. You have a natural sense of hospitality, and know how to make people feel comfortable and at ease immediately. You are diplomatic, friendly, and like to meet new people.

Of course you should enjoy tasting new dishes and even having a hand in creating them. Small business skills like accounting and marketing are vital for those in the restaurant business.

How to Learn It

Start by becoming a restaurant "mystery shopper." Eat in the types of restaurants that you envision yourself owning. Pay attention to details like ambiance, décor, wait staff, management presence, customer service, and menus. Even if you can't afford to eat out every night, many restaurants have their menus and other information on their websites.

A great way to prepare to own a restaurant is to spend some time working in one. Whether you are a chef, wait staff or management, getting real advice from people in the business will make the process of opening your own restaurant infinitely easier. You may even meet your future chef or manager this way.

While you don't need a degree to be a restaurant owner, if you've never worked in a restaurant and want to do hands-on work in yours, you will likely see the benefit of taking a few courses or training seminars. Almost every local college offers hospitality industry courses, and the National Restaurant Association (**www.restaurant. org**) offers research, training, and events for those in the restaurant industry.

Read restaurant magazines and other publications that support the restaurant industry. *Restaurant Business Magazine* (**www.restaurant biz.com**) is an excellent choice and will give you an overview of current industry news. There is also *Restaurant Startup and Growth Magazine* for those just getting started (**www.restaurantowner.com**).

Tom Hennessy, who has started ten restaurants of his own, is the author of the *FabJob Guide to Become a Restaurant Owner*, a step-by-step guide that shows you how to plan and open your own restaurant, including inventory and supply checklists, and systems to get the most out of your staff and keep your business running smoothly.

Fab Fact: Wolfgang Puck is the famous restaurant owner whose motto is, "Live, love, eat!" He has built a restaurant empire that includes celebrity hot spot *Spago* in Beverly Hills, about a dozen other fine dining restaurants, and more than 50 casual Wolfgang Puck Cafés or Express eateries. Wolfgang did not begin his training at a culinary school but instead worked as an apprentice at a number of eating establishments, including the famous *Maxim's* in Paris.

What it Pays

As with a number of merchant careers where you will be running your own business, what you will earn will be linked to the financial success of your venture. If you are the only owner of your business, your pay can be drawn (i.e. taken out) from your business after paying all expenses. If your business has more than one owner, your salary amount will need to be determined in advance as an ongoing expense, and you will also earn a percentage of the profits as your business grows. Many merchants choose to put most of the profits they earn in the first few years back into growing their business.

Secondhand Store Owner

If you love the thrill of hunting for retail treasures and are looking for a business that is relatively inexpensive to start, owning and running a secondhand store may be the right career for you.

What They Do

Secondhand store owners hunt for, clean, repair, and sell used items to customers, from a retail shop, a temporary booth or kiosk, or online. Your secondhand store could sell a mix of items, or specialize in clothing, CDs, children's items, sporting equipment, or anything that interests you and your customers.

Secondhand store owners may buy items and acquire an inventory of things to sell, or they may sell on a consignment basis. In the case of consignment you don't actually own the items, but you take a commission if and when the item sells. Therefore, consignment is an inexpensive way to acquire an inventory for your store. (If the item doesn't sell it is returned to the owner, or sometimes donated to charity if prearranged with the owner.)

As owner you will oversee all aspects of how your secondhand store is run, including acquiring inventory, setting purchasing policies, hiring staff, merchandizing, and guiding it to financial success. Your day as a secondhand store owner may include some or all of the following:

- Sourcing and purchasing inventory
- Considering items brought in for consignment
- Preparing used items for resale
- Setting the right price for each item
- Merchandising items into eye-catching displays
- Scheduling and managing staff
- Making bank deposits and paying bills
- Monitoring daily sales figures
- Greeting and assisting customers
- Organizing and maintaining your store
- Shipping out-of-town orders

Who is Likely to Succeed

Secondhand store owners are smart shoppers themselves. They love a good deal from a garage sale, and don't hesitate to clip coupons and scour the weekly store flyers. They have a knack for predicting what will be popular enough to sell, and are not intimidated by negotiating with buyers and sellers to get the price they have in mind.

Successful secondhand store owners have retail business sense, which they translate into unique store concepts, inviting displays, and creative promotions. Being good with numbers will help you calculate discounts and commission percentages off the top of your head.

How to Learn It

If you have time available, get a part-time job in a resale environment to see how the buying and selling works first hand. By networking with current secondhand store owners you may be able to find a mentor who will help guide you in your start-up phase. Look for someone who is selling a different product than you so they don't perceive you as competition.

Ask them questions about how they price items, how much they pay in overhead, and what sales have been like in the last few years in that area. You can also learn a lot just by shopping in places that sell the kind of items you intend to. Look in your local Yellow Pages, and then stop by to check out how and what they are selling.

If you already have a small inventory of items you'd like to sell, you can get experience by selling through online markets like eBay. Amazon.com and Yahoo.com also have marketplaces you can tap into for this purpose.

You can also host a garage sale, or take out a small table or booth at a flea market, which gives you the added component of negotiating price and meeting customers face to face. Print business cards and give them to all your customers as a reminder to come visit your bricks-and-mortar store when it is up and running.

If you don't want to come up with your own store concept and learn the ropes on your own, there is an appeal to opening a resale franchise business. Franchises come with ready-made systems, signage, and a customer base familiar with what your store offers.

The *FabJob Guide to Become a Secondhand Store Owner* by Lori Soard has a list of possible secondhand store franchises you can consider, as well a complete guidebook of insider tips and expert advice on opening a secondhand store of any kind.

What it Pays

As with a number of merchant careers where you will be running your own business, what you will earn will be linked to the financial success of your venture. If you are the only owner of your business, your pay can be drawn (i.e. taken out) from your business after paying all expenses. If your business has more than one owner, your salary amount will need to be determined in advance as an ongoing expense, and you will also earn a percentage of the profits as your business grows. Many merchants choose to put most of the profits they earn in the first few years back into growing their business.

Spa Owner

Spas offer health treatments and pampering to clients, who experience soothing, relaxing, enjoyment during their visit. Spa owners are the people who plan, design and operate these retreats.

What They Do

Spa owners are responsible for overseeing all aspects of their spa's operation. They are often onsite at the spa, keeping an eye on staff, monitoring business, balancing the books, and making sure customers are leaving satisfied. You might hire a spa director to run hands-on operations, or in smaller spas you may fill this role yourself.

Spas come in many different shapes and sizes, from mobile spas, to day spas, to resort spas. Some small spas are located as stand-alone businesses, in strip malls, or in shopping centers. Larger spas are often part of resorts, or resorts themselves, boasting exclusive services at exorbitant prices.

Each spa owner develops a unique menu of services to offer their clients. Spas usually offer massages and other physical treatments. Some offer hot stone therapy, reflexology, mud baths, aromatherapy, water therapy, or other therapies like Reiki. Salon/spas offer beauty treatments like haircutting and coloring, manicures, pedicures, waxings, and more. Some spas even have natural hot springs where clientele "take the waters."

As a spa owner you may do some or all of the following:

- Supervise and schedule staff
- Ensure that the spa is perfectly clean at all times
- Be highly visible and address guests' concerns
- Ensure all licenses and certifications are up to date
- Monitor daily and monthly sales figures
- Help develop your own line of spa products
- Set and adjust prices for each spa service
- Come up with creative and timely marketing ideas
- Stay aware of new trends in physical therapy and beauty

Who is Likely to Succeed

Successful spa owners are knowledgeable about the health and beauty industry, and have often worked in it in some capacity, or have visited their share of spas. They appreciate the role spas serve in our society, and will see spa-going as a necessity, not only a rare treat. They have an intuition that tells them how to best meet people's needs.

Many spa owners are calm under fire — they may give off the constant sense that they just had a massage themselves. And it's likely they did: spa owners believe in the mind-body connection and the ability of spa treatments to heal. As fun and funky as owning a spa can be, the best spa owners have a keen business sense as well.

How to Learn It

To begin your education in spa ownership, you should familiarize yourself with the treatments spas offer. Learning about the types of treatments is the first step to finding a niche for your spa.

In addition to excellent spa start-up information, the *FabJob Guide to Become a Spa Owner* by Jeremy McCarthy and Jennifer James has a detailed list of common spa treatments, the equipment and supplies used, the typical cost of the treatment, what staff is qualified to perform it, and what the benefits are to the recipient.

Don't forget to note how much each treatment costs too. You can browse the websites of spas online, or if you can afford it, visit the spas in your area and enjoy your research as you get pampered.

The International Spa Association (**www.experienceispa.com**) offers numerous resources, including an annual conference, a forum for spa owners and professionals to discuss business, and industry statistics you can use to support your business plan when you are looking for investors or funding.

If you have it, it can be very helpful to have prior experience in the industry as a massage therapist, an esthetician, or a manager in a spa. If you would like to get your feet wet in the spa industry before you make a commitment, try using the ISPA job board at their website listed above to look for a position.

If you have limited spa or service experience but want to open your spa as soon as possible, you may want to employ a spa consulting firm. The expertise of professionals who already have proven knowledge and industry success can be very useful, but a bit costly. You can also consider testing the waters by opening a mobile spa service. Mobile spas bring select spa services onsite to the clients' home or place of business, and so do not have as many overhead costs.

Did You Know? Medical spas offer medical cosmetic procedures such as Botox treatment, soft tissue fillers, laser procedures and acupuncture in addition to regular spa treatments, and have been the fastest-growing spa niche in the past few years.

What it Pays

As with a number of merchant careers where you will be running your own business, what you will earn will be linked to the financial success of your venture. If you are the only owner of your business, your pay can be drawn (i.e. taken out) from your business after paying all expenses. If your business has more than one owner, your salary amount will need to be determined in advance as an ongoing expense, and you will also earn a percentage of the profits as your business grows. Many merchants choose to put most of the profits they earn in the first few years back into growing their business.

Wine Merchant

A wine merchant shares his or her love of wine with fellow wine enthusiasts. You will buy or make wine, and then sell it by the bottle to take home, to vendors for resale, or by the glass in your wine shop or wine bar.

What They Do

Wine merchants are purveyors of wine. Some import wine from other countries or source it locally, while others buy the grapes and make it themselves. If they live in a region where the climate permits, they may even grow their own grapes and operate independent vineyards and micro-wineries.

Wine merchants either sell their wine to retailers and wholesalers, or they operate wine shops or wine bars where they sell their wine to the public. If the wine shop is located at a winery or vineyard, the merchant may offer tours and tastings as well as wine by the bottle. Most wine shops purchase wine at wholesale prices from importers or suppliers, and resell it at retail prices.

Wine merchants who operate wine bars will offer glasses and bottles of wine for onsite consumption, along with food, music and occasional entertainment.

As a wine merchant you will do some or all of the following:
- Make your own wine for sale to vendors and the public
- Purchase wine wholesale from suppliers
- Decide what prices are appropriate for the wine
- Merchandize your wine and accessories in a retail shop
- Stay abreast of trends in the wine industry
- Help customers make an informed wine selection
- Hire and train sales or wait staff
- Market your wine or wine shop to the public
- Work with sales reps. or vendors to promote your wine

Who is Likely to Succeed

Those who make their own wine are patient, and don't mind the challenging work of winemaking that results in a perfect glass of red or white. Wine merchants should have a well-developed sense of smell and taste, in order to differentiate between a great and a mediocre wine. You should of course have a love of, or at least an appreciation for wine itself. Maybe you have previous experience serving wine in a bar, or a collection of rare vintages yourself. You like to talk about wine with others, and are a natural host.

How to Learn It

If you want to sell wine you need to become an expert on the topic, so you can tell buyers how each style was made, where it was produced, and what they can expect in the taste. Learn who the major suppliers of wine are, and what types they produce. You can use websites like **www.wine.com** and **www.winespectator.com** to immerse yourself in wine culture. Making wine yourself will also deepen your appreciation for your product.

You should make an effort to sample wines with experts when possible, to learn how to taste like a pro. Larger wine shops often have free classes and tastings hosted by sales reps or other knowledgeable types, and your area may have a wine appreciation association or club you can join. Many cities have annual wine festivals where you can meet with the people who sell all kinds of wine locally and internationally.

If there are wineries in your state or province, see if they offer tours. Some wineries even offer educational courses about how their wines are made. You can also travel to important wine events like the Monterey Wine Festival (**www.montereywine.com**) to hobnob with others in the industry.

While you don't have to have a degree to be a winemaker, many professional winemakers get training in viticulture and enology. If you have never worked at a winery or at a vineyard, it is worth exploring this avenue — some offer short internships or apprenticeships to anyone who loves wine. And if you plan to open a wine shop or wine bar, you'll benefit from restaurant/bar or retail management experience and courses, or you can hire a wine industry consultant to help you set up shop.

What it Pays

As with a number of merchant careers where you will be running your own business, what you will earn will be linked to the financial success of your venture. If you are the only owner of your business, your pay can be drawn (i.e. taken out) from your business after paying all expenses. If your business has more than one owner, your salary amount will need to be determined in advance as an ongoing expense, and you will also earn a percentage of the profits as your business grows. Many merchants choose to put most of the profits they earn in the first few years back into growing their business.

HOW TO BREAK IN

Chances are you already have an idea for your business, but maybe you can't figure out where to start. Let's walk through each step in starting up a business: planning, getting some cash together, choosing a location, getting your paperwork in place, obtaining equipment and supplies, hiring staff, and getting clients.

Here's an overview of how you do it. For more information on each of these points check out the excellent resources in chapter 15.

Your Business Concept

The first thing you'll do is develop your business concept. This is where you brainstorm and then fine-tune your business idea, to make sure it can work the way you imagine it. To do this you'll want to choose a target market for your product or service. Try to narrow it down to a segment of the population defined by categories like age, interests, or where they live.

Also, take a look at your competition — where are they succeeding or failing? You can imitate their successful ideas, and use their shortcomings as inspiration for what your unique selling point will be. At this point in your planning you don't need to nail down specifics, but you should develop a general idea of where your business is headed and why your idea is a great one.

Your Business Plan

Here's where you get into the nitty-gritty of how your business will operate, by preparing a document called a business plan. You will present your business plan to bankers or investors to get start-up funding, and use it as a guideline to make business decisions. Remember to keep your ideas open to change as you prepare your plan.

Your plan will begin with a one- or two-page summary of your ideas. It will then cover how your business will run, what the market is like and how you plan to break into it, who will run your business, and what kind of profit you expect. This information is generally presented under these (or similar) headings:

- Description of Business
- Market Analysis
- Marketing Plan
- Management Plan
- Financial Plan & Statements

Your business plan should not be too hard to put together — it's really just putting all those thoughts floating around in your head onto paper. A business consultant can help you out with the market analysis and financial statements if you find facts and figures overwhelming.

Start-up Costs

Part of preparing your business plan will include estimating your start-up costs. While some businesses (such as auctioneering) can be started with a computer and phone out of a small office, others (such as restaurants or spas) will require a substantial financial investment. So how do you figure out what you need?

Your biggest start-up cost factors will likely be your lease payments or building purchase, your starting inventory, the equipment and supplies you'll need, and salaries.

> **TIP:** Don't forget some of the often-overlooked expenses like printed materials, insurance, licensing, and setting aside three to six months (or more) of money to cover your personal living expenses.

Some industry associations will help you estimate your start-up costs by providing an industry average cost per square foot of selling space. If your costs seem too high, look for creative ways to bring them down, such as leasing equipment, trading services instead of paying cash, and/or sharing a location with another business.

Financing

Once you have an estimate of your start-up costs, you will know if you will have to approach outside sources for money to start your business. Your first source of financing will be yourself: look at cash-ing out retirement funds, investments, your mortgage, and any personal savings you might have.

Other sources of funding include family and friends, investors, and lending institutions. If you plan to approach banks or investors, you will need to prepare a loan proposal, which basically states how much money you need and how long you'll need to pay it back. They will also look at your business plan and your personal debt situation. If you live in the U.S., the SBA (Small Business Association) may also be able to help you out by guaranteeing your loan. In Canada the BDC (Business Development Bank of Canada) fills a similar role.

Your approach for a loan can be a bit more casual with friends and family, but you should still always sign a contract. Also, think carefully before making investors into actual partners, or you may find you don't have the freedom to run the business the way you want.

Location

Depending on the type of business you are planning, you may need a location where you can manufacture and/or warehouse (store) your product, and sell products or services to consumers in a "retail" environment.

Choosing a location can be an especially crucial decision for retail businesses. Consider factors like the look of the building, traffic, parking, and crime rates. Visit the potential location at different times of the day, and talk to other retailers in the area. Make sure that it offers space to run your business now, and also to expand it in the future.

You may have the option of buying an existing location outright — this is the most expensive route upfront, but is an investment that usually pays off. Your purchase might also include existing inventory and equipment, which is a great way to cut costs.

If you can't afford to buy your location, you will need to find a space to lease. If you plan to renovate, talk to your landlord about footing the cost of the improvements, as many owners will pay at least a portion if the work you are doing improves the value of their building.

Legal Matters

Before you open your doors to the public, you have some legal matters to sort out. You will want to choose a unique name for your business, and register it with your state or provincial government.

You will need to choose and register a legal structure that suits your business, be it sole proprietorship, partnership, corporation, or limited liability company.

You will also need a business license from your city or appropriate level of government, and other licenses or registration that may be needed in your industry, such as food service, health inspection, liquor, etc. Once you have decided on a type of business, you can refer to the full-length FabJob career guide for specific licenses for that type of business.

For example, if you plan to sell products or services you may need a license to collect sales tax. If you plan to purchase items wholesale and resell them at a higher price, you will need a resale number (and sales tax license). If your business is incorporated or will have employees, you will need to obtain an EIN (Employer Identification Number) from the IRS, or a Business Number (BN) from the Canada Revenue Agency.

Running a business without adequate insurance is always a bad idea. Look into coverage for things like liability and property insurance, among others. You will also want to speak to an accountant about whether your taxes should be paid on your personal filing, or separately as your business.

Equipment, Supplies, and Inventory

If you are running a retailing business that sells a product, you will usually need to have a certain inventory of it on hand before you start up. Base your starting inventory on the financial projections in your business plan, and have enough on hand to cover you until just after your next planned order. Industry associations can provide you with inventory estimates that are common in your chosen type of business.

Monitoring your inventory is extremely important, so make sure you set up a system where inventory can be tracked by computer (or by hand) as it is bought or sold. Evaluate your inventory frequently, and look for innovative ways to keep products or services selling and maximize your profit. Always be aware of the margin you make on each and every item or service you sell.

Make a checklist of the equipment and supplies you will need to run your business. Consider where you will store inventory, where you will display your product to customers, and what you need to provide any services; as well as what is necessary to process payments, create promotional materials, and communicate with clients.

TIP: You can consider purchasing some used equipment, but bear in mind that certain types of equipment are better purchased new.

In most retail businesses the suppliers are eager for business and will contact you. You will need to get price sheets and determine who is going to supply what you need at your minimum quality for the best cost. You will likely use different suppliers for different types of items, and will need to include accessory supplies (things you need but can't be sold) like bathroom tissue and printer paper. Make sure you get arrangements for delivery and payment in writing.

Hiring Staff

If you are selling a service or product to the public, there is a good chance you will hire staff to assist you. If you don't want to be hands-on in all operations, your first hire will probably be a manager, who will run your business and report directly to you. From there you will hire the rest of the people you need to run your business at the pace you anticipate. You will need to fill out and file a number of IRS or Canada Revenue Agency forms for each employee, and make some financial contributions to appropriate agencies on their behalf.

You can figure out what to pay your employees by using online salary resources like **salary.com**. Because paying employees is expensive, look for ways for your staff to multi-task, and prepare a schedule that makes effective use of their time. In many types of businesses turnover is common, so be ready to continue the hiring process as long as your business will run.

Operations and Budgeting

A successful business needs operational procedures in place that are effective and consistent. Develop systems for regular maintenance of equipment and facilities, reward systems for employees, and service systems for doing business with clients. You should put these policies together in a series of manuals so that new staff can become familiar with them, and update them frequently.

If you are manufacturing a product yourself, you will need to arrange for product design and packaging, warehousing the product, importing supplies and possibly exporting your product, quality control, and streamlining your manufacturing process. You'll also need to be prepared for government inspections on a regular basis. A good manager (or several departmental managers) familiar with the industry and your product will be invaluable to you in a manufacturing environment.

To run a profitable business, you need to stay on top of the money coming in and going out. Review financial reports often so that you can analyze where you are at and what needs to change. Set fees for your product or service that not only cover your overhead expenses, but also allow you to make a decent profit. Be ready to change fees or prices when necessary, or look for ways to cut expenses to offset the difference. You'll also need to decide how much to pay yourself.

Retail sales businesses rely on daily sales reports and monthly or annual financial statements and sales projections to judge if they are on track, or if they are falling behind. Many retail industries, such as the restaurant business, have suggested profit percentages that may help guide you in setting your prices.

Finding Clients/Customers

Marketing your business begins even before you start up, and you should plan to reinvest a percentage of your profits back into marketing. Your business marketing plan will likely require "tools" such as signs and displays, business cards, brochures, and a website.

Traditional marketing routes you can consider for your business include advertising, mail-outs, and distribution of your brochures. Remember that your marketing should be geared towards who you believe to be your target market.

In some types of businesses the best marketing technique is picking up the phone (or having a sales representative do this) and arranging for a meeting with potential clients. Don't overlook the effectiveness of free publicity, in the form of press releases you send to media, seminars and other events you put on, and charitable donations.

Word-of-mouth (as detailed in Chapter 13) can also bring you a fair amount of business, especially if you offer an incentive such as a discount or small payment for each referral. Chapter 14, *Create Your Dream Job*, has some more marketing ideas for small business owners.

Once your marketing plan is in place, get ready to greet your clients and start selling your way to financial success!

8

Fab Relaters

Careers Working with People (and Animals)

Are you a "people person"? If your answer is a definite "yes!" this chapter is for you. Touching people's lives in a meaningful way is one of the greatest rewards a career can offer. If helping others just "feels good" to you, imagine being able to feel that way every day.

Maybe you already find ways to volunteer or get involved in making your community a better place to live, but what if you could make that your career, instead of squeezing it in during your spare time? There are a number of dream careers that will allow you to earn a living making people's life experiences richer, less complicated, or healthier; their families closer and happier, and their careers more fulfilling and successful. And if you're an animal lover, you can have a career making life better for animals as well as their owners.

This chapter includes information on 19 career options for individuals who like to be in service to and work with other people (or their animals). Following is a complete list of careers covered in this chapter, followed by descriptions of each.

- Animal Trainer
- Butler/Household Manager
- Clergy Person
- Concierge

- Cruise Ship Worker
- Daycare Owner
- Doula (Childbirth Assistant)
- Flight Attendant
- Funeral Director
- Life Coach
- Massage Therapist
- Personal Assistant
- Personal Shopper
- Personal Trainer
- Real Estate Agent
- Rescue Worker (Firefighter / Paramedic / Police Officer)
- Sports Instructor (Golf / Martial Arts / Ski etc.)
- Travel Consultant
- Veterinary Assistant
- Yoga/Pilates Instructor

THE CAREERS

Animal Trainer

If you feel like you have an almost psychic connection with your pet, you may have a special gift for working with animals. Animal trainers get to appreciate the beauty and unconditional love of animals every day while teaching them to respond to commands.

What They Do

Animal trainers are the kind, patient people who work with dogs, horses, dolphins, and other animals in order to teach them to perform certain tasks or behave in a particular way. You'll use positive reinforcement, such as treats and attention, to let animals know when they have done what you wanted correctly.

Animals can be trained to assist the disabled, protect or rescue people in danger, hunt down criminals, or simply show people how intelligent they are. Some animals (like dogs) are trained in obedience so their owners can be assured of their good behavior. And all kinds of animals can be trained to perform in movies and TV shows.

Animal trainers spend a lot of time with their animals, in order to bond with them and build trust. You will repeat the same procedure with the animal over and over until the response is timed just right. Some are actually "people trainers" too, since they teach owners how to get the desired response out of their animal companions.

A typical day for you as an animal trainer may include:

- Observing individual animals to learn more about their behavior
- Touching, talking to, and bonding with animals
- Using a variety of techniques to train and reward animals
- Traveling with trained animals to where their services are needed
- Playing with and stimulating animals
- Feeding, exercising and grooming animals
- Demonstrating your animal's abilities
- Teaching the public more about animals and their behavior

Who Is Likely to Succeed

Any animal trainer will come to this career with a love of animals in general, and maybe a special interest in a certain type or breed. You should be reasonably fit so you can physically interact with your animal. You are patient and don't mind repetitive tasks.

Animal trainers have a curiosity about animal behavior that propels them to question and learn. They are resourceful, are keen observers, and know that there is more than one way to motivate an animal — you will learn what works with each one. You are calm, gentle, and have a natural rapport with animals of every kind.

How to Learn It

To start, you should spend time observing and learning about animals. You can take a notebook and spend a few afternoons at the zoo, or keep a journal about your pet's behavior. Look at not just "what" they do, but examine the "why" behind it. Compare your observations with established information from books and websites on animal behavior.

Animal shelters, vet clinics, pet shops and zoos are often looking for volunteer assistants. You can also offer to walk, play with, and of course train other people's pets to get experience relating to different animal personalities. Assisting an animal trainer will help you learn techniques that work (and also those that don't). Offer to take some of the grooming and feeding tasks off their hands in exchange for watching them work.

A handful of North American universities and colleges as well as some independent institutions offer Animal Behavior programs that are a natural lead-in to this kind of work. Part of your training may involve an internship where you work with animals hands-on, or you can arrange this opportunity on your own with a zoo, marine center or other facility.

Certification is not mandatory, but several organizations offer training programs and certification for prospective animal trainers. If you want to work with marine animals, swimming and SCUBA training are also important so you can move comfortably in their environment.

What It Pays

Three out of five animal trainers are self-employed, which means you will set your own hourly or monthly rate (plus boarding fees) to train animals for others. Remember that you'll charge for each animal you train, even if training is provided in a group setting. You may also charge a fee for your trained animals to participate in TV shows or movies, which will be on a flat fee or daily basis.

According to the Bureau of Labor Statistics, median hourly earnings of animal trainers are $10.60, and the top 10 percent earned more than $20 an hour. The most sought-after animal trainers in the business earn more than $100 an hour for their specialized talents.

Butler/Household Manager

A butler or household manager is a trusted person employed by a wealthy individual or family to look after their household needs.

What They Do

A butler or household manager's job is to ensure that their employer's or client's everyday needs within the home are met. Since the employer is busy, they require a butler to free up their time for more pressing tasks. Some high-end hotels hire staff butlers to serve their guests as well.

Butlers are often on call much of the day and night. They may work in their employer's primary or secondary home, or even travel with them around the world. If there are other household employees on staff, the butler is usually their supervisor.

As a butler or household manager, your tasks may include some or all of the following:

- Shopping for groceries, gifts and other items
- Preparing and serving meals and snacks
- Laundering, maintaining, and repairing clothing
- Making travel arrangements
- Answering phones and correspondence
- Greeting and accommodating guests
- Organizing social events
- Supervising contractors and other staff for household maintenance and upkeep
- Driving household members to school and appointments
- Light housekeeping

Who is Likely to Succeed

A successful butler or household manager is a caring person who is genuinely devoted to their employer's well-being. Being cheerful, physically fit, and a good cook are also important. Beyond being a polite, caring personal assistant, they are organized, efficient and extremely detail-oriented. They must also be discreet and trustworthy in order to guard their employer's personal information.

If your particular job requires very long hours or travel, then you probably won't have your own family or home to manage. In some cases you will need to be willing to live in your employer's house (or in facilities meant for your accommodation) and available at a moment's notice, around the clock. Therefore you should be flexible, spontaneous, and quick to react, even at odd hours.

How to Learn the Job

The most direct path to learning how to be a butler or household manager is to attend one of several schools devoted to the profession such as Starkey International in Denver, Colorado (**www.starkey intl.com**). These courses will cost you several thousand dollars, so get value for your money and look for one that can help you with an internship or job placement. There is a list of butler schools available online at **www.modernbutlers.com/schools.html**.

You can learn butler skills by taking a job (paying or non-paying) in the hotel and restaurant industry. There you'll learn from maitre d's and hotel managers about the proper ways to serve food and attend to wealthy clients. Many hotels now offer butler services, and as a hotel employee you may be able to transition into this job, or convince an employer to create the position for you.

You can also offer your help as an apprentice for an event planner, caterer or personal chef — all of these professions encompass parts of what you'll need to know. You may attend cooking classes or culinary school to improve your kitchen skills, and courses in wine and beverage service so that you'll be able to offer knowledgeable assistance in these areas.

And of course you'll want to learn all you can about business and social etiquette, as your clients will rely on you to follow the rules of good social grace. Read magazines and other publications that appeal to the wealthy to get a sense of how they live, and network with the wealthy wherever possible — attend art auctions, charity functions, or wherever the wealthy congregate in your community. If you network successfully, you may even land a job this way.

Many butler schools use the book *Butlers and Household Managers: 21st Century Professionals* by Steven M. Ferry as a textbook for their courses. This excellent and comprehensive book on the art of household management is available through **www.FabJob.com**.

Fab Fact: Paul Hogan, the humble and witty butler on Fox's reality TV program *Joe Millionaire*, was an Australian diplomat and bed and breakfast owner before becoming a butler. As a condition of Paul's first butler position he was required to learn how to cook, so he took six months of culinary classes and followed that with three months of studying wine to round out his butler skills. He is now hosting the reality TV program *Groomed*, which puts soon-to-be-married men and others anticipating a big event through "gentleman's boot camp."

What It Pays

Butlers earn a salary based on their experience, how much training they've had, what their range of duties includes, and whether or not they live-in (are accommodated in their employer's home) or live-out (have their own household).

Experienced butlers with more than five years' experience earn between $50,000 and $150,000 per year, though the higher amount is exceptional. An entry-level butler can expect about $20,000 per year, however this figure may represent part-time wages of approximately $10 to $15 an hour to start.

Clergy Person

A clergy person is a person of influence in society. You will draw upon your spiritual faith to lead others with the same beliefs, and help them find ways to incorporate religious traditions into their lives.

What They Do

Clergy members act as spiritual leaders for their local community. Rabbis, priests, chaplains, preachers, and deacons are all clergy members. As a clergy member, you will be a respected community leader. You will play an important role in many people's lives, and be able to share your faith with others on a daily basis.

Clergy people may work independently, or may work in a house of worship or area assigned to them by a larger religious organization. They work with individuals and small groups, and speak in front of large groups gathered to worship. They have scheduled services every week, and are also on-call for individuals in need.

Clergy members are usually committed for life to the practice of their faith. They are paid either by donations from their congregation, by individuals for each service performed, or paid a salary by their church. As a clergy person, your tasks may include some or all of the following:

- Preparing for services and religious ceremonies
- Officiating at weddings, funerals, and other services
- One-on-one religious counseling
- Organizing events for the religious community
- Raising funds for projects related to the house of worship or community
- Visiting and comforting ill or bereaved congregation members
- Serving on committees for the community and social service organizations
- Meeting with other religious leaders
- Continuing to learn more about and practicing the faith

Who is Likely to Succeed

Clergy people are excellent communicators, listeners and counselors. As a compassionate, caring individual, you may already possess a desire to share your beliefs, and are comfortable in front of a large audience as a compelling, interesting speaker. You are confident, motivated, empathetic, and spiritually inclined.

Some religions have restrictions on who may become a clergy person, and may exclude individuals based on marital status, gender, sexual orientation, or level of education. Check with a leader in your faith to see what restrictions may apply.

How to Learn the Job

As an aspiring clergy member, you probably already hold strong beliefs related to a particular faith. You should learn all you can about your chosen faith, both by attending services and by reading your faith's holy books and interpreting their teachings.

Speak with established clergy members in your community, and discuss your desires to follow this path. You may apprentice as a junior member of the clergy, volunteer to help with services and activities of the religious organization, or, if there is one for your faith, attend the faith's training institutions or training programs.

Learn all you can about your specific religious community's history, concerns and belief structure. If your religion requires you to hold an undergraduate degree, you can improve your chances for success as a clergy member by doing that degree in theology, social work, philosophy or psychology.

You can learn some of the practical skills involved by practicing them in your daily life. Join a public-speaking group like Toastmasters to improve your ability to speak in front of crowds. Practice listening to others and communicating with them about their hopes, fears and concerns. Volunteer in your community as a lay counselor.

You can also work as a congregation secretary or records keeper (positions that may or may not be paid). You can take jobs in the related fields of social work and outreach, or volunteer with your local community in its homeless shelters, food banks and other social support systems. You can also travel to other countries as a volunteer for your chosen faith's missionary and human services work.

What It Pays

While some clergy members perform their duties unpaid, others are paid by their congregations, either by an annual salary or a monthly stipend. Salaries will depend on the size and relative wealth of the congregation. The median clergy person's annual salary in the United States is about $50,000, while an entry-level salary is about $17 per hour. In lieu of or in addition to pay, clergy may be compensated with free housing and a food allowance.

Concierge

A concierge is usually the friendly face that greets and assists the guests and residents of hotels, apartments, and offices. However, more and more independent concierge businesses are popping up across North America. These creative problem-solvers enjoy making sure everyone enjoys their day or stay to the fullest.

What They Do

A concierge is normally employed by a hotel, residents' association, or office building's management to meet various onsite needs of the guests, residents or employees. They typically work from an office or kiosk in the lobby of the building where they work. Hotel concierge shifts are usually around the clock, while apartments, office buildings, and independent concierge businesses may not need 24-hour service.

As a concierge, you'll enjoy meeting many different people and using your creativity, connections and inside knowledge to help them. Your help is often rewarded with tips or other gratuities.

As various requests come in from people, the concierge meets these requests promptly and efficiently. Requests will vary, and might include obtaining reservations at popular restaurants, procuring tickets to sold-out theater shows, or arranging transportation. Additional tasks may include any or all of the following:

- Greeting guests, residents or employees
- Sorting and delivering mail or messages
- Sending packages by mail and courier
- Arranging for transportation
- Booking appointments
- Opening building or car doors
- Providing umbrellas or other weather-appropriate gear
- Arranging for dry-cleaning services
- Offering advice on local entertainment, services or tours
- Keeping the lobby or entranceway tidy

Who is Likely to Succeed

The best person for a concierge career is someone who knows a little bit about everything. Maybe people already call you for opinions and advice, which you give in a non-judgmental way. You are observant, with a good memory for names and faces. You instinctively can tune into people's personalities and sense whether they need a funny story or sympathetic smile, or would prefer the silent treatment some days.

A successful concierge will be resourceful, trustworthy, organized, attentive, and discreet. They should be excellent communicators, and willing to go "above and beyond" in order to help their clients. They are well connected in their community.

How to Learn the Job

An entry-level or part-time job in the service industry such as a bus person, bellhop, baggage handler or messenger will teach you many of the skills needed as a concierge. Experience in related fields, such as restaurant or other service industry work, and even work as a tour guide can all help you hone your concierge skills.

Building a good knowledge of the businesses, entertainment and services available in the surrounding community is also important, so previous experience as a salesperson, a delivery person or box-office attendant will also help. Learn about the preferred restaurants, entertainment options and services in your area by reading local entertainment weeklies, which often profile the latest and greatest offerings.

You can contact special events coordinators or wedding planners in your area and offer your services as a helper or procurer of information or services. You can also arrange to meet with established concierges and ask them questions, or spend time watching them at work.

Working as a personal assistant will also give you in-the-field training, and may lead to connections who may be able to hire or recommend you. Develop your network of social and professional contacts, and your ability to schmooze with people, by attending business mixers and chamber of commerce events in your area.

In the U.S., you can also contact the National Concierge Association (**www.nationalconciergeassociation.com**) to learn about the nuances of the profession and keep up with trends in the industry.

What It Pays

The median salary for a concierge in the United States is approximately $25,000. However, concierges also receive tips based on client satisfaction and the level of difficulty of the tasks performed. Hourly wages for an entry-level concierge are about $9 per hour. Some concierges also receive commissions from tour operators, service providers and others to whom they refer clients. An independent concierge can charge between $20 to $50 per hour or more, depending on the services to be performed.

Cruise Ship Worker

Cruise ship workers are the hundreds of individuals who staff the floating resorts that travel around the world. They are responsible for feeding, entertaining and ensuring the safety of guests aboard the ship. So what's your special talent, and how will you use it at sea?

What They Do

As a cruise ship worker, you will manage or work at some aspect of life about a cruise ship, such as accommodations, shore excursions, food and beverages, entertainment, activities, or staff management. You will live aboard the ship for free for the duration of the cruise, while you meet the needs of the guests or keep the ship running smoothly.

Cruise ship workers can be hired on contract by small ships, luxury vessels, or private yachts, or they may be employed by an agency who freelances their services to a number of cruise lines. As many as 1,000 people may be needed to staff a single ship.

As a cruise ship worker, you may spend your days:
- Organizing onboard events and activities for guests
- Preparing or serving food and drinks
- Speaking on topics of interest
- Ensuring the satisfaction of guests
- Staffing the gift shop or casino
- Managing the dining facilities
- Taking tickets and handling accounts
- Singing, acting, dancing or performing in shows
- Taking guests on shore for excursions
- Operating the vessel
- Cleaning and maintaining the guest facilities
- Caring for and entertaining young guests
- Teaching fitness or sports classes

Who is Likely to Succeed

Cruise ship workers are spontaneous and love to travel. They have the personal flexibility to be away from home for weeks or months at a time. They are courteous and understand that the satisfaction of the guest is number-one. You are outgoing, enjoy socializing, and hopefully don't get seasick! Cruise ship workers with special talents or skill can move up from entry-level positions to those with more clout and more cash.

How to Learn the Job

For nearly all entry-level positions, no prior cruise ship experience is necessary. All you need is a passport, a physical exam, a background free of drugs and crime, and an age of 21 or greater.

If you are completely unfamiliar with cruising, there are a number of websites and publications that offer general information about this vacation option. Check out Cruise Lines International Association (**www.cruising.org**), which has general information about a number of popular cruise lines. *Porthole Cruise Magazine* (**www.porthole.com**) and *Cruise Travel Magazine* (**www.cruisetravelmag.com**) are both popular with cruise enthusiasts, and cost only $20 US per year for a subscription.

There are a number of skills that can help you land a cruise ship job. Customer-service experience is essential, and the more high-end your clientele, the better. If you don't have this experience, look for volunteer or part-time opportunities where you serve, entertain, or guide — local theme parks or tourist attractions are a logical crossover to cruising. You should also do a personal inventory of talent or experience you have that may translate into cruising.

Cruise ship guests come from all over the world, so speaking a second language is a definite plus. You don't need to be fluent, but knowing basic phrases in popular languages like Spanish and French may help you out in a communication pinch. You should also be up-to-date with first aid/CPR training.

The *FabJob Guide to Get a Job on a Cruise Ship* by Julie Botteri is an excellent resource to prepare you for a career in cruising. It has detailed descriptions of the positions available on a cruise ship, direct links to employers who are hiring, and tips for preparing an application package and landing the cruise job of your dreams.

What It Pays

Your income will depend on the cruise line you work for, what position you were hired into, and your experience. Typical salaries start at $1,500 to $2,500 a month. Once you have built experience, salaries can range up to $8,000 a month for top positions requiring highly qualified and experienced individuals. Some employers offer additional benefits like 401K plans, stock options, and profit sharing.

Daycare Owner

Daycare owners get to see the results of their caring and creative efforts every day. They are rewarded by the joy of children's laughter, and by watching them grow into independent, unique individuals.

What They Do

Daycare owners operate child care facilities where parents can bring their children to be looked after while they go to work, run errands, or exercise. The children cared for tend to be school age or younger, and are usually cared for during the day, although there are some exceptions. Daycares can specialize in caring for children with special needs, particular age groups, or offer a particular educational philosophy.

Daycare owners can run their business either from their home or another location. Most daycare owners interact with the children on a daily basis, although owners of very large daycares may strictly run the business aspects, and leave the child-minding to employees. Owners are paid, typically each week or month, by the parents whose children are cared for.

As a daycare center owner, your tasks may include some or all of the following:

- Supervising children's activities and play
- Helping children with toileting and hygiene
- Organizing weekly activity schedules
- Preparing and serving meals and snacks
- Soothing children's feelings
- Cleaning and sanitizing the daycare area
- Hiring, scheduling and paying caregivers
- Keeping track of accounts and business records

Who is Likely to Succeed

A successful daycare center owner is compassionate, caring and genuinely enjoys spending time with children. Perhaps you're a parent or an experienced babysitter, or come from a large family.

Daycare owners should be able to communicate clearly, and be willing to work at a job that requires a moderate amount of physical activity. A sense of enthusiasm and play is important, as is the ability to remain calm under busy, noisy conditions. Those with a criminal record may not be eligible for this career.

How to Learn the Job

You can develop your child-minding skills by offering to look after the children of friends and family members, or by volunteering at a local day home or community center. If they are happy with your services, ask for a letter of recommendation you can show to clients when you are ready to open your daycare.

You can learn more about different approaches to child-rearing and early education in some of the many books on parenting, and magazines such as *Parents* (**www.parents.com**) and *Today's Parent* (**www.**

todaysparent.com). Study up on issues such as growth and development, socialization and play, and types of discipline. Parents who are considering your child care services may want to see your philosophies on these issues in writing.

You can go online or to the library to find out plenty of ideas for age-appropriate activities and games. You should also research nutritional requirements for each age group, and acquire first aid/CPR skills for children.

Learn to communicate better with children by volunteering at a public library's story hour, or at a local elementary school. Some places of worship offer child-minding during services where you may be able to supervise or participate in the child care. If you want to get experience working in a licensed daycare, your state or province may require you to obtain a certain level of training and accreditation first.

The *FabJob Guide to Become a Daycare Owner* by Alisa Gordaneer has the contact information you'll need for local licensing authorities, as well as information on setting your fees and policies, instructions for setting up a fun and safe daycare space, a list of equipment and supplies, and much more.

What It Pays

Your pay will be determined by the number of children you care for and the rates you set. Anywhere from $25 to $50 a day per child is typical, as is a part-time hourly rate between $10 and $20 an hour. If you looked after four children, for example, that would be $800 per week, or as much as $41,600 per year — but don't forget you'll need to cover expenses.

Doula

Doulas support and guide pregnant women up to and during the childbirth experience, and help them to adjust to their role as a new mother in the days or weeks following the birth.

What They Do

Doulas are hired by hospitals, birthing centers, or pregnant women to assist new mothers before, during and after childbirth. Doulas understand the physical, mental, and emotional process of labor and delivery, and offer guidance and emotional support during this life transition.

Doulas may be trained nurses or alternative health practitioners, or simply caring people who desire to help women give birth. They do not replace the role of a husband or life partner, but complete the support team as a birthing expert. Doulas do not deliver babies or do any medical procedures, so they work in tandem with a midwife or delivery doctor.

Birth doulas focus mainly on the labor and delivery process, while postpartum doulas help out after a baby is born. This is a flexible job, as you can take on as many clients as you feel comfortable with. However, you must be available on call for each client when their labor is approaching.

As a doula, you may spend your days:

- Assisting mothers-to-be in preparing their birth plans
- Advising mothers-to-be about various childbirth options
- Assisting with pain control and breathing during labor
- Reminding midwives or doctors of the mother's birth plan
- Offering support and assistance with breastfeeding
- Preparing meals for the new mom and family
- Helping with light housekeeping, errands and childcare in the post-partum period

Who is Likely to Succeed

A successful doula is compassionate, a good listener, and able to focus their entire attention on the needs of another person for long periods of time. You are calm, organized, and are comfortable touching and holding people to give them comfort — you are always the first to offer a hug to an upset friend!

You believe in a mind-body connection, and may have an interest in alternative health care practices, such as Reiki or massage. And of course you should love babies, so your excitement with the 500th birth you attend is as apparent as with your first. Although the majority of doulas are women, some men choose this profession as well.

How to Learn the Job

You can study the physiology of labor by reading about it in books about childbirth, and watching videos of women giving birth. You can learn about massage, aromatherapy, Reiki and other means of support in books or training courses. *The FabJob Guide to Become a Doula* by Rachel Gurevich contains a wealth of information about learning doula work and getting hired, and is a well-respected resource in the doula community.

Formal doula training is a direct route to acquiring the skills to become a birth assistant. It also offers professional legitimacy, which may convince clients to choose your services over those of others. Doulas of North America (**www.dona.org**) is one of the major doula organizations, and offers training and certification.

Once you feel ready, you can set up an apprenticeship by offering to help a local midwife or doula. Meet with her (or him) to discuss your goals, and volunteer to assist for free at a number of births. Observe their techniques and degree of success, and where possible, assist hands-on.

You can offer your free assistance to any woman who is comfortable letting you attend her child's birth. Help family members and friends, or get to know the staff at local healthcare clinics and other social service agencies (like women's centers and community centers) that help pregnant women. Explain that you're working towards the goal of becoming a certified doula, and offer to help for free or on a sliding scale. As you gain more experience (at least 10 births), you can start charging for your services.

What It Pays

Most doulas charge a flat rate of anywhere from $100 to $1,000 per birth, depending on if they are offering pre-birth and postpartum services as well. For postpartum help, anywhere from $15 to $30 per hour is typical. Some doulas offer their services for free or on a "pay what you can" basis when they are working with women in crisis.

Flight Attendant

A flight attendant is a global traveler with a fun and flexible career. They meet the needs of airline passengers and ensure they are safe and comfortable as they fly from city to city, or around the world.

What They Do

Flight attendants work for an airline to provide safety and service for passengers on commercial flights. They work in aircraft traveling between cities serviced by the airline. Flight attendants may also be hired to work on private or corporate aircraft, on a permanent or on-call basis.

Typically, flight attendants work 12- to 14-hour shifts, which begin and end around the clock, but work a maximum of 135 to 140 hours per month, which leaves plenty of time off. You should be physically fit, energetic and able to spend long hours standing, as much of this job is done on your feet.

Your tasks as a flight attendant may include some or all of the following:

- Meeting with pilots and crew before each flight
- Ensuring supplies and equipment are ready for takeoff
- Greeting passengers and helping them find their seats
- Assisting passengers with stowing luggage and coats
- Explaining emergency procedures
- Serving meals and beverages
- Reassuring nervous passengers
- Directing passengers to exits in an emergency

Who is Likely to Succeed

A willingness to help, a sense of self-confidence and a cheerful nature are all qualities of a successful flight attendant. Most airlines require flight attendants to be a minimum height of 5'2" to allow them to reach overhead bins, and in good health with good eyesight (glasses or contacts are permitted). A good knowledge of geography and culture, plus at least one foreign language, will be useful if you are hoping to be employed on international flights. Many flight attendants in Canada speak both English and French.

How to Learn the Job

Once you're hired by an airline you will be trained to do the specific tasks needed for this job. But you can learn many of the skills involved before you even apply. To develop your customer service skills, you can work in retail, hotel and restaurant, or other service-industry jobs. In particular, working in restaurants will help you with the foodservice skills you'll need.

Working as a tour leader or tour guide will give you experience working with groups of people, and will help you with leadership skills. You can also volunteer to lead scout troops, classroom tours and other groups through cultural or historical sites.

You'll also need first aid skills as a flight attendant. You can learn these by taking a course offered through community organizations or your local Red Cross office.

Learn all you can about airport procedures, too, by going on field trips to airports or even on a few flights yourself. Don't forget to ask the flight attendants how they got started. You can also visit the website of the Federal Aviation Administration at **www.faa.gov**. Learn the codes for each airport (e.g. LGA for New York's La Guardia) and set your watch to the 24-hour time clock to get used to using it.

It's not possible to volunteer as a flight attendant, but you can volunteer or take part-time jobs in other related service industries in order to gain experience. You can also take a ground crew job at your nearest airport — working as a ticket agent or ramp agent are entry-level jobs that can get you in with airline unions.

What It Pays

Flight attendants are paid per "trip-hour" with entry-level attendants receiving about $20 per trip-hour. Benefits include health insurance, allowances for hotel rooms and meals on layovers, allowances for uniform maintenance, and free flights for flight attendants and sometimes their families and/or friends on the employing airline (though some fees or taxes may still apply).

According to the Bureau of Labor Statistics, the median annual income of flight attendants in the United States is $43,440. It can range as low as $15,550 for entry-level work at a small airline, and as high as $50,000 to $95,000 for an attendant with more than five years' experience.

Funeral Director

A funeral director helps people plan appropriate end-of-life arrangements and ceremonies for themselves and to mark the passing of loved ones.

What They Do

Funeral directors coordinate final arrangements for someone who has died, from paperwork to embalming to interment. They may be employed by a funeral home, or they may own their own business. A funeral director meets with individuals planning their own final arrangements, or with the family of someone who has died.

A funeral director will help the individual or family select a casket, plan a ceremony to celebrate the life, and decide how to prepare the body for final rest. They will also oversee events the day of the funeral. Not all funeral directors will train to embalm bodies — they can hire a mortician to do this work if they prefer.

As a funeral director, your tasks may include some or all of the following:

- Meeting with clients to plan funerals
- Coordinating with clergy or other officiants
- Writing obituaries and submitting them for publication
- Ordering caskets and funeral supplies
- Transporting the deceased
- Embalming and restoring bodies

- Arranging for cremation or burial
- Helping the bereaved with legal paperwork
- Greeting funeral attendees
- Overseeing funerals and wakes

While helping the bereaved or soon-to-die can be a challenging job, it is satisfying to those who do it because they are providing an essential and important service to their community.

Who is Likely to Succeed

A funeral director has real compassion and sympathy for those suffering a loss, but can remain distanced enough to conduct business in a professional manner. They are not squeamish, and accept death as a component of every life.

You should be tactful, discreet and calm, even in emotionally volatile situations, and an effective negotiator who can settle family disputes. Funeral directors are talented multi-taskers who can see the big picture, as well as handle the small details that are so important to the bereaved.

How to Learn the Job

Customer service is an essential part of this job, so any work that puts you in a position of looking after clients' needs — from retail to hairstyling to restaurant work — will help you gain skills needed in this industry.

Your ability to organize events, particularly at short notice, will help you as well. Volunteer to organize events for community, church or business organizations.

Learn about funeral rites in different cultures and in different religions. Libraries offer numerous books on this topic, or go online to research in depth. The *FabJob Guide to Become a Funeral Director* by Kelly Boyer Sagert offers information and career advice from successful funeral directors.

Taking courses or reading books about biology and human bodies will help you gain an understanding of what will be involved in embalming. And of course, you can also rent the DVD of the former television series *Six Feet Under* for a dramatized demonstration of what's involved.

Funeral directing is a licensed profession. The requirements for licensing vary from region to region, but the most common requirements are a high school diploma, having reached the age of 21, and passing a standardized exam. In some cases formal training from an accredited school is also required. There is a list of state associations to contact for more information at the National Funeral Directors Association website: **www.nfda.org**. In Canada you can contact the Funeral Service Association of Canada: **www.fsac.ca**.

Contact a funeral home in your area and offer your services as a volunteer, or contact an established funeral director to find out if they will take you on as an apprentice before or while you become licensed. Offer your informal services as a "funeral assistant," doing things like accompanying bereaved family members to and from the funeral home, helping them choose flowers and other services.

What It Pays

According to the Bureau of Labor Statistics, the median annual income for funeral directors is $45,960, but salaries can vary depending on experience. Entry-level is closer to $25,000, while experienced directors with more than five years' experience, living in larger cities and holding at least bachelors' degrees, can earn between $50,000 and $85,000. If you own your own funeral home, your income is determined by the scope and success of your business.

Life Coach

A life coach is someone who offers counseling to people who want to achieve a more fulfilling life, a more rewarding career, or more effective interaction with others.

What They Do

A life coach helps clients determine and achieve a variety of goals. They use coaching techniques to persuade, inspire and motivate people to change their lives for the better. Unlike therapy, which addresses what is wrong with the individual, life coaching is offered to generally well-adjusted individuals who would like to be more successful in one or several areas of their lives.

Coaching can be done face-to-face, by phone, in online sessions, or by email. Life coaches might specialize in a certain area of coaching, such as corporate/career coaching, relationship coaching, or spiritual coaching. Coaches may be hired by individuals or the companies they work for.

A coach will help clients close the gap between where they are (literally or figuratively), and where they want to be. They ask their clients questions in order to lead to the key issues that are presenting a challenge. Once they have identified work to be done, they help clients set goals that will bring them closer to personal satisfaction.

A life coach's day may include:
- Meeting with new clients to assess needs
- Preparing a proposal of services
- Analyzing client responses to written questions
- Conducting coaching sessions of 30 to 60 minutes
- Studying the latest coaching techniques
- Marketing coaching services to future clients
- Keeping track of accounting and billing
- Writing articles and books about life coaching

Who is Likely to Succeed

Life coaches are great at interacting with people. Many cross over to coaching from other "helping" careers, such as human resources or personal training. Even those who have no formal experience working with people but are simply social creatures who love to help others can become successful life coaches.

Coaches are positive, determined individuals who can motivate and inspire others to be the best they can and find the courage to take their lives in new directions. They are skilled listeners, and have a knack for coaxing honest answers out of people. They are critical thinkers who can analyze details and put them together to see the big picture.

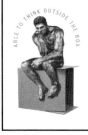

Did You Know? Although Anthony (Tony) Robbins is known for being a best-selling self-help author and motivational speaker, his work has also included coaching former world leaders such as Mikhail Gorbachev, Princess Diana, and several U.S. presidents, along with business people and sports professionals.

How to Learn It

In order to effectively coach others in your area of expertise, you need to become familiar with the well-known writers and speakers on your topic. Learn a variety of approaches to coaching, self-help and motivation to see which ones are the best fit with your personal style and beliefs. You should take note of exercises you come across that may be of help to your future clients, as well as develop a list of resources (books and websites) you will recommend.

There are a number of organizations and schools dedicated to training new coaches in this relatively young profession. The International Coach Federation accredits reputable coach training programs, and maintains a list of them at their website: **www.coach federation.org**.

The International Coach Federation and other coaching organizations hold annual conferences with various presenters, which range in price from a few hundred to a few thousand dollars. Most events are two to four days in duration, and are divided into seminars on some aspect of coaching. You can search for conferences put on by coaching organizations online or in trade magazines.

A good way to learn what a life coach does, as well as see coaching styles at work, is to be coached yourself. You can pay a coach or a few coaches for a number of sessions, or contact coaching schools and offer to be a "guinea pig" for their coaching students.

When you feel ready, you can develop your coaching skills hands-on by practicing with friends and family, or volunteering your services to those in need, in exchange for references or referrals. The *FabJob Guide to Become a Life Coach* by Allan M. Heller contains sample coaching techniques and exercises you can use, and explains how to build your business and find clients.

What It Pays

Fees for personal coaching services vary depending on the type of client, the experience of the coach, and other variables, but a typical monthly range is $200 to $600. Most coaches who are just starting out charge about $50 an hour, or between $200 and $300 for four half-hour sessions. You may charge extra for additional services such as email support.

Corporate clients pay more than individuals: anywhere from $1,000 to $3,500 per month, $300 to $400 an hour, or several thousands of dollars per day plus a development fee for training programs.

Massage Therapist

Massage therapists have healing hands. They use various techniques of touch on the body to help clients relax; ease pain, discomfort or illness; and experience a general sense of well being.

What They Do

A massage therapist is a trained health professional who uses his or her fingers and hands to provide massage to the soft tissues of the body. The person receiving the massage is usually lying down on a massage table, while the therapist moves around and massages the different parts of the body.

Most massage techniques fall into one of four categories: relaxation/spa, medical/clinical, sports, or onsite/corporate massage. Common techniques include Swedish massage, deep tissue massage, or hot stone therapy. A massage therapist may also specialize in pregnancy massage, massage for the elderly, or even massage for pets.

Some massage therapists open their own businesses, others join physical therapists, chiropractors, or doctors' offices as staff; some work at health spas or resorts. Massage therapists may pay rent and a portion of their hourly fees to operate their massage therapy business as part of an establishment offering related services.

As a massage therapist you will do some or all of the following:
- Set up your massage space and equipment
- Greet clients and get them settled in the treatment room
- Massage clients for a session of 30 or 60 minutes
- Continue to learn new massage techniques
- Keep in touch with past clients
- Market your services to new clients
- Network with other wellness professionals

Who is Likely to Succeed

Massage therapists possess a true affinity for people and a desire to help them feel better. They believe in a connection between physical well-being and a better life. They are professional with clients, and are skilled at making people feel at ease during a potentially vulnerable experience. Massage therapists must be okay with plenty of physical contact. You should be comfortable being on your feet for an hour at a time or more, and physically able to apply reasonable pressure during the massage.

How to Learn It

To get familiar with massage techniques and terminology, you can subscribe to some of the popular trade magazines for the industry, such as *Massage Magazine* (**www.massagemag.com**). If you have a massage specialty in mind, look for publications that are aimed at that style of massage.

You can test your early massage techniques on close friends and family — talk to them about what they do and don't like about your technique and about massages in general. You can develop basic skills by reading books or websites with step-by-step instructions.

In order to practice professional massage therapy, you will want to obtain training from a reputable program that specializes in the kind of therapy you want to practice. The Associated Bodywork and Massage Professionals organization (**www.abmp.com**) maintains a website with links to schools and training programs in each U.S. state.

Massage therapists are required to pass a state board examination and obtain a license in order to practice massage therapy in each region. Licensing requirements vary by region. There is a state-by-state/provincial list of requirements and contact information for each licensing board in the *FabJob Guide to Become a Massage Therapist* by Sharon Alfonso — along with great information on getting hired or setting up your own massage therapy business.

Some massage therapists get their first hands-on experience assisting or working for experienced massage therapists in their businesses. You can make contacts for therapists to assist by joining associations like ABMP listed earlier, or through the American Massage Therapy Association (**www.amtamassage.org**), which has a website with a section for massage therapy job seekers.

What It Pays

Often, massage therapists are independent contractors and charge fees for each massage or treatment they perform. You may choose to bill clients directly, or bill their insurance companies for them. Rates for self-employed massage therapists range from $40 or $50, to $100 per hour or treatment, plus a tip. According to the Bureau of Labor Statistics, median hourly earnings of massage therapists, including gratuities, are $15.36.

Personal Assistant

Would you like to assist busy, wealthy and/or famous people with the things they need to get done? Personal assistants are the behind-the-scenes lifesavers who know how to get things done in a pinch, quickly making themselves indispensable to their employers.

What They Do

Personal assistants function as organizers, coordinators, shoppers, errand-runners, and just about anything else you can imagine. Many personal assistants work for only one person, and may even be available to them 24 hours a day.

While there is some overlap between the work of a personal assistant and an executive (business) assistant, the main difference is that personal assistant work is… well, personal. Instead of typing business correspondence and sending packages, you may help your employer choose a color of dress to wear to an important event, for example.

Assistants are usually hired by people whose jobs are particularly demanding of their energy or time, such as movie stars, professional athletes, big-name speakers, famous authors, popular musicians, business executives, and politicians. In fact, anyone who is sufficiently wealthy may hire personal assistants.

What will you be doing as a personal assistant? Although this will differ from employer to employer (and even from day to day), your daily duties may include:

- Screening incoming phone calls
- Booking appointments and meetings
- Solving mini-emergencies with resourcefulness
- Shopping and buying gifts
- Planning parties or other events
- Responding to snail mail and email
- Managing household staff
- Minding kids and pets in a pinch
- Making travel arrangements
- House-sitting

Who Is Likely to Succeed

As a personal assistant you have to be a good communicator, a "get things done" kind of person, and cool under pressure. Ask yourself how you handle challenges and crises in your own life. Do you fly off the handle, or do you normally take a step back and think before you react?

The best personal assistants have an ability to move comfortably in the world of wealth and fame. Your appearance, etiquette skills and even your fashion sense may factor in here. You should be persuasive, a good negotiator, and your listening skills should be above average. You should also be extremely organized, a skilled problem-solver, and understand instinctively what types of information need to be kept in confidence.

How to Learn It

You can start today learning the skills of a personal assistant and building knowledge that will help you do this job. You should read up on or take courses in skills that will make you more attractive to a wealthy or famous employer, such as event planning, etiquette or international protocol, household management, and child care or pet care.

Make sure you are familiar with communication technology. From electronic organizers to cell phones to MP3 players, your employer will expect you to be able to make it work. Check online at the products' websites to view free tech-tutorials, or get some hands-on training from the helpful sales associates down at the electronics store.

You might also increase your comfort level by reading publications about or geared towards the famous or wealthy, such as *Town & Country* (**www.townandcountrymag.com**) and *Robb Report* (**www. robbreport.com**).

You can get paid to train as a personal assistant if you find temporary work as an executive assistant, nanny/butler, or concierge. As an added bonus, doing this type of work will put you into contact with the types of people who hire personal assistants, and you might just land your first gig just by doing an exceptional job for someone.

Can you keep a secret? If so, working with celebrities may be your thing. The *FabJob Guide to Become a Celebrity Personal Assistant* by John Havens has great information for anyone looking to land a personal assistant job, and specifically for those who are keen on working for a celebrity. It explains how to contact celebrities about working for them, and what to say (or not to say) in the interview to land the job.

What It Pays

Personal assistants to celebrities and other employers who need them to be available "as needed" generally earn an average of between $850 and $2,000 per week. Beginning assistants may earn as little as $450 a week, and the best assistants can earn $100,000 a year or more. Many personal assistants report that they frequently receive jewelry or other expensive gifts as a bonus from their wealthy employers.

Assistants who charge by the hour are likely to keep their fees in a range with personal concierge services: anywhere from $20 to $50 an hour, depending on the type of task they are asked to assist with.

Personal Shopper

As a personal shopper you will have a career that other people envy — getting paid to shop. While some personal shoppers specialize in a particular area such as fashion or gifts, others may shop for virtually any product or service their clients want.

What They Do

A personal shopper is someone hired to shop for other people. You will assist clients with selecting and purchasing items from one or several retailers. The shopper meets with clients to help them assess their needs and budget, and then heads out to the stores or online to find the items for them. They will purchase the items and bring them to the client, or arrange for their delivery.

There are also many boutiques and other retailers throughout North America that offer personal shopping services to their customers. A personal shopper working for a retailer will use their expert knowledge of their employer's merchandise to assist clients who make an appointment with selecting purchases.

As a personal shopper you may do some or all of the following:
- Help clients define their needs or wants
- Help clients determine budgets for their purchases
- Recommend specific purchases of goods or services
- Shop for or order goods or services
- Provide reminder services for seasonal or gift purchases
- Keep track of client preferences, sizes, etc.
- Handle delivery of items

Who is Likely to Succeed

As a personal shopper, excellent customer service will be part of your job on a daily basis. You will need to determine your client's needs and ensure those needs are met. To be truly successful you will go the extra mile for your clients — for example, keeping track of each client's important dates, and calling to remind them of occasions they may want to purchase gifts for. You will also have expert purchasing and product knowledge, a knack for negotiating the best price possible, and an ability to spot trends in advance.

How to Learn the Job

The great thing about this career is that you can make up your own course of study. You can take college fashion merchandising courses, or you can learn without taking any formal courses, but rather by constructing your own course of study using workshops, books, magazines, and even personal experiences of your own choosing.

The fun begins when you get to actually go to stores — a lot. Take notes about unusual items you see and ask sales associates for more information. Jot down the manufacturer information about lines of merchandise that you like. You are building a database of information to refer to when you need to find something for a client.

Acting as a personal shopper for friends and family is a great way to develop your skills. You may not be able to charge much – if anything – for your time and expertise. But you can sharpen your eye, improve your skills, and collect letters of appreciation to get you started.

The next step in educating yourself is reading books and periodicals in the field. Publications for consumers can give you some good ideas, but they generally will not contain cutting-edge information. You can get an excellent grasp of current trends in your field by reading periodicals for the retail or gift industries, such as *Women's Wear Daily* (**www.wwd.com**).

The *FabJob Guide to Become a Personal Shopper* lists a selection of good periodicals, books, industry associations and websites, in addition to comprehensive career information for getting hired or starting a business as a personal shopper.

What It Pays

A personal shopper working on salary or a combination of base pay and commissions can earn in the mid-$30,000s their first year, and will go up from there, especially as the shopper's client base grows. Shoppers working for retailers may also earn substantial discounts on merchandise. Independent personal shoppers can charge a percentage of the purchase price (usually 10% to 25%), or an hourly rate in the range of $25 to $100 per hour.

Personal Trainer

Are you a fitness buff or workout enthusiast? Personal trainers teach people how to exercise. They coach people one-on-one, providing motivation, inspiration, and encouragement like a good (and healthy!) friend.

What They Do

Personal trainers work with individual clients in gyms or in clients' homes. They meet with clients and instruct them in a fitness program. Unlike an aerobics class or group weight-loss program, a personal trainer's plans are specific to each client's needs and goals.

Personal trainers instruct in a combination of types of exercise, including weight training, core stability work, and aerobics. They suggest an activity or series of activities, and provide correction of techniques and encouragement to get the workout done. Many personal trainers are experts in nutrition, and offer their clients dietary or lifestyle advice as well.

Personal trainers work with a number of clients, and are either self-employed or work for an athletic club, gym or spa that offers personal trainers on staff. A few personal trainers work exclusively for one person — sometimes a very wealthy individual or even a movie or TV star.

As a personal trainer you will do some or all of the following:
- Assess a new client's fitness needs
- Plan personalized fitness routines for clients
- Lead clients in a workout routine of about an hour
- Assess your clients' weekly or monthly progress
- Provide lifestyle-based feedback to clients
- Maintain your own fitness level
- Market your training services to future clients
- Keep on top of trends in the fitness industry

Who is Likely to Succeed

If you love to work out and enjoy helping others succeed, a career as a personal trainer could be perfect for you. You should be healthy yourself so you can lead by example and motivate others. You likely have a knack for explaining tasks or demonstrating things hands-on to help people learn.

Personal trainers must be sensitive, and manage client relationships with discretion and tact. You should be able to communicate in a way that makes people feel positive, challenged, and supported — but never judged. You are a good listener, and can develop creative approaches to repetitive tasks that keep clients coming back.

How to Learn It

If you book some sessions to work with one or more personal trainers, you'll get to see the industry from a client's perspective, and at the same time give yourself a chance to study the techniques that other personal trainers use. Familiarize yourself with different types of exercise equipment and what they can be used for as well.

Many personal trainers, in addition to educating themselves about fitness, exercise, and nutrition from books or websites, get certified in the profession. Certification adds an attractive credibility to your profile, and will help you get hired by athletic clubs and gyms.

Types of certification vary, so if you have a particular employer in mind, call and ask them what types they require. You can check out classes at your local community college, or read the *FabJob Guide to Become a Personal Trainer* by Paige Waehner, which lists nine North American certification organizations and their contact information, including some that you can complete from home.

When you are ready to start honing your training skills, try to get hands-on experience any way you can. Approach gyms with ideas for new classes, or express your willingness to teach the early or late classes (or any time slots that no one else wants). Volunteer to teach fitness or do one-on-one training for seniors or other groups that would appreciate a beginner's efforts.

Attending clinics or conventions to see what other trainers or instructors are teaching is a great way to learn new skills and approaches. Many of the certification organizations offer these chances for ongoing learning to their members, as well as industry-related publications such as the American Counsel on Exercise's Fitness Matters Magazine.

What It Pays

Salaries for personal trainers employed at fitness clubs and gyms vary according to your clientele and where you live. For example, a trainer in New York City could expect anywhere from $70 to $150 an hour, while in Nebraska, you'd be more likely to earn between $30 and $60 an hour. Most independent personal trainers charge their clients between $40 and $60 an hour.

According to the Bureau of Labor Statistics, median annual earnings of personal trainers and group exercise instructors are $25,470, although they specify that earnings of successful self-employed personal trainers can be much higher.

Real Estate Agent

Real estate agents help people with buying or selling homes, buildings, and land. They are experts who make sure that their clients' best interests are protected in these big-money deals.

What They Do

Real estate agents are hired by people to help them find and purchase property, or get the best price selling property they own. These transactions can be complex and a lot of money changes hands, so the real estate agent is hired to make sure everything is done correctly.

Agents are expected to know what the real estate market is doing so they can negotiate the best price for their client. They also need to be familiar with the paperwork involved in transferring property from seller to buyer. They present offers and counter-offers from buyer to seller, and vice-versa.

Real estate agents can work independently, or they may be employed by a broker who is more experienced and has several agents under contract. Real estate agents have busy but flexible schedules, and will often work evenings and/or weekends. Real estate agents usually become members of the National Association of Realtors (**www.realtor.org**) in order to be able to call themselves "Realtors."

As a real estate agent you will do some or all of the following:

- Meet with buyers or sellers to assess their needs
- Monitor the market for new properties for sale
- Show real estate to buyers
- Advertise and otherwise market your listed properties for sale
- Host open houses for your listed properties
- Draft formal offers to purchase real estate
- Present offers and counter-offers to sellers and buyers
- Negotiate transactions with other real estate agents
- Market your services to new clients
- Assist buyers and sellers with paperwork and financing

Who is Likely to Succeed

Successful real estate agents are likeable, friendly, and generally enjoyable to be around. They are usually extroverts who enjoy a conversation or a crowd. They are skilled at "reading" people and assessing their unspoken needs and intentions. They are honest in all areas of life, and are able to communicate this integrity to others.

They are good listeners, and able to negotiate solutions that seem to leave everyone satisfied. It helps to be a good speaker and writer so you can present convincing offers and write intriguing sales copy.

How to Learn It

You can start preparing for a career in real estate immediately with a visit to the Multiple Listing Service websites located at **www.mls. com** (in the United States) or **www.mls.ca** (in Canada). These online marketplaces feature properties for sale across the country, listed by region or even by neighborhood.

By browsing MLS you can get a sense of what homes are worth in different areas of your town or city. You will also become familiar with the language agents use to describe properties for sale. You'll also learn a lot by visiting local open houses on the weekend and speaking with the selling agent, so you can see a real estate professional in action.

To become a real estate agent it is necessary to be licensed in all fifty states and all provinces in Canada. In order to obtain a license, an agent must pass a written exam. Exact requirements vary by region, so it is important to contact your state or provincial licensing board to find out what is necessary.

There are a number of reputable schools around the country that focus on real estate training designed to help students learn what they will need to know to pass the licensing exam. In some cases you can get your basic agent training in just a few weeks.

Real estate professionals can benefit from other sorts of training including sales and marketing courses, computer classes, and even architecture courses. If you decide to work with a broker, they may provide additional training as well.

What It Pays

Real estate agents' annual salaries are based on the commissions they earn when properties sell. According to the Bureau of Labor Statistics, the median annual earnings of salaried real estate agents are $35,670. Highly successful agents can make $100,000 a year or much more. Part-time and beginning agents may earn closer to $17,000 a year as they build their clientele. Income usually increases as an agent gains experience.

Rescue Worker

Rescue workers such as firefighters, paramedics/emergency medical technicians, and police officers are trained to saves lives in crisis situations by providing emergency assistance and preventing accidents before they happen.

What They Do

As a rescue worker you will prevent or treat injuries and save lives. Rescue workers are the first people called to the scene of an accident or crime. They provide medical attention at the scene of an emergency, as well as other specific duties such as investigating the cause, apprehending suspected criminals, extinguishing fire, and transporting injured people to the hospital.

Rescue workers are always on call to respond to any emergency that arises. Sometimes they remain at the site of a disaster for days at a time, rescuing trapped survivors and assisting with medical treatment. Between emergencies, rescue workers may patrol out on the streets, train to stay fit, learn more about rescue, prepare reports on emergencies, and increase public awareness of emergency prevention.

Depending on their specific position, a rescue worker may do some or all of the following tasks:

- Drive quickly to the scene of an emergency
- Assess people and situations to determine how critical they are
- Extinguish fires or otherwise respond to crisis
- Instruct or direct citizens or passersby in an emergency
- Administer minor medical attention
- Administer critical medical attention en route to a hospital
- Investigate the cause of accidents or emergencies

Who is Likely to Succeed

Are you the kind of person who runs into a burning building, or out of it? Rescue workers are brave, since they are often risking their own safety in order to save the lives of others. Far from reckless, though, the best rescue workers use their good judgment to quickly assess situations before they react, so they make the best use of their skills.

Rescue work is best suited to people who are strong and physically fit. When they need to react quickly they rise to the occasion, and don't get stressed out even in a crisis situation. They are good problem-solvers, and make decisions quickly and easily. They are strong leaders, but also work well as part of a team.

How to Learn It

You can start to learn about rescue work through first-hand accounts of those who are already working in the profession. Since they see so much action, many rescue workers write memoirs — books like *Paramedic: On the Front Lines of Medicine* by Peter Canning open a passage into the rescue worker's daily life.

Contact your local EMT service or fire/police station, and ask if you can meet with some working professionals for an informational interview. Ask if you can see the equipment and vehicles you'd be using. Some rescue services allow citizen ride-alongs (you ride in the rescue vehicle and observe the workers) to those who are genuinely interested in the career.

Rescue workers are required to pass a test that assesses their skill and suitability to the career. There are guidebooks that will help you prepare for these exams with practice questions and answers. You may be able to volunteer or apprentice for some rescue worker positions, or work in a related career such as dispatcher to learn more.

Would-be firefighters generally must pass a written exam; tests of strength, physical stamina, coordination, and agility; and a medical examination that includes drug screening. Community college courses in fire science improve your chances for appointment. The *FabJob Guide to Become a Firefighter* by Mark Armstrong offers insider advice on breaking in from a working firefighter/firefighting academy staff member.

Formal training and certification is needed to become an emergency medical technician (EMT) or paramedic. Training is offered at four progressive levels: EMT 1 (basic), 2, 3, and 4. EMT-Basic coursework emphasizes emergency skills, such as managing respiratory, trauma and cardiac emergencies, and patient assessment. Formal courses are often combined with time in an emergency room or ambulance. Graduates of approved EMT basic training programs who pass a written and practical exam earn the title "Registered EMT-Basic."

Physical examinations for police officers often include tests of vision, hearing, strength, and agility. Eligibility for selection usually depends on written exam scores, and previous education and experience. Many community colleges offer programs in law enforcement or administration of justice to boost your chances for success.

What It Pays

According to the Bureau of Labor Statistics, median annual earnings of EMTs and paramedics are $25,310. Median hourly earnings of firefighters are $18.43, while first-line supervisors/managers of firefighting and prevention workers earn $58,920 annually. Police and sheriff's patrol officers have median annual earnings of $45,210, while police supervisors earn $64,430.

Sports Instructor

Sports instructors are talented individuals who use their advanced skills to teach a particular sport or hobby to those who are just learning it, or improving their ability.

What They Do

As an instructor in your favorite sport such as tennis, golf or skiing, you will teach others one-on-one or in groups how to improve their skills. You may be self-employed, or you might work for a fitness or country club, a sports association, a training school or camp, a golf course or ski hill, or even at a resort or on a cruise ship.

An instructor demonstrates techniques for the students, observes them in action and takes note of where they can improve, and puts them through physical and mental drills to improve their overall performance. They may use recordings of the students to show them what they are doing right and wrong.

As a sports instructor you may do any or all of the following:
- Watch students participate in the sport
- Give verbal instructions about technique
- Explain basic rules and strategies
- Encourage a higher level of effort from the student
- Physically assist or correct students' form
- Plan exercises, drills and practice for the students
- Complete written evaluations of progress
- Market your instruction skills to new students
- Keep up with trends in the sport
- Give advice on equipment type and use

Who is Likely to Succeed

Like professional athletes, sports instructors are driven by a natural talent for and love of their sport. In fact, many people take up sports instruction after they retire from a career of active participation or competition in a sport. You have the unique combination of a healthy competitive nature plus a true sense of "team."

You are a natural leader and motivator, and can tap into people's personal motivation and get them to give their all. You are a keen observer, and can piece together the techniques used to succeed in your sport. You give good, clear direction, are patient, and are physically fit enough to keep up with your students for the purpose of instruction.

How to Learn the Job

Some entry-level positions for sports instructors require only past experience as a participant in the sport or activity. You need to have a certain level of talent and experience to be able to teach others, especially the higher the level of skill in your students. Study the performance of the best in the sport so you can see what techniques the elite participants use.

To get instruction experience, offer your services as a coach or instructor in your sport (or any sport you wish) at the amateur level. Community associations and junior leagues can benefit while you hone your ability to give instruction and motivate.

If you want to instruct professionally, you will likely need to be certified by the sports association to coach or teach. There are certifying organizations specific to the various sports, and their training requirements vary depending on their standards. Participation in a clinic, camp, or school usually is required for certification.

You should also take courses and develop skills in areas that will allow you to offer a holistic approach to instruction. Many athletes now use meditation and visualization techniques to perform at their best, and an understanding of nutrition as it relates to sports performance will help you help your students.

If you have the time and money for formal education, degree programs specifically related to sports instruction and coaching include exercise and sports science, physiology, kinesiology, nutrition and fitness, physical education, and sports medicine.

What It Pays

Some sports instructors are paid a salary, while others may be paid by the hour, per session, or based on the number of participants. Fees/wages depend on the sport and the level you are instructing at. The median annual wage for sports instructors or coaches is $26,350 per year, although many work part time or seasonally. Independent sports instructors charge anywhere from $10 or $15 hourly for group sessions to $100 an hour or more for private training.

Travel Consultant

People rely on travel consultants to help them get the most for their vacation or travel dollar. You'll use your knowledge of world destinations to help your clients plan their trips.

What They Do

As a travel consultant, you will help people plan vacations, business trips and tours to locations around the world. You'll determine the types of trips that are suitable for your clients, and using your organizational talent and expert knowledge, you'll help them plan their entire journey.

Travel consultants (also referred to as travel agents) learn about different recreational activities and the places in the world where those activities are offered. They monitor currency exchange rates and other international concerns, and advise clients on necessary visas, passports or immunizations required.

Agents may work on their own, as a member of a small or large travel company, or for an airline or tour company. You'll work in an office, using your computer and phone as lifelines to communicate with clients and travel service providers. You may work long hours during busy seasons, but will have opportunities to go on frequent vacations of your own.

As a travel consultant, your tasks may include some or all of the following:

- Speaking with clients in person or by phone
- Researching destinations and accommodations
- Booking hotel rooms, rental cars and specialized tours
- Developing itineraries (travel schedules) for groups and individuals
- Making reservations on airlines, trains and cruise ships
- Sending confirmation emails to clients with travel details
- Monitoring world news and weather
- Traveling to new places to learn about their amenities and attractions
- Developing package tours to specific destinations or countries

Who is Likely to Succeed

If you are a curious and adventurous person who seeks out new experiences to share with others, you'll likely make a good travel consultant. Personal travel experience is helpful, especially if you want to develop a specialty service. A good knowledge of world geography is important — you'll want to be familiar with the major destination options for your clients. Speaking a foreign language is a plus too. You should have advanced computer skills, since a lot of travel booking takes place online these days.

How to Learn the Job

Some of the skills needed to be an excellent travel agent can be learned on your own time. You can browse Internet sites like **www. expedia.com** to see what destinations are hot right now. Pick a destination and pretend you are booking all the arrangements to travel there. Compare prices and amenities of hotels, and see what the local attractions are. If you can afford it, plan trips for yourself and friends, organizing itineraries for various outings and recreational events at your destination.

You can start building a database or file folder of information about popular destinations. Read all the travel-related publications you can find, from the airlines' different in-flight magazines to destination-specific publications. Clip interesting articles and file them by destination so you have an "idea file" to share with future clients.

If you want to pursue formal training, you can enroll in a course or series of courses in travel consulting through your community college, or you may take a degree program in travel and tourism from some universities. There is even a correspondence course available from the American Society of Travel Agents (**www.astanet.com**).

Since making travel arrangements is no longer the exclusive domain of the travel consultant, you will need to offer specialized or exceptional services to your clients that save them considerable money or are worth the fees your charge. The Travel Institute (**www.the travelinstitute.com**) offers courses in travel specialties to help you develop a specialty service offering.

What It Pays

According to the Bureau of Labor Statistics, the median income for salaried travel consultants in the United States is $27,640, with a high of as much as $44,090. When they travel for personal reasons, agents usually get reduced rates for transportation and accommodations. In addition, agents sometimes take "familiarization" trips, at no cost to themselves, to learn about various vacation sites.

Earnings of travel agents who own their agencies depend mainly on commissions from travel-related bookings and service fees they charge clients. Income increases as you build your client base. There is the potential to earn more than $60,000 a year, as earned commission percentages can vary from 40% to 60%, or even 100% of a sale.

Veterinary Assistant

Veterinary assistants give care and attention to pets and other animals that are injured or ill, or that need a veterinary exam. They help make the experience less traumatic and more enjoyable for both the animal and the owner.

What They Do

As a veterinary assistant, your duties will include looking after a variety of animals in a veterinary clinic or hospital, or on location at farms, zoos, shelters, or other places where animals are kept. You will create a clean and comfortable environment for the animal, and offer food and water regularly. If the animal is ill or injured, you will watch for and chart any changes in their status.

You will perform your duties under the supervision of a veterinarian and veterinary technicians. You may assist the veterinarian and technicians with some procedures, and will look after the animals before and after surgeries. Part of your job will also entail contact with the owner or caregiver, in order to let them know how their pet is doing.

A typical day may include some or all of the following:
- Greeting clients and their pets
- Answering phones and scheduling appointments
- Feeding and watering animals
- Playing with or exercising animals
- Cleaning pens, stalls and cages
- Monitoring animals for signs of illness
- Restraining animals for examination or treatment
- Cleaning and preparing exam rooms
- Giving medication to animals
- Grooming and cleaning animals

Who is Likely to Succeed

You are kind and caring, and genuinely enjoy the company of all animals. You probably have had a number of your own pets, or worked with animals in some capacity. You do not hesitate to do tasks that must be done, and are able to cope with a job that sometimes requires you to deal with very ill, scared or injured animals.

Your ability to communicate clearly and calmly will help clients make informed decisions regarding their animal's care. You are practical and hands-on, and of course, free of severe allergies to pets. You are also patient, gentle and compassionate with animals and people who may be under stressful conditions.

How to Learn the Job

Your local community college likely offers courses in becoming a veterinary assistant, but this is a job that you can usually learn while you do it. You will have the opportunity to learn about handling different types of animals with different temperaments and needs, every day on the job.

Working at a pet store or apprenticing with a pet groomer are two ways that you can gain hands-on experience with animals. You can also learn many of the skills needed, such as handling, restraining and grooming animals by looking after your own or other people's pets. Volunteer as a dog walker or pet sitter to get experience interacting with animals.

You might also become involved in helping out at a humane society or animal shelter. The American Humane Association (**www.americanhumane.org**) and the Humane Society of the United States (**www.hsus.org**) both offer courses in animal care and other topics relevant to the industry. In Canada, the SPCA (Society for the Prevention of Cruelty to Animals) accepts volunteers to work with animals at their local shelters: **www.spca.com**.

If you want to get more involved with the medical aspects of animal care, you should consider becoming a veterinary technician or a veterinary technologist, both of which require a college degree and licensing. If you are hoping to work as a vet assistant in a zoo you may also need a bachelor's degree in biology, but this degree is not necessary for work in most veterinary clinics and animal hospitals.

What It Pays

Being a veterinary assistant is a job that's more about love than money, although you can make a living at it. You can expect a median hourly wage of $8.39, but this varies depending on the amount of experience you have and the type of facility in which you work. Top wages can be more than $13 per hour, and typically include benefits such as health insurance.

Yoga or Pilates Instructor

Yoga and Pilates (*puh-LAH-teez*) instructors teach physical and breathing techniques as they guide students through a series of related movements in a classroom or one-on-one setting.

What They Do

Yoga and Pilates instructors are experts in their chosen practice, and teach the principles of it to students. Yoga is an ancient physical practice based on mental and physical balance, centered on postures called asanas and breathing called pranayama. Pilates is a far more recent form of physical technique based on performing a series of small, strengthening movements.

Yoga and Pilates instructors hold classes averaging 45 to 90 minutes in length, in which they guide students through moves designed to strengthen the muscles and improve both physical and mental health. They give verbal instruction, motivate, and may also physically guide the students into a corrected position.

Yoga and Pilates instructors most often work as self-employed contractors at gyms, health clubs and spas, and even community college courses. Some yoga or Pilates instructors open up their own studios out of their home or off-site.

As a yoga or Pilates instructor you will do some or all of the following:

- Plan and practice classes in advance
- Greet students who are attending your class
- Teach classes of various skill levels and durations
- Attend conferences to learn the latest techniques in yoga/Pilates
- Maintain your own fitness level through personal practice of yoga/Pilates
- Market your services to new clients or employers
- Keep track of students' payments and issue receipts

Who is Likely to Succeed

Yoga or Pilates instructors discover within themselves a desire to teach others, and a talent for the practice of either yoga or Pilates. They are natural communicators who can use verbal and physical instructions to demonstrate accurately. They are likeable, non-judgmental, and are not embarrassed about getting up in front of a crowd.

Successful yoga and Pilates instructors are good businesspeople and have at least a basic understanding of marketing concepts that help them build awareness of their classes. And of course they are fit enough to do yoga or Pilates for several hours each day.

How to Learn It

To become a yoga or Pilates instructor you will need to be completely proficient in the techniques and practices that you plan to teach. You should take a number of yoga or Pilates classes and refine your own daily practice until your level of skill is classified as advanced. Your instructor can help you make this determination. You can also study in-depth principles of yoga and Pilates in books, magazines, and online.

There are various certification programs you can take through yoga or Pilates associations, schools, or community colleges that will help you improve your instruction skills and knowledge. Some specialized forms of yoga such as Iyengar require in-depth additional training and certification from accredited sources.

When you are ready to put your teaching skills into practice, you can ask one of your yoga or Pilates teachers if they would allow you to teach a portion of their class, and then offer you feedback about your teaching style and techniques. You can do this until your teacher feels you are qualified to teach on your own, at which time you can ask to be a back-up or substitute for them when they have to miss a class.

Self-evaluation can also be an important tool for you to learn from. If possible, record yourself guest instructing, or else pretending to instruct a class. When you watch the recording, check to see if the students were able to follow your instructions, or try to complete your instructions yourself as you follow along. Look and listen for any habits you have that might be distracting to your students.

You can jump right into teaching yoga or Pilates and learn from experience if you volunteer to teach for free. Seniors centers may benefit from you teaching a modified form of exercise, and those who would be unable to afford classes otherwise will be happy to learn while you do. A great resource to learn more in-depth information abut becoming a yoga instructor is the *FabJob Guide to Become a Yoga Instructor* by Sandy Hennessey.

Fab Fact: Mari Winsor, known for creating Winsor Pilates, is a highly successful and much sought-after Pilates instructor. She developed her first Pilates workout 20 years ago, and since then has introduced millions of people to Pilates through her books, DVDs and TV performances. Mari has also taught Pilates to celebrities such as Madonna, Danny Glover, Sandra Bullock, Melanie Griffith, Jewel, Vanessa Williams, and many more. Winsor owns and operates two Pilates studios in the Los Angeles area.

What It Pays

Pilates and yoga instructors usually charge by the hour or the class, and charge less for group classes than private instruction. Group classes range from $8 to $20 per session. Individual classes range between $40 and $70 per session. Yoga instructors' salaries average around $30,000 to $40,000 a year. Full-time Pilates instructors can make between $30,000 to $60,000 in annual income.

HOW TO BREAK IN

You may know in your heart that you would do well in one of the relater careers listed above. But how do you convince people to place important aspects of their life in your hands, especially when you are first getting started?

This section on breaking in will explain how you can develop your interpersonal skills to help you get hired and be successful. This section will also give advice on how to break in by using volunteer work to get practical experience and references to build your portfolio or resume.

While certain relater careers will require additional training or certification to enter into, rounding out your attractiveness with experience and excellent interpersonal skills is key. Whether you go into business for yourself and need to attract clients, or you approach an employer for a permanent position, the process we explain below will lead you to success.

Develop Your Interpersonal Skills

All the relater careers have something in common: they all require you to have better-than-average interpersonal skills. After all, who wants to hire a grumpy household manager, meet with an uncaring funeral director, or work with a real estate agent who doesn't listen and repeatedly shows you properties you don't like? You can have all the technical talent in the world, but if you can't relate to people, you will have trouble finding people who want to hire you.

Your interpersonal skills are the techniques you use to communicate with people. You can develop the ability to help people feel like you really listen to them, to get them to trust you, and to respond appropriately to whatever the situation demands. In this section we are going to focus on the four categories of interpersonal skills bulleted below:

- Relationship-building
- Listening skills
- Reading people
- Speaking skills

If you are considering a relater career, chances are you are already skilled in many of these areas, but remember there's always room for improvement when it comes to interpersonal skills, so read on.

Relationship Building

Building good relationships with clients or customers is the best way to get them to trust you, like you, hire you, and refer you to friends. Building relationships is also how people will grow to become comfortable with you and your skills. When it comes down to choosing between two equally qualified and attractive service providers, people are going to select the one they get along best with. And clients who like you will often transfer that positive feeling and impression to your work.

To build a relationship, you want to really connect with people, and have them see you as trustworthy, friendly, and sincere. The challenge in building relationships is that no two people will respond to the same approach, so your attempt to be likeable has to be genuine, not rehearsed. A positive attitude is also key to having people enjoy being around you. It sounds simple, but a smile helps too.

Being sincere is an important factor in relationship-building — people can spot a phony when it comes to friendliness, and will back off like they would from a pushy salesperson. It's not that hard to find common ground with most people, or at least identify how they want to be interacted with. The information that will follow on listening skills and reading people will help you figure out what people want from you.

Many relater careers involve people sharing personal details with you, and they'll want to feel safe doing this. To build trust, let clients or customers know that you respect their privacy — you can even sign an agreement to this effect. An even better way is to showcase this quality in yourself by not gossiping, criticizing, or disclosing private information about other people.

If relationship-building is an area you want to improve in, a great resource used by many professionals is the book *How to Win Friends and Influence People*, by Dale Carnegie. In it, he relates both his personal experiences and stories told to him about what people want in a friend, acquaintance, or business relationship, and how to be that person.

Listening Skills

"What was that again?" If you're like most people, listening is just an interruption before you get to speak. Many people like to think they are good listeners, but in reality their skills actually need some work. You may not be an ideal listener if you:

- Plan what to say while the other person is speaking

- Don't acknowledge the other person's point before making your own
- Have a tendency to interrupt
- Like to help people "get to the point"
- Assume that you know what people are going to say
- Are distracted by events around you during a conversation

Be honest — how many of these poor listening habits do you have, even from time to time? You may even strive to be a good listener, but forget listening etiquette in the excitement of the conversation. If you want to pursue one of the relater careers, now is the time to start improving this skill. While your friends and family may be more forgiving, missing crucial details from clients or customers (or even giving the impression you aren't listening) can be a career-killer.

Listening skills are like what they say about games like poker or chess: they take a moment to learn, and a lifetime to master. The good news is that you have an opportunity to practice listening every day.

If you catch yourself not paying attention to someone speaking, apologize, and ask them to start again. You can also tell family and friends that you are trying to improve your listening skills, and ask them to point out when you are being a less-than-perfect audience.

If you find your attention wandering, a useful technique is to ask questions to make sure that you understand what the other person has said. This forces you to listen attentively, and gives the other person the satisfaction of feeling like their point has been made. You can also summarize the other person's comments before you move on, such as: "So what you're saying is …" Making appropriate comments can help the speaker feel acknowledged and better understood.

Reading People

In addition to hearing what people say, a skilled communicator also notices non-verbal communication. Being able to "read" people will not only help you get jobs, it can help ensure you keep your clients satisfied. Although body language can't tell you precisely what someone is thinking, it can give you clues so you can ask follow-up questions, even as basic as, "How do you feel about that?"

If you feel like people are a mystery to you, or are often confused by people's responses or reactions, you can find some excellent advice in books such as *Reading People*, by Jo-Ellan Dimitrius and Mark Mazzarella. A successful jury consultant, Dimitrius shares in this book how she is able to see through people's words to what they are truly revealing about themselves.

Speaking Skills

When we think of speaking skills we usually think of public speaking, but even the conversations you have one-on-one require a certain amount of skill. Consider the following with tips on projecting a professional image from the *FabJob Guide to Become an Image Consultant*.

Vocabulary:	A large vocabulary will help you express yourself. You can subscribe to "word-of-the-day" emails or listen to vocabulary-building cassettes, but the best way to boost your vocabulary is to read a lot, with a dictionary by your side. Look up any words you don't understand, or even those you are unsure of. When you use your new words, make sure you use them correctly, or you'll sound less intelligent than if you had used a simpler word. Also be aware that using large words unnecessarily can be perceived as pretentious. If someone wants to appear down to earth and likeable, it may be preferable to speak simply and directly — for example, "I drove across town in my car" instead of "I traversed the community in my automobile."
Pronunciation	In addition to ensuring words are used correctly, they also need to be pronounced correctly. When someone hears a speaker pronounce nuclear as "nucular," probably as "probly," or espresso as "expresso," they may assume the speaker is not well-educated.
Grammar	Using proper grammar lends credence to a message. It also speaks to the intelligence and class of a speaker. Speakers may be judged harshly if they make grammatical errors such as using the word "none" instead of "any" (e.g. "I don't want none") or the word "seen" instead of "saw" (e.g. "I seen my friend yesterday"). The first step to overcoming grammatical errors is to become aware of them, then practice using correct English. Even replacing "yeah" with "yes" can help someone make a more positive impression.
Fillers:	Conversation is often cluttered with unnecessary filler words and phrases. While an occasional "um,"

"ah," or "like" will go unnoticed, when your speech is filled with them people will wonder if you are nervous or unsure of yourself — plus, they can be irritating to the listener.

Words to avoid: Swearing reduces a speaker's credibility and distracts from the overall message. Slang should be eliminated or, at least, selectively used. Jargon or acronyms (abbreviations) should only be used if everyone present understands their meaning.

Your voice: You will want to find a pace of speaking and a level of loudness that is suitable to the conversation. Other vocal qualities that can create a poor impression include nervous laughter, breathiness or raspiness, and whininess (think Fran Drescher, a.k.a. *The Nanny*).

Again, your family and friends are your best allies in discovering what speech issues you may have. You can also record yourself in conversation with someone, and then play it back later and take note of anything you do that may be a turn-off to future clients. (And yes, you really do sound like that!)

How to Get Experience

A key to breaking in to a relater career is to get experience and build your resume by volunteering your services. This is how you get around the problem of "How do you get a job without experience and how do you get experience without a job?"

Of course you aren't likely to get hired into the top position without experience, there's no mystery there. But if you are willing to do some volunteering for little or no pay, you are building for the future, and adding valuable experience to your resume.

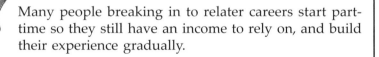

TIP: Many people breaking in to relater careers start part-time so they still have an income to rely on, and build their experience gradually.

Work for Family and Friends

One of the first people you'll probably "work for" for free will be yourself. You can get valuable practice in the skills you'll need by improving your own life the way that a service provider would.

For example, if you want to be a fitness instructor, you can design and do your own fitness program. If you want to be a household manager, you should take over all the duties in your own home related to this profession. While you won't put these experiences on your resume, doing the tasks will help you develop skills and systems to use with clients in the future.

Your friends and family will be the next place you look for people to help. They are usually willing to have you use them as guinea pigs, and are more likely to be honest in their feedback.

When you work for friends and family, don't cut corners — go through all the same steps you would if they were a client. This way you will be getting a full rehearsal of what you'll be doing on the job from start to finish.

When you have completed the job, ask for a letter of reference, and if appropriate, take photos or otherwise detail what you did for the person. You can add these to your portfolio of experience that will help you get paying jobs down the road. Read Chapter 6's "How to Break In" section for more information about putting together a portfolio.

You can also ask friends and family to spread the word that you are looking to build your resume and will offer your services at a reduced price. When you are working for "friends of friends," though, you may want to charge a small fee, or else you risk getting a reputation as someone who always works for free. Not charging for your services might also lead people to see your work as less valuable because you don't attach a value to it.

Offer Services to Those in Need

People who have limited resources are also a good place to begin working with little or no experience. Contact the volunteering association in your region and see what not-for-profits are a fit with your career plans.

For example, if you are interested in becoming a veterinary assistant, you can get excellent hands-on experience by volunteering for an animal rescue foundation while a would-be yoga instructor can teach modified yoga at a seniors' facility.

TIP: You may need to get a background check in order to volunteer in certain settings. This process can take several weeks, so be sure to arrange this in advance of applying.

Assist Professionals in the Industry

One of the best ways to get some experience is to assist professionals in the industry. This may be either as a volunteer or paid assistant, depending on the career. For example, busy real estate agents rely heavily on assistants to get their day-to-day work done, so they may pay a minimal fee to an assistant.

Being a good assistant can really help kick-start a career. It will give you an opportunity to experience what the job is like without the pressure of doing everything alone. It's also a chance to learn from a senior member of the profession, so make sure you ask a lot of questions when the time is right.

A capable assistant will establish a reputation as such, and may even be able to assist more than one person, depending on the nature of the work. And if the assistant is talented, these professionals may begin sending work to him or her when they become too busy to take on more work.

To become an assistant, you will want to approach the profes-sional you'd like to assist in a business-like manner. You can offer to take them out to lunch and discuss assisting them informally, or you can prepare a letter explaining your intentions that you can drop off or email.

This letter will be a lot like a cover letter (see chapter 12 for some examples), except you will mention in it that you are willing to work for a specified amount of time for little or no pay. You can also write out notes that you can adapt into a phone script, and call the person to offer your services.

You can also try to get assistant work from any networking con-tacts you have made (we'll explain networking in depth in Chapter 13). If you meet with someone working in the field you respect and find you "click with" right away, you can conclude or follow up your meeting with a request for work. Ask if they would be willing to take on an assistant, and make it clear that you are willing to do menial or even unrelated work in exchange for a chance to help them on the job.

If they don't have a way for you to assist, ask them for a referral to someone who does. If they tell you to keep in touch for future work, call every so often, but not to the point of pestering them. Take cues from how they respond to determine if you might assist them in the future. If they aren't willing to share their time, someone else will be!

Once you find someone who is willing to take on an assistant, it's important to set ground rules early on, and respect their business and their time. Make sure you make it clear that you will not waste their time, get in their way, or embarrass them in front of clients.

TIP:  If you want to impress even more, offer the professional some assistance of your own, based on whatever you are good at. If you are good with organizing you can possibly get their office paperwork in order, or maybe you can run some errands for them on the side.

When assisting, it's important to get a sense of how comfortable the person is with having you "around." Some would prefer if you were in the background getting coffee, while others will want you at arm's length when needed. If you're not sure, ask, but always have anything you need on hand to do the job just in case.

When you are working as an assistant, treat it as a paid job, which means being on time and professional. There is also a certain etiquette to assisting you should be aware of — be willing to do menial tasks without complaining, don't try to "steal" work for yourself, and accept that you have a lot to learn. If you are taking training courses, don't use your knowledge to try to correct the person you are assisting — save it for when you are working in the business yourself.

Internships and On-the-Job Training

In some types of relater careers an internship or temporary placement in on-the-job training (sometimes called "co-op education") is likely to be part of your formal education. You may have to seach yourself for a company to take you on, or else you may be placed with someone chosen by your educational provider. These types of positions are very similar to being an assistant, and may be paid or unpaid.

Internships are often advertised on company websites, with most available only to current students. Your educational provider may also have a list of businesses that work with interns or co-op students that you can choose from. These placements usually last about a few months, and you will work the same hours as the regular staff.

An important tip about internships: don't assume that being an intern will automatically lead to a job for you with that company, because there will not necessarily be a position open when you complete your internship. The best way to boost your chances of getting hired from an intern or assistant position into a full-time role is to create your own job by showing your employer you are valuable, as we'll explain in Chapter 14.

Sample Relater Resume

Chris Goulet

123 My Street
Mytown, USA 11111
(111) 555-1212
chrisgoulet@internet.com

Objective

I am passionate about sharing my love of snow sports with others, and eager to provide attentive, positive training to those looking to improve their skiing ability at any age or level, in either a private or group setting.

Highlights

- Advanced-level skier with more than 10 years' experience
- Current CPR and First Aid Certification
- Recently certified with PSIA (level 1)
- Prior experience teaching skiing professionally

Experience

Private Ski Instructor
Winter 2005/2006

Taught eight and nine year olds from Sir Flemming Academy the basics of skiing every Monday afternoon. Worked with all kinds of experience levels. Parents commented on noticeable improvement in their children's ability by end of season.

Sir Flemming Academy, Teacher's Assistant
2004/2005

Volunteered to give children more one-on-one help with their studies and organize special events for children, since teachers were short-staffed. Recognized by teachers as "valuable assistant" at end-of-year celebration.

SportStuff, Sales Associate
2002/2004

Assisted shoppers in finding the correct type and fit of sporting equipment to suit their needs, including skis and snowboards. Named "Associate of the Month" three times.

more...

Education and Training

2005 — Professional Ski Instructors' Association Level 1 Certification
2002 — SportStuff sales training/customer psychology course
1999 — St. Stephen's High School (honor student)

Related Skills and Experience

- Co-captain, Mt. Snow Ski Racing Team
- Capable ski-doo driver
- Experienced snowboarder and cross-country skier
- Familiar with local ski conditions and safety
- Physically fit

9

Fab Brains

Careers for Critical Thinkers

When you watch a movie, do you figure out what is going to happen long before it's revealed in the plot? While it can be annoying to friends and family if you spoil the ending, you should feel proud of this special and rare talent. Someone who can figure out how all the little details fit into the big picture has a bright future in one of these brainy careers.

People who are suited to these types of careers are true critical thinkers. Maybe you are good at mind puzzles or board games. You probably have an excellent memory, and you notice the little details that others miss. People may call you intuitive when you showcase your talents, but as far as you're concerned, it's just common sense.

Well, it's time to get paid to use that big brain of yours, by pursuing one of the dream careers listed on the following pages:

- Archaeologist
- Editor
- FBI Agent/Secret Agent
- Financial Planner
- Food Writer
- Forensic Specialist

- Interpreter/Translator
- Mystery Shopper
- Nutritionist
- Pilot
- Private Investigator
- Professional Organizer
- Researcher
- Stock Broker or Trader
- Travel Writer
- Treasure Hunter
- Web Designer

THE CAREERS

Archaeologist

If you have always dreamed of unraveling the mysteries of the past like Indiana Jones and unearthing clues to our very existence, the intriguing world of archaeology is calling your name.

What They Do

Archaeologists study past cultures by looking at the things they left behind (called artifacts), and coming up with theories about how lives were lived. Archaeologists experience the thrill of discovery as they look for and excavate artifacts at dig sites around the world.

Archaeologists will plan out an approach to the excavation first, and get any permissions required from local authorities. They also theorize about what might be found at the excavation, and then see how the discoveries match their expectations.

On site they will supervise crews of up to 50 excavators, making sure the project is carried out according to plan. They may also participate in hands-on tasks such as surveying the land, excavation, artifact collection, and preparing artifacts to be taken to the lab for analysis.

As an archaeologist, your day may include:
- Overseeing activity at the excavation
- Excavating, cleaning and studying artifacts you or your team discover
- Solving unforeseen challenges with the excavation

- Writing reports or articles about your discoveries
- Speaking with local authorities about your progress
- Meeting with botanists, geologists and other specialists
- Researching the history of an area and its culture
- Keeping up with the latest discoveries of your peers

Who is Likely to Succeed

Archaeology is best suited to people who have an existing interest in science and in studying the past. People already working in other scientific careers will make an easier transition into archaeology. And if you like hiking, photography, studying maps, and/or examining rocks, you already have some of the skills you need.

You should enjoy traveling and learning about different cultures, and believe that there is value in preserving the past. It also helps if you have advanced writing and speaking skills so you can tell the public and fellow archaeologists about your exciting discoveries.

How to Learn the Job

While volunteers are not always accepted in every profession, archaeology takes volunteers in with open arms. There is plenty of hands-on work to be done at an excavation, and you can learn the physical tasks involved with the career.

To find volunteer opportunities in archaeology, you can contact your local college or university and speak to someone in the anthropology department. For fieldwork openings all over the world, visit the Archaeological Institute of America's website (**www.archaeological. org**), which lists hundreds of opportunities by region.

You can also look for part-time or volunteer opportunities with your local museum. Working at a museum will expose you to many artifacts and help you learn their history, and may even present networking opportunities with archaeologists in your region.

You can learn about archaeology on your own through books and websites as well. Develop a personal plan where you learn about different regions of interest one at a time and build your knowledge of culture and geography, as well as the great discoveries of the past. Your region may even have an amateur archaeology society you can join. The *FabJob Guide to Become an Archaeologist* by Robert Larkin explains in detail how to prepare for and break into this career.

You can work with only a high school diploma in archaeology as a lab assistant, excavation laborer, or field technician, but if you want to be involved with more challenging tasks, you will want to look into obtaining an education in anthropology — either a BA, an MA, or a PhD.

The American Anthropological Association (**www.aaanet.org**) publishes the AAA Guide to anthropology departments, which will help you find the best program for you.

What It Pays

Principal archaeologists who lead an excavation have a general salary range of $30,000 to $50,000, or more as they progress in their careers. Field directors who work under the principal earn $25,000 to $45,000 annually. Crewmembers doing the manual work of an excavation earn anywhere from minimum wage to $12 an hour.

Editor

Editors are the people who shape what the world reads. They decide which pieces of writing are interesting or worthy of publication, and then they tweak, alter and adjust them into a readable form.

What They Do

Editors are the technical experts of the publishing industry. They take "raw" manuscripts and articles and make them fluid, organized, and error-free. They help writers to see the parts of their manuscript that need rewriting or restructuring. They also decide whether written work is publishable, or if it should be returned to the writer.

Editors work on books, newspapers, and magazines; corporate material such as websites, brochures and annual reports; and even academic papers. Anything that is written by someone who is eager for the reader to understand and enjoy it is usually subjected to an editor's eagle eye.

The editor may oversee groups of other editors and proofreaders and assign jobs for large editing projects, or they may do any or all editing work themselves. Editors can work on staff for a publishing company, or they can work with individual writers and companies on a freelance basis.

As an editor you will do some or all of the following:
- Review proposals for articles or books
- Assign projects to writers and photographers
- Plan the editorial content of a magazine, newspaper or book
- Proofread manuscripts and articles for typos and grammatical errors

- Fact-check details in books and articles
- Meet with art or marketing departments regarding projects
- Communicate with writers and give them feedback about their work
- Reorganize or rewrite portions of books or articles

Who is Likely to Succeed

Have you ever had that "Aha!" feeling when you catch a typo in a book or newspaper? Editors are curious, critical thinkers who question why things are a certain way. You may be somewhat of a perfectionist, but are able to be diplomatic when it comes to pointing out the errors of others.

You don't mind redoing or correcting things, and would rather be right than speedy. You are an avid reader of not just books, but everything from advertisements to road signs. You are systematic and self-disciplined, and when a deadline is looming, you step up and get things done.

How to Learn It

While there isn't a strict requirement for editors to have post-secondary education, many editors have studied journalism, communications or English at the college or university level. However, even if you haven't gone or don't plan to go to school, there are many ways to develop a natural talent.

Begin by refreshing your knowledge of grammar and style. (If you had a negative reaction to that last sentence, this probably isn't the career for you!) In addition to your dictionary and encyclopedia, editors use stylebooks such as the Chicago Manual of Style, or the CP Stylebook. These are fun to browse, and you'll learn the standards of the industry.

You can also take editing, writing, or technical writing classes at your community college. Editing courses should cover the tasks of writing or editing, as well as related issues like copyright law, layout and design, and the business of publishing. You can also subscribe to industry publications, and read the *FabJob Guide to Become a Book Editor* by Jodi Brandon.

The publishing industry is known for its availability of internships. These may be paid or unpaid — even unpaid is worth it if you will be working with people who can advance your career, or the company is well-known and looks good on your resume. If the internship is paid and/or with a smaller company, make sure that you will get hands-on experience doing the type of editing work you are most interested in.

If you want to jump right into doing everything editorial on your own, start your own magazine, 'zine, website or e-zine that you publish or update frequently. Hire writers and edit their work, then use this experience to build a portfolio you can show to future employers or clients.

What It Pays

According to the Bureau of Labor Statistics, median annual earnings for salaried editors are $43,890. The lowest 10 percent earned less than $25,780, and the highest 10 percent earned more than $80,020. Freelance editors are paid per assignment or per word, with assignment pay ranging from several hundred to thousands of dollars, or from a few cents to a dollar per word.

FBI or Secret Agent

An FBI or secret agent investigates suspicious or criminal activities, with a mandate to protect the people of their country from terrorism and crime.

What They Do

Federal Bureau of Investigation (FBI) agents are the U.S. government's principal investigators, responsible for investigating violations of more than 260 statutes and conducting sensitive national security investigations. They assemble the evidence into reports that are presented to federal authorities for consideration.

In Canada, the Royal Canadian Mounted Police (RCMP) fills a similar role. Special agents are also hired by the U.S. Secret Service, the Central Intelligence Agency (CIA) and several other federal agencies to investigate criminal behavior under their jurisdiction.

The FBI investigates organized crime, public corruption, financial crime, fraud against the government, bribery, copyright infringement, civil rights violations, bank robbery, extortion, kidnapping, air piracy, terrorism, espionage, interstate criminal activity, drug trafficking, and other violations of federal statutes.

As an FBI or secret agent your day might involve:
- Conducting surveillance
- Monitoring court-authorized wiretaps
- Examining business and computer records
- Working in tandem with local law enforcement

- Tracking the movement of stolen property
- Collecting evidence of spy activity
- Participating in undercover assignments

Who is Likely to Succeed

Secret agents are resourceful problem-solvers who can assemble many bits of evidence into a convincing "big picture." You are brave, patient, and don't mind working behind the scenes, since other members of the team may move in to make the big arrests. You have the personal flexibility to travel and be away from family and friends for weeks or months at a time with little or no notice.

You believe in justice and doing the right thing, and have a background free of criminal activity or drug use. You should be fit and healthy, with good vision and hearing. To be considered as an FBI agent you must be between the ages of 23 and 37 and have a minimum educational level of a four-year degree.

How to Learn It

Much of your specific agent training takes place in an academy once you are accepted to the FBI, RCMP, or other agency. However, you can look for ways before you apply to make yourself a more desirable candidate with skills already in place.

The FBI is currently most interested in applicants with the following skills: accounting/finance, computer science/IT, engineering, foreign languages, intelligence or law experience, law enforcement, military or investigative experience, and physical sciences. Look for courses and training in these areas to boost your chances of being accepted to the academy.

If you don't have education in one of these areas, look for ways to get part-time, entry-level or volunteer work and do some hands-on learning. Take courses in possible on-the-job skills such as gunmanship and self-defense. You can also volunteer with community organizations to demonstrate your commitment to helping the public.

Working in a related capacity such as security work or with the local law enforcement is also a good step, and will help you learn some of the language and techniques you'll need on the job.

Visit the FBI's website (**www.fbi.gov**) or the RCMP's website (**www.rcmp-grc.gc.ca**) to learn more about these agencies' mandates and what they are looking for in an applicant. Applications for other agencies such as the Secret Service (**www.secretservice.gov**) can be obtained from each agency's website.

What It Pays

FBI special agents start out earning $43,441* annually when they are accepted into the academy for training. Once you graduate, you receive what's called law enforcement availability pay (LEAP) — equal to a 25 percent bonus — because you are expected to be on call at all times. You may also receive "locality pay" depending on where you are sent to work. FBI supervisory, management, and executive positions can pay more than $100,000 per year (including LEAP).

RCMP officers are hired out of the cadet training program at an annual salary of $43,428*, and within 36 months of service, your salary will increase incrementally to $70,366* annually.

*Note: These numbers were accurate as of date of publication.

Financial Planner

People are becoming more concerned all the time with saving, protecting, and growing their wealth. Financial planners are the experts who help people manage their wealth and financial security.

What They Do

Financial planners are money experts who teach clients how to build financial health and wealth through proven savings, debt-reduction, tax management and investment techniques. They help clients assess their goals for educational and retirement planning, investments, insurance, estate planning and more. They use statistics and data to convince clients of the value of the products they sell.

Financial planners can work independently or for financial planning firms. They can also work for banks, brokerage firms, and insurance companies. Financial planners who work independently run their own small businesses, pursue their own leads and charge fees. Those who work for large companies often work on commission, and because of this need to be expert salespeople.

As a financial planner you will do some or all of the following:

- Aggressively pursue new leads for potential clients
- Assess clients' current financial situations and goals
- Present a written financial plan for clients
- Answer questions about financial products and their value
- Research investment opportunities for clients
- Offer suggestions for long-term financial planning solutions
- Help clients complete application paperwork
- Finalize the sale of financial products to clients

Who is Likely to Succeed

Financial planners should have a thorough understanding of the financial products available and their benefits. They build trust and rapport in order to be able to sell these effectively to clients. They are curious about money matters, good with quick calculations, and have their own finances in order with a plan for the future.

You are an excellent communicator, don't mind pursuing and winning clients to build your own business, and have the perseverance and financial flexibility to work on a commission basis. You have a flexible schedule in order to meet the availability of your clients.

How to Learn It

The place to start is exploring your own financial situation and what your options are. Most financial planners are happy to meet with you and explain the products they sell. Experimenting with the financial products that are on the market is a good way to learn how to assess who they are suited for.

You can work out theoretical calculations to see where your money should go, and then compare your data to what the financial planner brings to you. Ask questions until you fully understand what you are buying. You can also ask close friends and family about their financial decisions to look for current trends or good value.

There are many community college courses that are helpful for financial planners, including sales and marketing courses, economics, finance, and computer courses. Courses in investments, taxes, estate planning, and risk management also are helpful.

Some financial planners have previous experience in business, accounting, finance or related disciplines, and are able to translate that experience into giving solid financial advice.

Some of the big financial service companies such as Edward Jones (**www.edwardjones.com**) offer on-the-job training once you decide to affiliate yourself with them. Training with these companies ranges from courses of a few months in duration to weekend seminars, and may also include written material for you to study on your own.

Some individuals choose to become Certified Financial Planners to add to their industry knowledge and credibility with clients. The CFP Board-Registered Education Program is available at nearly 300 colleges and universities across the U.S. Attendees may take the Certified Financial Planners exam for a fee of around $600.

The Financial Planning Association can help you learn more about the industry. Their website (**www.fpanet.org**) offers numerous resources for those considering a career in financial planning, including an excellent overview of the industry, and a calendar of financial-planning related events.

Fab Fact: Suze Orman is the host of *Suze Orman's Financial Freedom* and CNBC's *The Suze Orman Show*. She is a well-known financial advisor, and author of the bestsellers *The 9 Steps to Financial Freedom* and *The Courage to Be Rich*, as well as many other finance-related books. Suze, whose philosophy is, "People first, then money, then things," attended the University of Illinois to get a BA in social work.

What It Pays

According to the Bureau of Labor Statistics, median annual earnings of personal financial advisors are $62,700. Personal financial advisors who work for financial services firms are generally paid a salary plus sales bonus.

Financial planners who work for financial-planning firms or who are self-employed either charge hourly fees for their services or charge one set fee for a comprehensive plan, based on its complexity. Advisors who manage a client's assets usually charge a percentage of those assets. A majority of planners/advisors receive commissions for financial products they sell.

Food Writer

Food writers lead delectable lives. They are the people who sample and write about the best foods, recipes and restaurants from around town or around the globe.

What They Do

Food writers specialize in writing about food and drink. They get a chance to dine out, travel, research, and often invent and test recipes. They might work as food critics or reviewers, food columnists, or they can even be cookbook writers.

Food writers are often self-employed freelance writers. However, they might work for newspapers, magazines, or television shows as on-staff writers or editors. Some food writers, especially those with published books, hit the lecture circuit and give talks about their favorite cuisine or cooking style.

As a food writer you will do some or all of the following:

- Write critiques of restaurants you visit
- Write articles about a particular food or cuisine
- Develop recipes to share or put into cookbooks
- Send query letters to food-related publications
- Monitor the food and dining industry for new trends
- Attend food-industry events
- Speak publicly about food, dining or cooking

Who is Likely to Succeed

If you are already planning your next meal out with gleeful anticipation, and love to write almost as much as you love to eat, you may find the life of a food writer perfect for you. Food writers are lifelong learners. They are observant of small details, and very tapped into their highly tuned senses of smell and taste.

Food writers can boost their marketability by learning about foreign cultures and their cuisine, fine-tuning their journalism skills, and taking up photography. The best of them can generate excitement about their ideas, so they can effectively sell them to editors.

How to Learn It

You already have the makings of your very own food writing training program in your home. Check out the Food Network (**www.foodtv.com**) and other food-related programming to get started. In your kitchen, dust off the cookbooks you haven't used in a while, and look for recipes that call for ingredients you seldom use to broaden your horizons.

Use the Internet to learn about food — everything from information about restaurants to massive websites devoted to the food industry are at your fingertips. Read what other food writers have to say about interesting cuisine, recipes and foods.

If your town or city already has a food critic, read his or her reviews regularly, and follow up with a visit to a restaurant they recently wrote about. Compare your experience to the critic's — what would you have written about this restaurant? Did they miss anything interesting or unusual? The *FabJob Guide to Become a Food Critic* by Pamela White explains the steps of writing a restaurant critique, as well as how to sell your work and succeed.

Some food writers obtain a degree in home economics, or journalism, but a college degree is not required for this career. There are courses in the hospitality industry and writing courses you can take, as well as hands-on cooking courses — both in traditional college settings and at cooking schools.

Start writing about food consistently by developing your own food blog. A blog is an online journal that many writers use to publish their own writing on the Internet — you can use it as a portfolio to direct potential employers to, and you will get feedback on your content from people who come across it. Set up a blog at **www. blogger.com**.

Does your neighborhood have a community newspaper? Maybe your child's school has a newsletter, or the PTA needs a volunteer to put together a cookbook of family recipes from the student population. You can gain a wealth of food writing experience and learn by doing at the same time.

What It Pays

Freelance food writers make anywhere from $50 to a few hundred dollars for a newspaper article (depending on the size of the publication), and $500 to $2,000 per article for a magazine. Staff food writers make salaries from $20,000 to $80,000 annually, and may have their expenses paid as well.

Food-related book authors can work for a flat fee or royalties (normally 10 to 15 percent of a book's sales). Beginners can make from $10,000 to $20,000 in royalties for a successful book, and experienced authors can make much more.

Forensic Specialist

Are you fascinated by TV shows like *CSI* that feature specialists using science to solve crimes? Forensics is not for the squeamish, but will definitely get your pulse racing as you help bring criminals to justice.

What They Do

Forensic specialists take the methodology of science and apply it to finding and interpreting crime scene evidence, in an attempt to prove how a crime was committed and who did it. They may work for the government, police departments, hospitals, coroner's offices, or independently.

Forensic specialists look for, analyze, and categorize criminal evidence. They work in forensic laboratories conducting scientific tests on physical evidence. They also work at the scenes of crimes, sometimes gathering evidence from violent crimes or homicides.

Forensic specialists may test for levels of poison, or use the principles of mathematics and engineering to interpret crime scene events. They gather fingerprint evidence and collect DNA samples from crime scenes to see how they match up with databases.

As a forensic specialist you will do some or all of the following:

- Visit crime scenes to gather and preserve evidence for analysis
- Work in a lab analyzing evidence
- Catalog evidence using a computer database
- Theorize about what happened at a crime scene
- Work in tandem with law enforcement officers
- Appear in court to give evidence
- Stay current with new forensic techniques

Who is Likely to Succeed

Forensic specialists must be well versed and knowledgeable about their scientific specialty, as well as general principles of science. They have a great deal of nerve, and the ability to deal with disturbing situations or violent crime scenes without letting their emotions get too involved.

Forensic specialists are both logical and creative thinkers. They are precise, orderly, and thorough in their work. They are extremely observant people who have a knack for interpreting human behavior. They are curious, and don't always accept the obvious answer as the right one.

How to Learn It

To break into this field, you'll want to start with an education in science and criminology, since you will likely cross over into forensics after some experience in one of these two areas. A Bachelor of Science degree is a perfect start, if you have the time and money — emphasize courses in chemistry, physics, and biology. You can also see what is available at your local community college — most have courses in criminology, and may even offer training in forensic science.

While pursing formal training, you can also learn more on your own. The American Academy of Forensic Science (**www.aafs.org**) publishes the *Journal of Forensic Sciences,* and hosts the Young Forensic Scientist Forum, designed to help new and beginning forensic scientists establish themselves in the field.

Develop your observation skills in everyday life. Take mental notes on each person on the bus on your way home, or try to figure out where your roommate went based on what they left lying around before you read the note they left. Ask a friend to test your memory of small details in a movie after you watch it. You can carry a notebook with you to improve your shorthand as well.

You may be able to get hands-on experience as a forensic specialist by working as a forensic intern. Colleges and law enforcement agencies offer a variety of internships, some paid, some unpaid. For example, the New York State Division of State Police offers intern positions for beginning forensic specialists. Use the Internet to check out possibilities in your region.

What It Pays

According to the Bureau of Labor Statistics, median hourly earnings of forensic science technicians are $21.16. Entry-level forensic specialists can make anywhere from $20,000 to $40,000 in annual salary. The most experienced and highly respected forensic specialists can make $100,000 or more annually. Independent forensic consultants charge on an hourly basis, from $100 to $500 an hour.

Interpreter / Translator

Interpreters and translators assist people who don't speak the same language in understanding each other, both verbally and in writing. As the global marketplace continues to evolve, their role is becoming ever more vital to the economy.

What They Do

Interpreters work with people who don't speak the same language, usually in a live conversation setting. They first listen in one language, and then communicate what was said to one or more listeners in another language. A translator does similar work, converting important documents from the language in which they are written to another.

Both interpreters and translators have superb English skills and a near-perfect understanding of another language. They find ways to communicate not just literal meanings, but ideas and figurative concepts that may be specific to a particular culture. Some interpreters specialize in converting spoken languages into sign language.

Some interpreters or translators are employed by multinational corporations, consulates, or other large companies that need them full time. Other interpreters and translators sign on with agencies that place them. One in five interpreters or translators is self-employed.

As an interpreter or translator you will do some or all of the following:

- Interpret statements after the speaker has finished
- Interpret ongoing speech simultaneously (the speaker continues to talk)
- Travel with clients to meetings, appointments, and even internationally
- Listen to recorded speech in another language, and then explain it to listeners
- Translate documents from one language into another
- Testify in court about interpretations of language
- Market your services or apply for assignments

Who is Likely to Succeed

Successful interpreters like to work with people in fast-paced environments, enjoy travel as part of their jobs, and have a genuine regard and sensitivity for other people's cultures and customs and nuances of language. A good memory is also an asset.

Successful translators don't have to be as proficient in people skills, but must be superb wordsmiths in both English and another language. Of course, the more languages you are proficient in, the better. Asian and Middle Eastern languages are particularly in demand at this time.

How to Learn It

Some people who have foreign-born parents have been interpreting and translating for them since childhood. This hands-on working knowledge helps many interpreters and translators even before they begin using their skills to make a living.

Begin by determining which language, other than English, you want to focus on. This will probably be easy to decide if you come from a bilingual family or already know a second language. Enroll in language classes that are appropriate to your level of skill.

It is generally agreed that the best way to learn a new language is to immerse yourself in it as much as possible. Ideally, you should travel to the region where the language is spoken and stay there for several months. When you are forced to use the language daily, the learning process is fast-tracked. If you have a basic knowledge of the language, ask questions about words or phrases that have complex meanings.

If it's not possible to travel, then listen to radio and TV programs in the foreign language in order to get used to the cadence of speech and accents. Read books that are familiar to you in foreign languages, and compare the texts to see what words are used. For a win-win exchange, you can also teach or volunteer to work with ESL (English as a Second Language) students or anyone who is new to the country.

Many interpreters and translators pursue college educations, and focus on one or several different languages. Also, don't neglect your English skills. You can learn more about careers in interpreting and translating from the American Translators Association (**www.atanet. org**).

What It Pays

Interpreters' and translators' salaries depend on specialty, experience, and whether or not they work full time, for an agency, or freelance. Salaried interpreters and translators have median hourly earnings of $16.28. According to a salary survey by the American Translators Association, Chinese and Japanese interpreters and translators earned the highest median hourly rates, ranging from $45 to $50 an hour. Self-employed interpreters charge from $40 to $80 per hour, and some freelance translators charge by the project or by the word.

Mystery Shopper

Do you always fill out the feedback forms to comment on the customer service you received? Put this habit to use as a mystery shopper, working undercover to help businesses evaluate their level of service.

What They Do

Mystery shoppers are paid to act like customers and shop at stores, stay at hotels, and dine at restaurants. They provide feedback to companies about various areas of their businesses, such as customer service, cleanliness, store appearance and staff efficiency.

Only five percent of customers actually register complaints when they are dissatisfied, while the other 95 percent simply never return. Because of this fact, companies hire mystery shoppers to find out what an average experience in their store or restaurant is really like, without the artificial preparations that often happen when the boss is around. The companies use this feedback to improve their standards of service.

Mystery shoppers are usually independent contractors who work from home when they are not out on assignment. They apply and are selected for mystery shopping assignments. They will visit the business in question, and then fill out a questionnaire with questions about cleanliness, service, staff's product knowledge, and efficiency. In some cases, shopping assignments may even take place online.

As a mystery shopper you will do some or all of the following:
- Apply for mystery shopping jobs
- Schedule assignments into your week
- Review assignment details to prepare for your visit
- Prepare questions to ask service providers
- Visit the selected business and discreetly note appropriate details
- Fill out and submit a report about your experience
- Keep records of completed assignments and payment

Who is Likely to Succeed

The best mystery shoppers have excellent powers of observation, good judgment, integrity, and the motivation to seek out assignments regularly. They are not easily flustered, and don't mind traveling to jobs within about a 60-mile radius. They are colorful writers who can truly paint a visual picture of an experience.

If you are organized, on time, and reliable, you already have three of the most desired characteristics in this industry. Many mystery shopping companies prefer to hire shoppers that have retail or customer-service experience.

How to Learn It

The next time you have a remarkably good or poor shopping, dining, or service experience, don't just brag or complain to your friends about it. Instead, write up a detailed report about your experience, including the date and time of your visit, and a description of what happened. Use interesting language, and include as many details as you can remember.

What you do with your practice reports is up to you. You can send them to the store manager or company headquarters — chances are you might even get a reply or some free coupons in the mail for your effort. You can also post your reviews on websites like

www.epinions.com for other consumers to read and comment on, or combine them into a mystery shopping website or blog that you update frequently.

The Secret Shopper Company (**www.secretshoppercompany.com**) and The National Center for Professional Mystery Shoppers & Merchandisers (**www.justshop.org**) offer online learning opportunities and conferences where you can learn the basics of the business and get certified. You can also learn a lot by visiting mystery shopper chat boards, where shoppers come together to ask questions and discuss experiences.

You can begin work as a mystery shopper as soon as your application is accepted by an agency or company (in the state of Nevada mystery shoppers must be employed by a private investigation company). The *FabJob Guide to Become a Mystery Shopper* by Lauren Morgan has all the details you need to learn the ropes and land your first assignment.

What It Pays

Mystery shopping payment can range anywhere from $10 to $1,000 or more per assignment, or may simply come in the form of reimbursement of your expenses. You can easily make $500 to $1,500 a month working part time, and some full time shoppers make in excess of $50,000 a year.

Nutritionist

As more people are beginning to realize the impact of proper diet on good heath, they are turning to experts for help planning and preparing what they eat. Nutritionists advise people on the best foods for their lifestyle and overall heath.

What They Do

Nutritionists help individuals analyze what and how much they eat, and explain how it is affecting their overall health. They help people with health problems choose foods that are better for them, help overweight people plan diets to slim down, and help athletes choose foods that will help them perform at their best.

Nutritionists work in conjunction with doctors' offices, holistic health centers, or retail businesses that emphasize health, or they may work in private practice. Some nutritionists specialize in helping a certain group of people who have distinct dietary concerns, such as the elderly, children, or pregnant women.

Nutritionists start by meeting with clients to determine their overall heath. They ask questions, examine clients, and sometimes order tests to determine how they can best assist them. As a nutritionist you will do some or all of the following:

- Meet with clients to explain your services
- Review client test results and questionnaires
- Plan nutritionally sound menus for clients
- Advise clients on specific food choices that are good or bad
- Stay on top of recent medical discoveries related to nutrition
- Work in tandem with medical or other professionals
- Assess clients frequently and give them progress reports
- Write articles or speak about nutrition

Who is Likely to Succeed

Nutritionists are truly interested in helping people make healthier food choices. Maybe you developed an interest in the science of food while you planned your own weight-loss program, or cooked healthy meals for your family.

You are a kind person who can give advice without sounding like you are criticizing, and are a natural teacher and motivator. It helps if you are a talented cook so you can develop or recommend recipes that your clients find both enjoyable and healthy.

How to Learn It

To develop your knowledge of nutrition, become a label-reader. It might surprise you to read that most breakfast cereals are a good source of iron, or that they are now adding calcium to old favorites like orange juice. Read books and online informational websites about nutrition. Start keeping a mental (or actual) list of the key dietary requirements of human beings, and what foods are good sources of them.

As you learn more about nutrition and are ready to try out what you have learned, approach friends and family members (and even use yourself) to test your theories and diet suggestions. Perhaps you have a family member who is dealing with a health issue that requires a special diet — develop a creative meal plan they can try for a week, and ask them for feedback on your choices and the first week's results.

There are a number of courses and degree programs available for those interested in learning about nutrition, some of which are offered as distance learning programs or self-study courses. If you want to work for hospitals or other regulated institutions you will likely need a four-year degree, but employers such as spas, gyms and holistic centers will not necessarily be as stringent.

The National Association of Nutrition Professionals (**www.nanp. org**) hosts a variety of ongoing continuing education courses for nutrition professionals as well as an annual convention and trade show.

One online community geared toward dieticians and nutritionists that provides a forum for those new to the industry is Dietician Central (**www.dieticiancentral.com**). This online community offers an expert's corner with a number of high-level experts who will address your questions in the form of online posts.

If you want to get a comprehensive education in nutritional issues, consider studying to become a RD (Registered Dietician – four years of school) or DTR (Dietetic Technician, Registered – two years of school). You can learn more about nutrition careers at the American Dietetic Association website (**www.eatright.org**).

What It Pays

The typical nutritionist annual salary ranges from $25,000 to $60,000 a year, with an average in the $40,000 range. Nutritionists who are in private practice typically charge $50 to $250 or more per 30- to 90-minute appointment.

Pilot

As a pilot, you will have the exciting and high-flying responsibility of operating a plane or helicopter. You will transport people and cargo safely, or carry out specialized tasks that can only be done from the air.

What They Do

Pilots fly jet planes, propeller planes, seaplanes and helicopters; transporting people and cargo from place to place. Some are employed by large commercial airlines to fly passengers across the country or to exotic destinations. Others may fly small planes for corporations or wealthy individuals, or to dust crops, transport mail, fight fires, or rescue people.

Some pilots fly stunt planes in air shows, or pull advertising banners behind their planes. Helicopter pilots may fly helicopters for tour companies, for TV or movie productions, or to transport executives and personnel for police, weather and news organizations.

Working as a pilot allows you to travel around the world or around your region. You have the tremendous responsibility of ensuring passengers and cargo get to their destinations safely, and must be able to remain calm and cool-headed in stressful conditions.

As a pilot, your duties may include some or all of the following:

- Deciding on appropriate routes and altitudes for each flight
- Creating and logging flight plans
- Ensuring that cargo is loaded correctly
- Checking the plane's or helicopter's equipment and systems before flight
- Meeting with flight crew to discuss the day's flight
- Working in tandem with a co-pilot
- Communicating with control towers, flight crew and passengers
- Monitoring instrument panels in the aircraft's cockpit
- Reporting on weather and other conditions you have observed from the air
- Responding appropriately in case of emergency

Who is Likely to Succeed

You are probably adventurous and mechanically inclined, and enjoy the workings of machinery. You're responsible and detail-oriented. You are flexible in your schedule and willing to spend long hours and sometimes even days at a time away from home.

To get a private pilot's license you must be at least 17 years old, meet medical and training/experience requirements as established by the Federal Aviation Administration, and pass a written test and flight exam. If you have had previous military training as a pilot, you may be more likely to land the higher-paying jobs, as this experience will have exposed you to more sophisticated technology and aircraft.

How to Learn the Job

Learning the basic skills of flying an airplane or helicopter must be done with the help of an accredited instructor. You can become a pilot either through the military (by joining the navy's pilot training or the air force), or by taking pilot training at civilian flight schools or with the help of a private instructor.

Any of these routes will teach you to operate aircraft, to file flight plans and perform maintenance on aircraft. You will undergo practical, hands-on learning in real aircraft as well as learning in flight simulators. You will also write written exams to ensure you know about aircraft maintenance, flight plans and weather conditions, among other topics.

Once you are able to operate an aircraft, you need to log at least 250 hours of flight time before you are able to qualify for a commercial pilot's license through the Federal Aviation Administration (**www.faa. gov**). Many pilots start their jobs as flight engineers or first officers, and gain additional flying experience this way. You can also qualify for additional ratings (such as flying jet planes or flying with instruments only) by logging more hours of flight experience.

You can study books and websites to familiarize yourself with the types of aircraft in existence, and visit air shows that have planes and helicopters on the ground that you can go inside and examine. Practicing at home with flight simulation video games will help your reflexes and responses, and can contribute to your overall skill.

Fab Fact: John Travolta, star of such films as *Saturday Night Fever*, *Pulp Fiction* and *Broken Arrow*, is an accomplished pilot licensed to fly several types of aircraft, including his own Gulfsteam II and Boeing 707 jets. John is an Ambassador-at-Large for Qantas airlines, and at his home in Florida he has a 1.4-mile runway and hangars to house a couple of his planes.

What It Pays

Earnings of aircraft pilots and flight engineers vary greatly depending whether they work as airline or commercial pilots. According to the Bureau of Labor Statistics, median annual earnings of airline pilots, copilots, and flight engineers are $129,250. The median annual earnings of commercial pilots (such as crop-dusters, test pilots, and helicopter pilots) are $53,870.

Those working for large airlines are typically members of unions, while those working for smaller, regional airlines or corporate clients may earn less than the median. Pilots flying sophisticated jet planes can expect higher salaries. Benefits like free travel and health insurance are standard.

Private Investigator

Private investigators use their critical thinking and observation skills to help people find out the truth about events in the present or past.

What They Do

Private investigators are hired by individual clients or companies to perform specific investigative and detective work. They are skilled at observing people unnoticed, and may also use interviews and research to build a case of evidence that supports a particular theory.

Private investigators often find themselves performing surveillance work such as waiting at a stakeout location to secretly snap pictures, or observing a suspect's activities. There is also a market for private investigators who are computer and research experts who spend much of their work time logged on to the Internet searching for hard-to-find information.

Types of assignments include searching for missing people, arson investigation, background investigations, employee theft, insurance fraud, or surveillance for any number of purposes from suspected adultery to criminal behavior. As a private investigator you will do some or all of the following:

- Meet with clients to determine their needs
- Explain to clients what your services entail
- Use surveillance techniques to covertly observe people
- Research for relevant facts in libraries and online
- Take pictures or video that will be evidence
- Work in tandem with law enforcement officials
- Write reports of what you have learned
- Bill clients and manage your bookkeeping
- Keep on top of the latest technology and gadgets

Who is Likely to Succeed

If you are an expert researcher, curious, adventurous, patient, and determined, you have many of the characteristics of successful private investigators. You have a healthy dose of skepticism, and take nothing for truth until it's proven.

You have a knack for finding out information that is difficult to track down. You are sympathetic and a good listener, discreet and ethical. You are a creative problem-solver to whom no task is impossible. You notice details others tend to miss, and are a good judge of character.

How to Learn It

While some private investigators transition into the work from careers in law enforcement or military careers, it isn't necessary to have these to break into this career. If you have studied or plan to study psychology, English, sociology, business law, computers, or criminology, any of these are logical transitions into the work a PI does, and may allow you to develop an investigation specialty.

There are numerous detective schools and training programs for private investigators, ranging in price from hundreds to thousands of dollars. Distance learning courses are also available. Ensure that the program you choose is reputable, and that the curriculum is up to date. You can also learn how to do the job and how to get hired or start your own investigation company in the *FabJob Guide to Become a Private Investigator*.

You might consider conducting an investigation into a personal matter in order to learn the ropes in a forgiving environment. Perhaps you have a cousin who is adopted and would like to find her birth mother, or you have a friend who suspects his sister-in-law is having an affair. You can offer your investigation services in exchange for a letter of recommendation if you are able to uncover the truth.

You can get experience in surveillance and other investigative tasks by working as a store detective or security guard, or even in paralegal work or insurance claims investigation. You can also volunteer your investigation services for little or no pay to a law office or investigation agency, with the understanding that, if they are satisfied with your work, future investigation will be on a paying basis.

Many regions have an association for private investigators, and there are dozens of different associations and organizations that speak to specific areas of the industry. Most associations have conferences and other opportunities for learning and networking for private investigators.

Most states and provinces require private investigators to be licensed. Check with your state or region for education, work experience, and licensing requirements, which vary.

What It Pays

Beginning private investigators make around $30,000 annually, and those more advanced make $55,000 or more. Self-employed sleuths must determine a fee structure including hourly rates, retainers and expenses. Hourly rates range from $40 to $75 an hour for basic investigation, and $150 or more per hour for an established expert.

Professional Organizer

Clutter... chaos... confusion... professional organizers love these words, because they know it means there is work to be done. Professional organizers create organizational systems for people in their homes and businesses.

What They Do

Professional organizers help people get their daily lives in order. They use systems of categorizing and arranging to sort people's physical, mental and virtual spaces into user-friendly domains. They help people develop ways of doing and organizing things that are intuitive and user-friendly, to help them save time and aggravation.

Organizers are hired by individual clients to help them organize rooms in their homes; and by both individuals and businesses to assist them with their computer or actual filing systems, their time or schedules, and their systems for getting things done. Many organizers focus on a specialty like small businesses, closets, garages, moving/ relocation issues, or Feng Shui.

As a professional organizer you will do some or all of the following:
- Meet with clients to discuss their needs
- Analyze information from your client to work out systems for them
- Purchase organizing equipment and supplies for clients
- Assist clients with de-cluttering their space
- Determine what items, if any, can be removed or stored
- Implement organizational systems hands-on
- Create marketing materials for your business
- Bill for services and keep your books
- Write or speak about organizing to promote your business
- Network with other professional organizers

Who is Likely to Succeed

Professional organizers have a passion for order. They lead orderly lives themselves, and are always looking for a more efficient way of doing things. They use their critical thinking skills to identify problems and present solutions.

Sympathetic and good listeners, organizers can point out where people's systems are failing them without sounding critical or judgmental. They are positive, motivating people who inspire their clients with a can-do attitude. They are great networkers, and find most of their clients through getting out and talking to people about what they do.

How to Learn It

Start by assessing the organizational skills you already have or use. Look at the already-existing organizational systems and methods you have created in your own home, office and life. Perhaps you have a talent for organizing closets; perhaps you are a whiz at computer databases. Once you have defined your skills, you will be able to refine them and package them to share with clients.

You can begin hands-on learning immediately by helping your family and friends with their organizational challenges, or even in your own home. Apply the principles of organization you are already familiar with to each situation.

Take before-and-after pictures of your early work, and ask for testimonials you can use to attract more paying clients. You should also use your early experiences to develop questionnaires and exercises so you will be able to help future clients based on your expert knowledge.

You will find more than 250 pages of organizing advice and strategies, along with forms and checklists to use with clients in the *FabJob Guide to Become a Professional Organizer* by Grace Jasmine, along with tips on setting up your business and finding clients.

You can join the National Association for Professional Organizers (**www.napo.net**), which is the largest association for professional organizers in the world. They have 20 local chapters across the U.S.A. so you can attend monthly chapter meetings in your area. In Canada, Professional Organizers in Canada (**www.organizersin canada.com**) fills a similar role.

You can also get great ideas for reducing clutter and organizing different spaces by watching TLC's *Clean Sweep* on television.

What It Pays

Professional organizers are mostly self-employed. Annual incomes are based on their levels of expertise, their reputations, and the type of clients they pursue. Most professional organizers charge an hourly rate of anywhere from $25 to $200 or more. For jobs where the work involved is straightforward, you can also offer a flat fee or square-footage rate. Organizers' annual salaries range from $20,000 to more than $100,000.

Researcher

With the world's collection of information constantly expanding, experts in tracking down hard-to-find information — a.k.a. professional researchers — are in high demand.

What They Do

Researchers search the Internet, books, archives, computer databases and other sources of information to locate precise details their clients or employers want, such as how many people attended the 1999 World Series, or what past case law supports a recent court decision. Sometimes they will look at the information they have tracked down to draw interesting conclusions about what the data tells them.

Researchers or "information professionals" work in colleges and universities, libraries, for TV producers and book publishers, government offices, corporate think tanks, dedicated research companies, and as self-employed consultants. Some of the specialty jobs researchers may hold are research assistant or clerk, research librarian, fact-checker, and archivist.

As a researcher you will do some or all of the following:

- Assist a writer or other professional in compiling research
- Work as part of a research team or think tank
- Use computer databases to locate existing knowledge
- Use the Internet and libraries to search for information
- Write reports or research papers
- Compile bibliographies of existing books and periodicals on various subjects
- Categorize notes, and construct databases of information

Who is Likely to Succeed

If you get a thrill out of finding out the tough answers, and always have general trivia to share with your friends, this may be the career for you. Perhaps you yearn for your school days, when tracking down information was part of your daily routine. Well, researchers are lifelong learners who love knowledge for knowledge's sake.

You are curious and resourceful — "I can't" is not in your vocabulary. Although a basis of general knowledge is helpful, it helps to have an interest in a research specialty, such as medicine or law. You don't mind quiet days spent with your nose in a book or in front of a computer screen — in fact, these are probably already some of your favorite pastimes.

How to Learn It

While a large number of researchers are academics at various stages of their undergraduate or postgraduate work, it is still possible to be a researcher with no credentials other than a proven talent for finding out information.

Begin to expand your horizons in a place where all researchers love to hang out — a university or research library. These libraries usually make library cards available to the general public for a fee. You can ask for help learning (or take a short course in how to use) powerful information databases like LexisNexis, or browse the periodicals collection to familiarize yourself with what they offer.

If you are thinking about getting a formal education, take an inventory of your existing knowledge and expertise. Determining what areas of research you consider your strengths will help you gear your education in the right direction.

Information technology, technical writing and library studies are all logical transitions to this career, and also put you in a position to network with people who need your researching help. Courses in statistics will help your career as a researcher, as well as higher education in an area you hope to specialize in. You may even be able to find courses in research techniques at your community college.

To get hands-on experience, look for opportunities to contribute to some of the growing online information databases, or work on updating projects for them. Entry-level work as a fact-checker for a newspaper or magazine will also teach you where to go for hard-to-find information, and introduce you to copyright laws and other researching concepts. Check out the Association of Independent Information Professionals at **www.aiip.org** for information about the profession.

What It Pays

Beginning researchers earn in the range of $18,000 to $30,000 annually. On the other hand, an academic researcher with an advanced degree can make from $50,000 to $75,000 a year or more. Self-employed consultants charge rates of $25 to $120 an hour (with $55 being average), or $300 to $800 dollars for a day's work.

Stockbroker/Stock Trader

Are you a calculated risk-taker with an eye for trends and a mind for money? Stockbrokers and stock traders ride the volatile wave of the stock market, with the intention of making more money than they put in, through smart buying and selling.

What They Do

Stockbrokers and stock traders invest money in the stock market. Brokers invest their clients' money for them in stocks and bonds, as well as purchase mutual funds and insurance. They must be a member of the stock exchange to buy or sell, so they work for brokerage firms.

Stock traders, on the other hand, invest their own money to buy and sell stocks for themselves. They are often self-employed, and earn a living by successfully trading stock.

Both stockbrokers and traders must have an expert understanding of the stock market. They must be able to analyze the market itself, the business climate, the ramifications of world events, and the companies that have stock in play, and use this information to make decisions that pay off.

As a stockbroker or stock trader you will do some or all of the following:

- Meet with clients to discuss their investment possibilities
- Advise clients by phone on possibly lucrative moves
- Analyze the stock market daily
- Meet with other brokers to discuss market trends
- Stay on top of current events that may affect stock value
- Watch hourly fluctuations in the market on your computer
- Give orders to buy or sell your own or clients' stock
- Fill out related paperwork
- Aggressively market your services to new clients

Who is Likely to Succeed

Stockbrokers and stock traders share an interest in the stock market that goes beyond a desire to make money. They are interested in how the market fluctuates, and excited by trying to predict where it will go. They are level-headed and cool under pressure, and decisive when they need to be.

Stockbrokers must be superb salespeople with the ability to network, and the finesse to pursue high-income, extremely busy potential clients. Stock traders must have the intellect of analysts, money to invest, and nerves of steel. Past experience in real estate or financial planning are natural transitions to trading stocks.

How to Learn It

Potential stockbrokers and stock traders should get started watching the stock market. It's time to start paying attention to those cryptic tickers along the bottom of the news channel screen — familiarize yourself with at least the more common stock market symbols, as well as recent and past trends.

Browse the business sections of the newspaper for stories of national or global interest. As you read, think about how the events in each report could affect stock prices for better or for worse, and then follow up with those sectors of the market in the next few days or weeks to see if you were right.

An easy and free way to get experience investing in the stock market is to "trade paper." Trading paper is doing all the research and carefully watching a fictitious portfolio as if you had invested a set amount of money. Don't just track your results, instead think about why your stocks have responded the way they have. This will help you predict future changes more accurately.

Some future stockbrokers start out with finance or economics degrees. If you don't have a college degree there is still much you can do to prepare yourself for either career, including topical courses at your local college campus or distance-learning courses available online.

Stockbrokers in the U.S. must complete exams to have the legal authority to advise their clients. First they must be employed by a broker or dealer, register with the securities industry regulators, and then study for and pass an exam called the Series 7. Additionally, most states require that stockbrokers take the Uniform Securities State Law Examination (Series 63 exam), and the Uniform Investment Advisor Law Exam (Series 65 exam). In Canada, you need to complete the Canadian Securities Course and become registered with the Investment Dealers' Association to trade stocks, bonds and other securities.

What It Pays

Stockbrokers often make a commission on each stock purchase they arrange for their clients, and traders make their money by investing in stocks when they are low in cost and then selling them for more. Successful stockbrokers average between $80,000 and $150,000 or more a year. Successful traders make widely varying amounts based on their ability to invest initially, and the success of their trades, but the potential to make big gains is present.

Travel Writer

Travel writers stay in fabulous hotels, enjoy wondrous sights, eat spectacular cuisine at excellent restaurants, and savor exotic cultures

— all while being paid to share these pleasures with others through their writing.

What They Do

Travel writers are people who write about the places they have visited for magazines, newspapers, books, and travel guides. They share their unique global experiences with their readers, and open doors in people's imaginations. Travel writers feed the sense of adventure in us all.

Travel writers are often freelancers, although they may work exclusively for one publication. Sometimes they shop their completed articles or manuscripts around to different publishers to see who will buy them, or else they can approach editors with their concept, and then hopefully get the assignment to pursue their idea.

As a travel writer you will do some or all of the following:
- Prepare to visit, and travel to interesting locations
- Take notes about your travel experiences
- Refine your notes and flesh them out with research and facts
- Brainstorm unique angles to write articles from
- Learn about different cultures and regions
- Submit query letters or proposals to editors
- Communicate with editors and/or agents
- Rewrite portions of your work as requested
- Read other travel writing to keep up with the market
- Negotiate payment for your writing
- Help promote your work

Who is Likely to Succeed

You don't need a degree in journalism or creative writing to be a great travel writer. If you have the ability to tell interesting stories, a love of travel, attention to detail, and an interest in and respect for other cultures, you have the makings of a great travel writer.

You should also be someone who is naturally organized and good at planning ahead, adapt easily to changes in plans, and motivated to make traveling for a living your career. You'll increase your marketability if you can take excellent photos to accompany your writing.

How to Learn It

You can develop your travel writing skills by practicing writing descriptively about the world around you. Try bringing a journal with you when you go out, and describe what is going on around you, even in your own town or city.

Attend local cultural events, and then imagine how you would describe them to someone who was unfamiliar with the culture. Try to paint a picture with your words. Think about any areas that really interest you — these have the potential to become your travel writing specialization.

If you want help with your writing, chances are there are numerous writing classes offered in your community, or you can join writing critiquing circles online. Foreign language classes are also a great idea to increase your versatility. Check out the catalog of your local community college, or visit a website like **www.writers.com**.

Of course, the more traveling you can do early on in your career, the better you will be familiarized with a variety of locations and cultures. If you can't afford to travel internationally, then visit local areas of interest. When you can't get away, immerse yourself in written material and TV shows devoted to travel and distant locations.

You might also try to get related experience by working with a travel agency or as a tour guide. Even volunteering in a museum or historic village will give you experience learning about cultures and working with the public in a "storytelling" capacity.

What It Pays

Beginning travel writers are usually paid a flat fee per article or per book. Payment for a travel article ranges from $10 to a few thousand dollars, plus a small sum for your pictures.

Most book publishers pay a flat fee, such as $10,000. Your travel expenses may also be covered. In some instances you can work out a royalty arrangement with your publisher, where you get a percentage of what each copy of the book sells for. Book royalties are typically six to 10 percent of sales.

Treasure Hunter

As a treasure hunter, you will search both the physical world and historical records to discover rare and valuable items that have been hidden, lost or forgotten. If you loved *The Da Vinci Code*, got hooked on the show *Treasure Hunters*, or can't get enough of your *Raiders of The Lost Ark* DVDs, this may be your dream career.

What They Do

Treasure hunters search for coins, gold, minerals, jewelry, historical artifacts or man-made objects. You'll use your intelligence and curiosity to figure out where objects might be hidden, and do extensive research to support your theories.

Treasure hunting can be physical work done mainly outdoors, or sometimes in unusual locations around the world. However, some treasure hunters look for valuable but overlooked objects that are hidden in plain sight, and base their work on knowing the financial, historical or cultural significance of particular items.

Treasure hunters use specialized equipment, such as metal detectors, to search for coins and other metal objects, and may specialize in a particular type of treasure hunting, such as deep-sea or scuba diving around sunken ships.

Treasure hunters may be employed on a contract basis, working for various individuals, or may work for an archaeological firm or other company that does a lot of work in excavation. In some cases they are self-employed. As a treasure hunter, you may find yourself doing some or all of the following:

- Referring to and interpreting maps
- Researching in libraries and archives for historical information
- Interviewing people who may have historical information
- Identifying found items through research
- Sifting and sorting through items to find what you want
- Traveling to a location where you plan to hunt
- Using technology such as GPS to guide your search
- Searching for treasures

Who is Likely to Succeed

You love mysteries, and enjoy figuring out puzzles. You're probably interested in history, and have a good understanding of human nature. You are determined and passionate about your work, and can't rest until you've accomplished your goals. In addition, you're patient, diligent and detail-oriented, and probably have a good memory for stories and images.

You'll be a successful treasure hunter if you can combine your deep curiosity about a particular era or type of treasure with both the research abilities needed to uncover information about where valuables might be stored or hidden, and the physical search skills needed to uncover them.

How to Learn the Job

Treasure hunters don't need any professional training or qualifications, but some education in history, archaeology or even anthropology can help you find a niche, or figure out a type of treasure or valuable you might want to look for. Read historical documents, geological surveys, and shipping records and maps. Learn how to find your way around libraries and archives, and develop your research skills by studying photographs and written records.

There are a variety of magazines and books, such as *Western and Eastern Treasures Magazine*, which can help you learn more about particular items and topics relevant to treasure hunters. Treasure hunter and explorer Stan Grist offers training courses and treasure guides at his website **www.stangrist.com**.

You can also attend meetings and conventions with other treasure hunters to learn new techniques and share stories. Start by joining treasure hunting associations and clubs in your area, where you can meet with other members who can help you learn.

Developing your knowledge of an historical era (such as the Gold Rush) or culture can help you think like someone who might have hidden treasure. Developing your related skills, such as observation of detail and research, and physical abilities, such as digging, sorting and even scuba diving, can help you with your actual hunts.

What It Pays

If you work for yourself, treasure hunting doesn't pay a thing until you've found your prize. You may be paid for the actual searching time if you are working on behalf of a client, in which case you may negotiate a flat fee of hundreds to thousands of dollars, depending on the complexity of the search.

Fab Fact: Mel Fisher has been named the "World's Greatest Treasure Hunter." He searched for more than 16 years for a shipwrecked Spanish galleon that sank along with seven other ships near Key West, Florida during a hurricane in 1622. In 1985, all the searching that Mel and his team of treasure hunters had done finally paid off when they found more than 40 tons of gold, silver, emeralds, coins and precious artifacts valued at more than $450 million.

Found objects are usually sold to a collector, museum or through auction. Depending on the item's worth, you may make a few hundred dollars or millions of dollars from any given find. For example, *Smithsonian Magazine* reported in 2004 that American treasure hunter Robert Graf stands to make $200 million or more on a treasure he's tracking in the Seychelles.

Web Designer

Nearly everyone knows how to use the Internet, but relatively few people have the skills required to create each of the websites that make it up. Web designers are the sought-after, high-tech artists who design each web page and make it functional.

What They Do

Web designers create web pages and manage websites for their clients. They work with clients to discuss a website's content, and then use design programs to create what is desired, from moving images to easy-to-read text. They interconnect each of the pages in a way that is user-friendly, and may be required to troubleshoot for and correct programming or navigational errors. Those who focus on programming may have the job title "web developer."

Sometimes designers start a website from scratch, and do it all. Other times they work with clients who have existing sites or content, and help them to take their raw and unedited ideas and design concepts and build these into an effective web presence.

Web designers hold a variety of jobs. Some work in departments of large corporations, dedicating their work solely to their own company's website development and design. Others work for companies that have constantly changing content and design needs such as online newspapers or magazines, while others become freelance designers.

As a web designer you will do some or all of the following:

- Meet with clients or other departments to discuss their needs
- Stay up-to-date with web trends and advances in technology
- Learn new design techniques and programs
- Market yourself to new clients
- Prepare proposals to land freelance design jobs
- Help clients write or edit their content
- Do hands-on design using software and programming languages
- Revise web content and design based on client feedback
- Update websites frequently to reflect the client's desired changes

Who is Likely to Succeed

The most successful professional web designers combine several major areas of talent: expert computer knowledge, writing, editing and graphic design talent, and sometimes marketing, advertising and business skills.

If you love to study and create web pages, consider yourself an expert computer user, and have an eye for what looks good and works in a website, you may find that a career as a web designer is an excellent choice for you. Web designers have excellent customer service ability and good listening skills to accurately interpret their client's needs.

How to Learn It

Learning to be a web designer is something you can begin today. All you will need is your computer, an Internet connection and your own creativity, talent, and business skills.

Even though you don't need a college degree to pursue a career as a web designer, you will definitely need to know what you are doing. Most community colleges offer courses on a variety of web design topics, some geared to specific software. There are many distance-learning opportunities for web designers as well.

Start by building your own website, and incorporate as many unique features as possible to give yourself a broad range of experience. If you are thinking about going into business for yourself, make it a site that sells your services and demonstrates your talent. Study your favorite websites for inspiration, and take note of design elements that you could improve on.

If you are not sure what design software you want to use, work with a variety of them. See if they have free online trials you can download, or student versions you can purchase while you are learning. You should also work on building a reliable network of resources (people and reference books) to help you with design-related challenges.

Begin on-the-job training by using your friends, family, and volunteer contacts as a way to get started building experience immediately. If you have a family member or friend who needs a website built, offer your services for free in exchange for a link on their new website to your web design business.

What It Pays

According to the Bureau of Labor Statistics, average annual salaries range from $51,750 to $74,520 for web developers. Freelancers typically charge by the hour or the project, and hourly rates average from $25 to $100 an hour. Web designers working on contract for large companies can charge even more than that.

HOW TO BREAK IN

Once you have decided which "brainy" career is right for you, it's time to plan your steps to breaking in and succeeding in it — and as a critical thinker, planning should come fairly naturally to you.

As you'll see on the following pages, no one's path to success in a particular career is ever the same as the next person's. You will draw on your unique abilities and experiences, and round them out with study or training where you fall short. When you approach employers or clients, you are selling them the complete package of "you," so make sure you are attractive to them by:

- Getting experience
- Showing off your talent
- Selling yourself effectively

The rest of this chapter will guide you through these three steps.

Getting Experience

Depending on the career you are pursuing, you may require formal training, learning on your own, or a mixture of both that is compelling to an employer.

Formal Training and Education

Pursuing formal training in a career is ideal for those with more money than time, since you will be handed the appropriate textbooks for learning, get help arranging internships or apprenticeships where appropriate, and learn the skills necessary in the least possible amount of time — as little as a weekend for some of the careers listed. For those of you with more time than money, informal training (as described later in this chapter) may be a better route for you.

Before looking into any formal training in your career, the first thing you'll want to do is find out if your career is regulated by local or federal agencies. This means that you will need to be licensed or certified to be a professional in the career.

Licensing agencies can provide you with their requirements for licensing, and you can use these requirements as a "checklist" when you prepare for your career. Many agencies or associations certify or endorse certain educational providers, so there's no point in taking a particular training course only to find out that you needed a different one to earn your certification.

In some of the careers listed above, such as editor or professional organizer, certification will be not required, but voluntary. Voluntary certification can benefit anyone who is new to a career, or those with limited experience in the field, and especially anyone who will be working directly with clients. Your certification just might be the deciding factor in hiring you over the competition. It gives the client or employer the impression that you take your job seriously, and that you are fully qualified in your profession.

When you are considering a training program, make sure that you are getting value for your money by asking some or all of the following questions of the educational provider:

- Are the teachers working professionals? If not, you may run the risk of someone teaching you skills, styles and techniques that are out of touch with today's industry.
- Is the curriculum up-to-date, and also advanced enough for your level of skill? Ask questions about what the most recent changes or additions have been to the curriculum, and ask if there are both beginner and advanced levels, or if everyone is lumped into the same group.
- If the class or program is a longer one, does it offer on-the-job training, co-op programs, or job shadowing so you can learn the "etiquette" of your future job environment?
- Does the school have any kind of published placement rate of its graduates?
- How big is the average class? The pace of information can move quickly in a three-week course, and if there are 40 students, there's little time for individual questions.

If you are applying for a longer program (six weeks or more) it is realistic to ask if you can sit in and "audit" a class for a short time to see what the teacher and material are like. If the school says no, this should send you a clear message that they are cranking out graduates and don't really care about helping you.

Make sure the program has a cancellation policy in place, and find out what it is. If they don't get enough students for a session and cancel it, you will want your money back right away to reapply elsewhere. Make sure you don't have to wait until the next session is scheduled in three or six months.

Find out if there are past graduates you can talk to. If the school won't help, that's another red flag. If they do supply a list, ask any of them you talk to for a referral to someone else they graduated with. One degree of separation is more likely to get you an honest review.

Informal Training

Learning on your own, at your own pace, is a popular option for anyone who wants to break into a new career gradually or part-time, or who plans to forego formal education and jump right into the thick of things.

The first step to learning on your own is the Internet, bookstores, or your local library. You can begin researching your career and learning the skills you'll need. Chances are, because you have an interest in your career, you may already have learned a bit about it on your own. Bookmark your favorite websites, subscribe to related newsletters, pick up some books or magazines, and make yourself a true "fan" of your new career.

Once you have learned a reasonable amount from reading, it's time to take up your career as a hobby or part-time pursuit. If you want to become a food writer, it's time to visit restaurants and practice writing reviews. If you want to be a forensic specialist, see if your local police force allows ride-alongs. You get the idea — you have to put your book-learning into practice, and get a feel for the work environment.

When you are trying to build experience informally, it's important to not wait for opportunities to fall in your lap. You will need to take initiative and create positions for yourself. This might mean joining volunteer associations, contacting professionals in the field and offering to assist them for free, or even creating your own groups or associations to head up.

As you learn more about the career and get some experience, you are bound to make connections in the industry. Never throw a business card away, since these people may have room for an assistant or be able to refer you to someone who does, so you can learn the ropes first-hand. (Chapter 13 of this book will have more detailed information on finding a job through word of mouth.)

Showing Off Your Talent

As you acquire experience in your career, you don't want to forget to keep track of it. This is the proof that you'll have to show employers and clients that you have the skills to do the job.

For each job you do early on in your career (paid or volunteer), you'll document the experience in an appropriate way. You can keep a logbook or journal where you can make an entry for each experience. This will be mostly for your own records, so you can jog your memory later. Write down the date or dates your performed the job, the name and contact information of the employer or client, the nature of the work, and the results you achieved.

TIP: If appropriate, take pictures or document your results somehow — "before and after" pictures or other documentation work well to show results in many careers.

When a job is complete, another way to document your results is to get a letter of recommendation or testimonial from the person you did the work for. This letter should document what you did, what results were achieved, and how you exceeded expectations.

To make it more likely that you will get a letter from a client or employer who is very busy, you can draft an outline, or even the entire letter for them. Most people you did great work for are happy to recommend you, but might have trouble finding the time to draft a letter to that effect.

When you are ready to look for work, you can assemble your documentation in a format that suits the career you are pursuing. For careers like nutritionist or stockbroker this will be in the form of a standard resume (see a sample resume on the next page), while for someone like a professional organizer, a scrapbook or portfolio with pictures and comments might be appropriate.

For careers involving writing or publishing, make sure you get and keep a copy of anything you worked on that is published. (Ask for a written credit or byline where possible to increase your visibility.) You should photocopy or burn these materials to disc to present them to potential clients or employers so they can take them away and read them later.

If you don't yet have any published material, you can type up your articles or excerpts and lay them out in a way that makes them look like they were published. Include appropriate photos and your byline. You don't have to lie about whether or not they were printed — you are just showing that your work lends itself well to a professional format.

Sample *"Brains"* Resume

CHRIS J. GOULET
123 My Street
Mytown, USA 11111
(111) 555-1212
cjgoulet@internet.com

OBJECTIVE

To help build a solid reputation for the private investigation agency I work for by providing thorough investigation work that leads to concrete answers for every client.

PROFESSIONAL SKILLS

Security and Enforcement

- Have current professional experience as an overnight security guard
- Familiar with electronic surveillance equipment and techniques
- Have been able to successfully prevent crime using security techniques

Research Ability

- Have helped families trace their backgrounds as a volunteer at the town hall archives
- Assisted Mytown mayor with research for speeches and presentations

Exceptional Analytical Skills

- Helped clients with satellite dishes troubleshoot technical problems using a systematic approach
- Researched and wrote portions of training manual to explain protocol to other satellite service agents

Sales and Service

- Developed promotional ideas that saw home accessories store increase sales by an average of 20% when promotion was on
- Have a unique ability to convert browsers into buyers
- Top "save percentage" (retaining and satisfying irate customers) at telecommunications firm

Chris J. Goulet

WORK HISTORY

2005 – present:	Binder Building Management Security Guard Mytown, USA
2003 – 2005:	Norelco Telecommunications Customer Service Mytown, USA
2002 – 2003:	Candles and Such Sales Associate Smallton, USA

RELATED TRAINING

2004–Present:	Volunteer, Mytown Town Hall
September 2005:	Photography course at Mytown Collegiate

For careers where you might be working directly with clients (private investigator, professional organizer, researcher, translator, financial planner, etc.) an effective presentation medium is PowerPoint, which creates a computerized slide show to accompany your proposal to do work for a client.

A PowerPoint presentation can set you apart from the competition, who will be fumbling with papers and notes. You can take PowerPoint classes at an adult education institution or college.

You may also want to build a website to promote yourself, where you can upload your bio, experience, achievements, photos, and anything else you may need to sell yourself effectively to employers or clients. And if you are applying to become a web developer or designer, this step is a must!

If writing is your business, you can possibly forego the website and instead write a "blog" (weblog), which is an online journal of personal experiences and observances. You can see samples at **www.blogit.com** or **www.blogger.com**. Other people are free to browse your blog, and you can direct people to it as an example of your writing style. Even in non-writing careers, you can use your blog to document progress on jobs and promote yourself and your services.

Selling Yourself Effectively

Selling yourself in a "brains" career can be a challenge since you are used to being judged by your ability, not your salesmanship. You may be thinking, "If they'd just give me the chance to prove myself, I would do an amazing job," but you have to realize that it's hard for employers to take that chance.

There are big risks in taking you on: the employer will have to commit time, resources, and money into training you, and has to hope that your skills will be up to the task. Then they have to hope that you will be a credit to their reputation, that you will make good decisions, and that you will stay with them at least long enough to balance out the time taken to train you. (Bet you never thought about it that way — although maybe you have, given your analytical skills!)

As we'll elaborate on in Chapter 13 (Create Your Dream Job), employers and clients are usually looking at a simple equation: will you ultimately bring them more value than you will cost them up front? Here are five ideas to help you help decision-makers take that leap of faith.

1. Offer a "free trial."

Offer to work for a reduced fee (or for free) for a period of time so the employer can evaluate your abilities. This lets you get in the door and demonstrate the quality of your work.

2. Have proof of your value.

If you have assembled your materials as described earlier in this chapter, you will have evidence to show that you have exceeded expectations in the past. If you work directly with clients, put together some figures to show them that you will save them more money, time, or bring them value to exceed your fees.

3. Be enthusiastic and persistent.

Your attitude can be a swaying factor in making a decision to hire you. Smile, express interest and enthusiasm, and keep in touch after any meetings. Even if your skills or experience are lacking, this is where you can shine regardless. Just make sure that you respect the distinctions between enthusiastic and desperate; persistent and downright annoying. You don't want to come across looking like a stalker.

4. Go the extra mile.

This may take some creativity, but that's what you're good at. Something as simple as calling before your meeting at the cafe and asking how the client or employer takes their coffee so you can have it ordered and waiting for them could just shock the person into hiring you on the spot.

5. Be willing to start at the bottom.

This is especially important when you are first breaking into a career — expect some unglamorous days of hard work. Express your willingness to learn. You may not get hired for a senior position right away, but an employer might be willing to create a junior position for you, or keep you in mind when one opens up.

10

Fab Movers

Careers for People Who Make Things Happen

Ever since you were young, you've known that you like to make things happen. You're not a casual observer in life — you like to get involved. Movers like to shake things up, and are interested in helping people and organizations get results. People turn to movers for their expert advice on important matters such as politics and the legal system, as well as any area of business where it's critical that things are handled in a specific way.

The careers in this chapter will allow you to make changes in your world, and see the results of your hard work impact people's lives for the better. The challenge in breaking in lies in communicating to clients that you are qualified to give advice, and showing co-workers and supervisors that you are talented, poised and savvy. This chapter will explain how you can smoothly transition into one of the 12 mover careers listed below.

- Activist
- Business Consultant
- Congressional Aide
- Ethics Officer
- Etiquette Consultant
- Human Resources Professional

- Image Consultant
- Legal Assistant
- Mediator
- Public Relations Consultant
- Recruiter
- Sports Agent

THE CAREERS

Activist

As an activist you will use your communication skills, your passion for your beliefs and your determination to help change the world socially, politically, or environmentally.

What They Do

Activists are people who work to advocate causes that are powerful and important to them. Activists work for social change, lobbyist or environmental organizations, such as Amnesty International or Mothers Against Drunk Driving (MADD), in an effort to improve issues on a global level. While all activists have their passion for and commitment to their causes in common, each contributes to their cause with their unique talents and skills.

Organizations that hire activists need people who can perform many job functions. Activists do some everyday tasks like stuffing envelopes, making phone calls, and office work, and some major activities, like staging awareness events, working with the press, and raising money to support their causes. Some travel to remote and dangerous parts of the world.

No matter what set of skills you bring to your job as an activist, you will find most activists doing some or all of the following:

- Learning constantly about the issues that affect your cause
- Keeping up with political changes that could affect your cause
- Speaking to others about your beliefs
- Recruiting and inspiring people to join your cause
- Organizing and leading volunteers
- Fundraising to support the cause
- Planning and staging a variety of events to raise awareness
- Getting attention for the cause through advertising and press coverage

• Writing about your beliefs for print and electronic publication

Who is Likely to Succeed

The most important trait of successful activists is their passion for the causes they believe in. They are dedicated to helping others, altruistic, and generous. They are wonderful communicators, enjoy working with volunteers, and relish the possibility of making the world a better place.

Successful activists don't mind moving out of their comfort zones to approach their work. They are patient and deal well with conflict. Activists are team players and keep the big picture in mind.

How to Learn It

Breaking into a career in activism is a process of exploring the causes that are meaningful to you, and assessing the skills you have that you can use to join the cause. Use the Internet to research websites of activist organizations that interest you and attend meetings and events for organizations that you find the most interesting.

Some activists pursue higher education in political science or social studies, or through courses like those offered by the Institute for Policy Studies' Social Action and Leadership School for Activists in Washington, DC (**www.hotsalsa.org**). This program offers courses in areas like Starting a Successful Nonprofit, and Techno-Activism.

One advantage of a career in activism is that you can begin today even without formal training, just by following your inclinations and passions and getting involved in organizations that interest you — even for a few hours a week, or month. Work for social change in your own community, or get involved in local politics.

Each nonprofit organization has a variety of jobs that need to be done. Getting a job as an activist is a process of matching your passions and your talents to an organization that needs them both. Many activists who work in paid positions began their careers by joining the organizations as volunteers or interns. Some volunteers and interns who prove themselves are invited to take paid positions.

There are also a variety of valuable books available that can benefit the beginning activist. *Good Works: A Guide to Careers in Social Change* by Donna Colvin provides more than 1,000 activist organizations that have job opportunities for those interested in social change.

What It Pays

Salaries for activists vary depending on education, location, the organization, experience and special skills. Annual salaries start in the $20,000 to mid-$30,000 range. High-level positions at major nonprofit organizations pay anywhere from $40,000 to $90,000 annually.

Business Consultant

Business consultants (also known as management consultants) help business leaders and owners deal with everyday challenges such as employee management and staffing issues, project, time, and work-flow management, and technological or industry-specific concerns.

What They Do

Corporations and small business owners hire business consultants to help them over rough spots, growing pains, special situations and industry-specific concerns that challenge all businesses at one time or another. They pay business consultants to analyze a situation, and then give them expert advice.

Many business consultants have extensive backgrounds or knowledge in some aspect of business. Business consultants can choose to focus on their specialties — the heath care or insurance industries, for example. Further, some specialize in a specific role in a company, like accounting or human resources.

Business consultants traditionally work in one of two ways: either as employees of consulting firms, or as independent self-employed consultants. However, some are employed full-time by large organizations. Some of those who have their own consulting firm prefer to work with clients that are large companies; others work with start-up operations or small business people.

As a business consultant you will do some or all of the following tasks:

- Meet with clients to assess their needs
- Research background information on a situation or issue
- Write proposals to land contracts with clients
- Present your proposals to clients
- Help clients implement changes
- Analyze data to look for trends and findings
- Write detailed reports of your findings and present solutions to clients
- Network to meet with potential clients
- Keep up with trends in business and your industry

Who is Likely to Succeed

The most important attributes you will need are expertise, talent or experience to draw on to qualify you as a business expert, and the ability to communicate ideas and concepts to individuals and groups. If you love the excitement of the business world, consider yourself a natural facilitator and instructor, and are motivated by helping people improve their businesses, working as a business consultant may be the perfect job for you.

How to Learn It

While you don't need an MBA to become a business consultant, what you do need are business-savvy and experience. This fact makes this dream career an excellent choice for people who are looking for new challenges after a successful career in some aspect of the corporate sector, or after owning their own successful small business.

Breaking into business consulting is a matter of assessing your skills and determining your potential market. If you already have an area of business you consider yourself an expert in, it would be a natural move for you to consult to others on that topic.

If you are just getting started in business, you will probably want to pursue business and management courses or programs at a local college or university. To get started learning right away, start reading the business section of the newspaper, and keep up with respected periodicals such as the *Harvard Business Review* and the *Wall Street Journal*.

Take stock of your own resume — think about what you have mastered and what skills you have that you can share with others. Even if you don't have years of experience in another business, if you have expert ability in some useful skill, you can market this skill as a management consultant.

You can connect with The Institute of Management Consultants, USA (**www.imcusa.org**), a national network with opportunities for networking, career education and certification. The organization has local chapters so you can connect with other consultants in your area. In Canada, contact the Canadian Association of Management Consultants at **www.camc.com**.

Before you get out on appointments with your first client companies, consider volunteering your services to family members or friends with businesses or nonprofit organizations that are eager for assistance. Use these opportunities to fine-tune your presentation to clients, to determine your rates, and to get comfortable by actually getting out there and doing it.

The *FabJob Guide to Become a Business Consultant* by Craig Coolahan offers additional information including advice on how to do consultations, including preparing proposals, how to get hired as a business consultant, and how to start a consulting company.

What It Pays

Depending on their geographic area and expertise, self-employed business consultants may earn from $35 to $350 or more per hour. Those who work as data collectors or analysts typically charge less than those who are highly skilled technical experts, or industry experts who deal in complex projects. Business consultants employed by large firms average earnings between $50,000 and $100,000, depending on their area of specialization.

Congressional Aide

As a congressional aide you will make a difference in life, not just for yourself but for generations to come, as you work with a member of congress at the federal or state level of government.

What They Do

Working in a congressional office offers all kinds of exciting possibilities for travel, important responsibilities, and career advancement. Congress, which consists of the House of Representatives and the Senate, is responsible for making the laws of the country. You can have a direct effect on how laws are made in your country, and get a chance to see how the legislative system works first hand.

Members of congress need to staff their offices with qualified workers. Members of congress have staff in at least two offices: one in Washington, DC, and one or more in their district or state.

Congressional aides (also called legislative aides) are responsible for a wide variety of tasks. The most junior position, the staff assistant, is responsible for clerical tasks and errands, possibly tours, and other support tasks. As a congressional aide advances they get more involved with the legislative process.

As a congressional aide you will do some or all of the following:
- Provide administrative support for the office
- Conduct tours of the congressional office
- Field phone calls, emails, and letters from constituents
- Attend meetings, compile and synthesize information
- Communicate with the press
- Supervise or assist interns

- Assist in researching and writing bills
- Meet with constituents and lobbyists

Many congressional aides use this career as a stepping stone to more advanced political careers, since the experience they get as a Capitol Hill staffer gives them a serious leg up on the competition.

Who is Likely to Succeed

Successful congressional aides are adaptable. They tackle both mundane tasks and challenging assignments with the same high energy. Many congressional aides are young, with few personal commitments – the average age is 31 – and being in or around Washington, DC will give you the most opportunities.

If you are flexible, tireless, and a team player; and if you are motivated, organized, and have excellent communication skills, a career as a congressional aide may be an excellent choice for you. Congressional aides need writing, research, and computer skills. Understanding politics, government and the legislative process are also key in developing your career potential.

How to Learn It

To begin with, refresh yourself about how the U.S. government works by spending some time online or at a public library reviewing how the three parts of government – executive, legislative and judicial – work together.

Spend some time learning about the internal workings of the legislative process by logging into Congressional Quarterly House Action Reports, which you can access through the Congressional Quarterly website listed below. With this online publication you can learn everything about the bills that will go before the House.

Even though you don't need a degree to pursue a "hill" job, you may find that some of the opportunities provided by universities and colleges are worth investigating. Many congressional aides have college educations or have studied political science, history, or law.

One excellent way to get your foot in the door in a congressional office is to take advantage of the many intern opportunities that are available. Opportunities for internships as well as other positions can be found online at *Congressional Quarterly Magazine* (**www.cq.com**), which features a section called Hill Jobs.

Finally, the *FabJob Guide to Get a Job on Capitol Hill* by Stephanie Vance is a full-length guidebook that explains the different jobs available working for members of congress, and gives insider tips on how to break in and get hired for one of them.

What It Pays

Congressional staff assistants often start below $20,000 annually. Aides with more legislative responsibility attract salaries in the range of $25,000 to $30,000. Assistants working directly with their member of congress researching and writing legislation make more: in the House from $30,000 to $40,000, and in the Senate as high as six-figures.

Ethics Officer

An ethics officer will establish and implement a code of ethics (a set of principles or values) for a company, and help them ensure that they do business with their ethics policies in mind.

What They Do

Ethics officers are the moral watch dogs of a company. They oversee the value-driven decisions in a firm, and help employees to determine whether they are acting in accordance with the principles that the company has determined should guide them.

An ethics officer helps people in a company define ethics. It is the job of an ethics officer to make sure that everyone in a company is on the same page about what are right and wrong business practices, and that the actions of the company reflect its ethical code.

As an ethics officer you will spend time doing some or all of the following:

- Talking to business leaders about their perception of ethics
- Working in tandem with an ethics team to develop policies
- Consulting with legal and human resources departments
- Developing and writing codes of ethics
- Creating and implementing ethics training for executives and employees
- Offering ongoing ethics consultation
- Investigating allegations of ethics violations
- Acting as an arbitrator in ethical conflicts
- Measuring and reporting on progress to company leaders

Who is Likely to Succeed

An ethics officer has a finely tuned sense of values. They are mature, experienced business people with a commitment to integrity. They believe that problems should be resolved, not ignored.

Do you have excellent public speaking skills, the ability to lead training sessions, and a good teaching ability? These are some of the skills an ethics officer will use frequently. It also helps if you are an excellent writer, enjoy research, and consider yourself diplomatic and sensitive. Successful ethics officers have a thorough understanding of the industries they work in, and the legal and regulatory issues that affect it.

How to Learn It

Start by assessing your experience so far and seeing what you have done that will lend itself to a career as an ethics officer. To become an ethics officer you will need to have experience managing others and acting in a supervisory position. You will also need to have perfected your communications skills, your presentation and public speaking skills, and your writing and research skills.

Some colleges and universities offer extension courses in ethics education, and some offer certificate programs. For example, the Colorado State University College of Business offers an online business ethics course called Essentials of Business Ethics: Foundations and Best Practices. Check with local colleges to see what is available to you.

The Ethics Officer Association (**www.eoa.org**) has more than 1,000 members, including many Fortune 100 companies. Their website boasts a great deal of interesting information that, while directed at the experienced ethics officer, is extremely useful for someone contemplating the career, and includes links to educational opportunities.

The Institute for Global Ethics offers seminars and a free newsletter which you can subscribe to at **www.globalethics.org**.

Many ethics officers are promoted within companies from other positions. Getting a position in the HR department of a company that you are interested in working for is an excellent start to move forward into a career in ethics. Many human resources professionals take on ethics as a part of their jobs. Another way to break into ethics in a large company is as part of the legal department, which lends itself to a natural transition.

What It Pays

Ethics officers' salaries vary based on career experience, position longevity, and the size and location of their company. Ethics officers can expect to make an annual salary of $40,000 to $90,000, depending on experience and responsibilities. In the highest paying job markets an experienced ethics officer can make $125,000 or more.

Etiquette Consultant

An etiquette consultant's love for good manners and social graces can be the basis of a fun and lucrative career, as they advise people on the correct protocol for social and business situations.

What They Do

Etiquette consultants are experts in one or several areas of etiquette protocol, such as business etiquette, children's etiquette, communication etiquette, dining etiquette, international protocol, social etiquette, and wedding etiquette. They advise their clients on how to ensure their behavior is acceptable to the people they spend time with or want to impress.

Many etiquette consultants are self-employed and run their own businesses, although some are on staff at larger companies. Some even work for government offices, helping VIPs ensure they adhere to protocol with dignitaries from other cultures.

An etiquette consultant may work with brides to consult regarding the etiquette concerns of weddings, or with business people helping them train their staff on anything from polite telephone manners to business meeting tips. Many teach classes or give seminars on etiquette-related topics as well.

As an etiquette consultant, you will spend time doing some or all of the following:
- Keeping up with etiquette trends
- Broadening your existing knowledge of etiquette
- Researching etiquette protocol for specific situations or cultures
- Marketing your services to new clients
- Meeting with clients to determine their needs
- Teaching etiquette classes and seminars
- Developing etiquette training materials
- Networking with potential clients and explaining what you do
- Writing on etiquette topics for newspapers and magazines
- Holding one-on-one training sessions with clients

Who is Likely to Succeed

If you are the person at your family get-togethers who loves to set the table and you never question which way to place a knife; if you think an afternoon spent reading Emily Post is one well spent; and if you instinctively handle potentially awkward situations with good taste and common sense, you may find that a career as an etiquette consultant is perfect for you.

The most successful etiquette consultants are diplomatic with their clients, resourceful in finding information, and have a good personal presentation. They are comfortable speaking with people one-on-one or to groups, and are confident self-promoters.

Fab Fact: Emily Post, who lived from 1873 to 1960, is known as *the* authority on etiquette. Emily, who had a lively writing style, began writing both fiction and non-fiction in the early 1900s. After her 1922 book *Etiquette* became a bestseller, she then focused most of her work on etiquette, although she also had a passionate interest in interior decorating. She even wrote magazine articles about decorating and an interior decorating book called *The Personality of a House*, which was published in 1930.

How to Learn It

You don't need a college education to be a successful etiquette consultant. What you do need is a broad knowledge of proper etiquette for any given situation, and the ability to convey that knowledge to your clients successfully.

There are a number of excellent books that cover just about every conceivable issue regarding etiquette and protocol. Start with books that give you a general overview, such as *Miss Manners' Guide to Excruciatingly Correct Behavior, Freshly Updated* by Judith Martin.

Does your mother have a business meeting with a client from another country? Does your best friend have an upcoming interview, or a party that she wants to go off without a hitch? Start by honing your skills with friends and family to practice and work out in your own mind how you will present your information to paying clients.

Also, consider volunteering your expertise for nonprofit organizations that will help you build your professional resume in business situations. Make sure to ask those to whom you donate services for testimonials to aid you in getting paying clients.

Consider the area of etiquette that you may wish to specialize in, and see if there is training specific to it. Many successful etiquette consultants start their own training programs for other consultants, such as Gloria Starr's Success Strategies (**www.gloriastarr.com**). The *FabJob Guide to Become an Etiquette Consultant* lists a number of training programs you can choose from, and is an excellent source of etiquette guidance itself.

What It Pays

Consultants often charge clients by the hour, with rates that average from $40 to $60 for a beginning consultant and $100 to $200 for an established consultant. Etiquette consultants may work part time or full time, drawing annual salaries of between $15,000 and $50,000 or more. When you develop training programs, a per-attendee fee or flat project fee that rings up in the thousands of dollars is quite common. The most experienced consultants will earn six-figure salaries for their etiquette services.

Human Resources Professional

Human resources (HR) professionals are people who help businesses and organizations manage their staff. They serve as an essential communications link between management and employees.

What They Do

Human resources professionals assist businesses with their staffing and personnel needs. They may be employed exclusively by one company to meet all its needs, or by a human resources specialty company that provides HR help to a number of smaller clients.

Basically, a human resources professional recruits, hires and fires employees on behalf of a company. They also help with the ongoing maintenance of employees' needs, including overseeing salary and benefits packages.

They may organize motivational events, training sessions and other employee functions, and act as a liaison between the employer and the employee. Some may specialize in particular fields that are unique, such as information technology. As a human resources professional, your tasks may include any or all of the following:

- Meeting with managers to talk about staffing needs
- Advertising open positions and reviewing resumes
- Conducting prescreening interviews
- Checking references and backgrounds of potential employees
- Conducting staff orientations

Sample "Mover" Resume

Christine Goulet

123 My Street
Mytown, USA 11111
(111) 555-1212
cjgoulet@internet.com

Summary of Key Abilities

- Ability to quickly assess situations, develop solutions and follow through
- Competent in any position or function – finance, marketing, purchasing, operations, research, etc.
- Solid understanding of the importance of the bottom line
- Willing and able to put in the extra time and effort to ensure success

Experience

Jan 2005–Present

Community Programs Coordinator, Heart & Stroke Foundation

Coordinated the February Heart Month door-to-door canvassing campaign for the Mytown area, enlisting and managing more than 100 volunteers. Developed business plans for all community-based programs for the office. Also responsible for development of media strategy for the region, and coordination of the community presentations programs.

Winter 2004 (internship)

Sales Department, Lynx Multimedia

Learned the inner workings of the department with a senior sales director, including prospecting, relationship management, and proposal development. Helped develop marketing plans and sales materials.

2001–2003

Manager, Music City, Mytown

Increased sales of CDs and tapes by 8 percent from 2001 to 2003. Performed all aspects of running this location of the Music City chain, including ordering and pricing product, managing a staff of six, merchandising, putting on promotions, handling complaints, bookkeeping and bank deposits. Was originally recognized and promoted from a part-time position.

- Designing and implementing training programs
- Completing and filing benefits and wage paperwork
- Helping resolve staff concerns or issues
- Terminating employment of staff
- Handling some negotiations with unions
- Keeping records of staff salaries, benefits, vacations and sick days

Who is Likely to Succeed

You're probably already a people person — and this is one of the ultimate people person jobs. You're understanding and sympathetic, with a good grasp of human nature and common sense. You should have a good understanding of the needs of businesses, coupled with an ability to negotiate.

You should be an excellent listener and a good judge of character, as well as a skilled interviewer. You'll be meeting many kinds of people, and you will need to be able to ask questions about them — curiosity is essential. You'll also need to assess answers and prepare detailed reports, so being good at record-keeping and communication is vital.

How to Learn the Job

In this job, you may be working for any number of different types of industries, and for a variety of companies. Therefore, it helps to have a wide range of background experience, in a variety of positions.

You can take formal training in business management and HR practices at universities and colleges, but you can also learn the basic skills of the job — interviewing, assessing and networking with people — by practicing them in your everyday life. Focus on your ability to ask questions and on being an impartial judge. Practice your skills in determining both sides of an issue or story.

The American Management Association (**www.amanet.org**) offers a wide variety of human resources seminars and conferences for you to develop your skills, and an increasing number of colleges and universities are now offering human resources courses, certificates, and degree programs online.

Learn about a broad range of careers and occupations so that you'll be familiar with industry needs — you may even want to contact local companies' HR offices to ask advice of their HR professionals. The *FabJob Guide to Become a Human Resources Professional* by Tara Foote is a great resource for those considering this career.

You can offer to sit on hiring committees or personnel-related committees for local societies or community organizations to gain a greater understanding of the relations between management and staff, and to further demonstrate your interest in these relations. Learn as much as you can about legal and labor issues that will affect the staff you will manage.

What It Pays

According to the Bureau of Labor Statistics, median annual earnings of human resources managers are $81,810. Median annual earnings of compensation, benefits, and job analysis specialists are $47,490, and median annual earnings of training and development specialists are $44,570. As a part-timer or contractor, you can expect to make in the range of $20 to $30 an hour.

Image Consultant

An image consultant is a professional who advises individuals and companies about their image. As an image consultant, you will get paid to help people look fabulous, be more successful, and feel good about themselves.

What They Do

An image consultant works with clients to help them maximize their image potential. The image consultant will meet with clients to assess their physical appearance and communication style, including makeup, hairstyle, fashion choices and mannerisms. They make recommendations for improvement in these areas.

Image consultants also help clients who need to appear before the public, whether they are politicians, public speakers, sales and marketing professionals, or others who need to present themselves in the way that will help them to be successful.

Many image consultants run their own businesses, although some work for image consulting firms. Some image consultants speak before groups in seminars or workshops, while others write books or magazine articles, and some appear on television.

As an image consultant you will do some or all of the following:
- Meet with clients and businesses to assess their needs
- Stay in touch with image-related and fashion trends
- Market your services to new clients
- Help clients shop for new wardrobes and accessories

- Demonstrate or advise clients on image improvement
- Refer clients to other image professionals for assistance
- Maintain a top-notch personal image

Who is Likely to Succeed

Successful image consultants need to be great at showcasing the image skills they are selling to clients with their own personal presentation. They have an eye for what will come across well in personal image.

If you know how to present yourself, have a flair for fashion and are a pro at communicating, you may find that you are a natural at image consulting. Image consultants are most often talented networkers. Many are writers and public speakers who promote what they do constantly to those around them.

How to Learn It

You can get great information about image consulting as well as opportunities to learn from professionals already in the business from the Association of Image Consultants International (**www.aici.org**). Their website will give you access to a number of educational and training resources, including an international annual convention as well as books and courses designed for beginners in the industry.

While it isn't necessary to have a college education to be an image consultant, many image consultants get training specifically for this career. The *FabJob Guide to Become an Image Consultant* is a fantastic resource for up-to-date college and certification training program details, as well as all the information you need to get started in this line of work.

You can learn skills hands-on by recruiting friends and family to be your very first clients. Invite your friends to an image and makeover party and practice on the group — you can get feedback at the same time. Or consider donating your time. Nonprofit organizations that offer image and business clothing makeover services to underprivileged women trying to re-enter the work world are often eager for volunteers.

Related work can also be helpful to assist you in building your skills. Employment at a makeup counter, a fashion retailer, as a personal shopper, at a beauty salon or spa, a weight-loss center, or even ad and marketing agencies will give you valuable experience, and may connect you directly to paying clients.

Fab Fact: Stacy London is the spunky and quick-witted fashion expert and female co-host of TLC's *What Not to Wear*. She is the ultimate image consultant who, along with co-host Clinton Kelly, gives unsuspecting "friends" an image makeover. She began working in the fashion industry in 1991 as a fashion assistant at *Vogue* magazine. Stacy is college-educated, and holds degrees in both philosophy and German literature, although her career path led her to fashion.

What It Pays

Newer image consultants charge anywhere from $25 to $50 an hour, while more experienced consultants may charge $75 to $250 an hour or more, depending upon the client, the situation, and the specifics. For example, an experienced image consultant with a good reputation might charge $150 for a 45-minute telephone consultation, while a newer consultant may charge significantly less.

Presenting a seminar for a corporation is likely to earn you in the range of $500 an hour, or a full-day rate of several thousand dollars. You may also bill your corporate clients for travel and expenses.

Legal Assistant

A legal assistant helps busy lawyers complete the many tasks involved in providing legal services to their clients. While not lawyers themselves, they will often find themselves assisting in an important way in the legal process.

What They Do

Legal assistants, also known as paralegals, work with attorneys in law firms as well as in corporations and nonprofit businesses. They may have a general base of legal knowledge, or specialize in any of a number of areas of law such as litigation, criminal law, corporate law, family law, real estate, personal injury, bankruptcy, intellectual property, or probate.

A legal assistant can be required to provide a broad range of services to a lawyer — just about anything that makes them better able to serve their clients quickly and effectively. They may review relevant documentation and prepare a report for the lawyer, or they may do additional research to help the lawyer investigate a situation or prove a point.

They are often involved in drafting legal paperwork, and will organize documents for the lawyer. What a legal assistant cannot do by law is anything that would be considered practicing law themselves, such as advising clients or presenting cases in court.

As a legal assistant you will do some or all of the following:

- File client information and legal information
- Research legal information and analyze it in a report
- Draft letters, contracts, memoranda, and briefs
- Interact with clients
- Assist in preliminary investigations and interviews
- Aid lawyers during their court appearances or elsewhere

Who is Likely to Succeed

The most important thing a successful paralegal needs is an understanding of the law — and a particular understanding of their legal specialty area, if they choose to have one. Some paralegals decide to study law to become attorneys. Other paralegals are actually law school grads waiting to pass the bar exam.

You should be organized, good at prioritizing tasks, and precise and thorough; you enjoy the process of research and discovery, and have outstanding writing skills. Successful paralegals are tactful when working with clients and confidential information. Since much legal research is done by computer these days, building your online research skills is a good idea.

Successful legal assistants with good management skills can also move into the position of legal assistant manager at larger organizations, where they will manage the legal assistant department.

How to Learn It

To become a legal assistant or paralegal it is important to know the law. Some employers will train paralegals on the job, hiring college graduates with no legal experience or promoting experienced legal secretaries. California is the only state in which legal assistants and paralegals must meet specific requirements.

Check out approved educational courses at the American Bar Association Directory of Approved Paralegal Education Programs website (**www.abanet.org**). You can also connect with your local college and find out about their paralegal course offerings.

Many paralegal programs have job placement services or internship programs. Before you sign up for a paralegal program inquire about their job placement services and ask to talk to recently placed graduates. A reputable organization will have no problem letting you contact former graduates to hear their success stories.

You can build your knowledge if you help your family or friends research their legal issues, although you can't charge them for legal advice. Some nonprofit legal aid services use the help of volunteers. Look through your phonebook or check online for legal aid or free legal services to find out if this is an option for you.

Although most employers will not require you to be certified, earning a voluntary certificate from a professional association may improve your job prospects. The National Association of Legal Assistants (**www.nala.org**) provides continuing education and development programs, and can award the distinctions of Certified Legal Assistant or Certified Paralegal.

What It Pays

Salaries for paralegals depend upon experience, education and location. Salaries start in the range of $30,000 to $35,000. Overtime is usually expected, but, depending on the type of employer, is typically paid. Overtime pay can make a relatively small beginning salary more appealing on payday. Experienced paralegals make more money, ranging from $50,000 to $90,000 or more for legal assistant managers.

Mediator

Mediators assist people who are having disagreements to come to a mutually acceptable solution, by helping them better communicate with each other. They try to resolve issues without the need for the parties to go to court.

What They Do

Mediators are the ultimate facilitators. They are employed by two or more parties with a dispute to guide them towards an agreement by getting them to move from their adversarial positions and work together in a goal-oriented and problem-solving manner.

People choose mediators because they want to settle their disputes out of court. Disputes that are brought before judges can be time-consuming, emotionally draining and expensive. Unlike an arbitrator or judge, the mediator does not pass judgment, and will remain completely objective and nonpartisan.

Mediation can take place anywhere parties agree to meet — inside schools, legal buildings, churches or community rooms, or at the mediator's office. Some mediators specialize in divorce, business, insurance disputes, or landlord/tenant issues — or even more diverse specializations based on their background and education.

As a mediator you will do some or all of the following:

- Keeping up with changes in the laws that affect your area of expertise
- Learning new techniques in conflict resolution skills
- Meeting with clients and explaining the process of mediation
- Assisting clients in breaking down disputes into manageable issues
- Helping clients to come to agreement about lesser issues
- Facilitating clients in the process of explaining their position
- Listening and reframing remarks so that parties can understand each other
- Helping the parties involved to reach agreement
- Marketing your services to new clients

Who is Likely to Succeed

As a mediator the most important trait you can bring to the career is your expert ability to guide people in the process of conflict resolution. Perhaps you are an excellent communicator. You are positive, patient and calm. You have a knack for understanding and explaining issues. You are adept at reading nonverbal cues.

Successful mediators have the ability to put their personal judgments and emotions aside. They are poised and professional, organized, and clear thinking. They are confident, intelligent, well informed, diplomatic, and have genuine respect for their clients.

How to Learn It

While some mediators are former lawyers and judges, it does not take a law degree to be a mediator. There are courses you can take in mediation at the college and university level, degrees available in related disciplines like conflict resolution, and there are a number of excellent workshops, courses, and certification programs too.

Contact organizations and associations that will provide you with training opportunities, workshops, and a forum to learn more about mediation. The Association for Conflict Resolution (**www.acrnet.org**) is very helpful for the beginning mediator, and they offer internships as well. While an internship usually only pays a stipend, it will give you valuable job experience.

To start the learning process right now, look at how you handle conflict in your own life. See if you can help people around you like friends, family, and coworkers resolve their conflicts using conflict-resolution techniques. Perhaps you can even get friends or family members to be willing to let you try out what you have learned and give you feedback.

Another way to get involved in mediation is to offer your services free of charge. Offer to instruct your child's classroom in peer mediation techniques, or speak to a club or organization you are involved with on the subject, once you have done some learning on the subject and techniques.

What It Pays

Some mediators are employed by others and receive a salary, others are self-employed and set up a private practice. Most mediators charge by the hour, although some charge a flat fee or by the day. Most mediators charge $50 to $300 an hour, based on experience and clientele. According to the Bureau of Labor Statistics, arbitrators, mediators, and conciliators earn a median annual salary of $54,760.

Public Relations Consultant

As a public relations (PR) consultant you will have an exciting job informing, influencing, and persuading people to take action. In this fast-paced job, you will use your creativity and communications skills to come up with cutting-edge solutions.

What They Do

Public relations consultants help organizations work to create positive and productive relationships with the public. They understand people, and listen and respond to both the goals of a company and how a company is perceived in the world.

It is the job of a public relations consultant to help an organization understand the impact its goals and reputation have in the public sphere, and to adjust these goals to create the sort of public relationship it desires. They recognize that the relationship organizations have with the public directly relates to their success and profitability.

Public relations consultants work in corporations, government agencies, hospitals, schools, and nonprofits — basically, any organization that needs qualified professionals to help them analyze, assess, and address public relations issues. Some public relations consultants work for companies that are dedicated PR firms, and others work for advertising agencies. Others work as self-employed consultants.

As a public relations consultant you will do some or all of the following:

- Meet with clients to assess their needs
- Analyze public opinion about an organization
- Gather and interpret data about the client's company
- Design a PR plan for companies
- Write press releases, presentations and other documents
- Build relationships with the media to create positive press opportunities
- Work in tandem with advertising departments to design marketing materials
- Produce presentations and reports that measure PR success
- Market your services to new clients

Who is Likely to Succeed

Successful public relations consultants need to be both analytical and creative. They combine these two qualities to not only assess and understand a client's relationship with the public, but also to plan original and creative ways to help companies achieve the relationships they want.

Public relations consultants must have business and marketing savvy — and superb interpersonal skills. They are excellent communicators, and can get their ideas across effectively. They have professional presentation skills as well.

How to Learn It

Most public relations consultants have a broad range of knowledge and skills. Because of this, some PR professionals do choose to get degrees. However, if you have the natural attributes needed to be a PR expert — an ability to communicate, and business and marketing sense — you can teach yourself many of the skills needed.

Develop your writing skills with community college or online courses. You should study other PR writing to see the type of language and techniques that are commonly used. Learn to vary your sentence structures and avoid repetitive phrases. You may also want to take courses in computer skills and presentation skills. The *FabJob Guide to Become a PR Consultant* by Lynne Bliss has great tips on developing your skills, as well as insider advice on breaking into the career.

Contact the Public Relations Society of America (**www.prsa.org**) to learn more about the public relations industry. This organization, which is the largest and most successful professional association for

PR professionals in the world, has chapters around the U.S. as well as student chapters at college campuses. In Canada, the Canadian Public Relations Society (**www.cprs.ca**) is the one to contact.

If you are hoping to work with a smaller or independent firm, or open up your own public relations consulting business, contact NAIPRA — the North American Association of Independent Public Relations Agencies (**www.naipra.org**).

What It Pays

Public relations consultants who work for major or midsize public relations firms earn average starting salaries of between $35,000 and $45,000 annually. More experienced public relations consultants can make from $65,000 to $100,000 or more.

Self-employed PR consultants charge their clients by the hour, ranging from $20 to $75 an hour for beginning consultants, to $100 or $200 an hour (or more) for PR experts. Some public relations consultants will charge a minimum monthly fee or a retainer for long term clients based on the expected monthly work, and others will charge by the project for one-time jobs.

Recruiter

As a recruiter you will use your people skills and analytical ability to meet and assess potential employment candidates, and offer fabulous job opportunities to those who are best qualified.

What They Do

Recruiters spend their time searching for perfect candidates to fill open or hard-to-fill positions with employers. Some recruit for their own company, while others work as third parties (often for recruitment firms) to match employer with employee. Recruiters work in conjunction with a company's human resources department.

Recruiters sometimes fill positions in branch offices around the world, or travel to college campuses to locate qualified applicants. Some recruiters work independently as small business people out of their homes; others telecommute as employees of large executive search firms around the country. Still others work in their company's offices and spend "face time" with client companies and prospective applicants.

As a recruiter you will do some or all of the following:

- Contacting new companies to sell your recruitment services
- Speaking to client companies about their staffing needs

- Networking in order to meet potential candidates
- Meeting with potential candidates and explaining what you do
- Working in tandem with HR departments to set salaries and benefits
- Explaining career opportunities to candidates
- Administering tests and conducting background/reference checks
- Extending job offers to candidates

Recruiters have the satisfaction of knowing that they are making people's lives easier and better by creating win-win scenarios for both the employees and the employers.

Who is Likely to Succeed

Successful recruiters know how to sell. They enjoy connecting people with each other, and finding that perfect employer/employee match. They are motivated and competitive. They understand the business marketplace, and they feel as comfortable talking to a senior vice-president as they do to a company receptionist.

If you are an extrovert, and if you enjoy talking on the phone for hours at a time, recruiting might be a fit for you. It helps if you are imaginative, open, friendly, and energetic. Successful recruiters know persistence is the key to their success. It helps if you are already well connected in an industry or community.

How to Learn It

Recruiting is often a "learn-by-doing" career. Recruiters tell stories of how, on their first day, they were given a phone and a database of leads and they simply picked up the phone and began to make calls. If you are the right person for this job, this task won't seem daunting, it will be fun. You will be able to carve out your own network from day one, and learn as you go.

Some recruiters have college degrees in business, sales and marketing, or human resources, although a degree isn't necessary to be a recruiter. There are courses you can take at your local community college to improve your business skills.

Focus on sales, telemarketing, and courses that will help you with your communication skills like public speaking. Work to enhance your general business skills. Knowing how to use a computer and the Internet will make you a better recruiter too. Books on sales and telemarketing are abundant, and the *FabJob Guide to Become a Super Salesperson* is an excellent resource on the topic.

Some employment services may employ you to work for them as a temp and then hire you permanently based on your performance and position availability. This will give you the chance to learn the job without pressure or commitment. You could also see if you could spend a day with a recruiter to observe their techniques and ask about the job.

What It Pays

Most recruiters work for commission. Experts make six figure incomes, and beginners make substantially less. According to the Bureau of Labor Statistics, median annual earnings of employment, recruitment, and placement specialists are $41,190.

Some recruiting firms will pay recruiters a draw against commission that is repaid as commissions are received. Other firms offer base salary for several months until recruiters have begun to place employees at client companies.

Sports Agent

Sports agents are the marketing-savvy deal closers who work representing professional athletes to get them big-money contracts and endorsement deals worth millions of dollars.

What They Do

Sports agents work much like other agents do — they represent talent, work out deals for their clients, and then take a percentage of each successfully negotiated deal when it closes as their payment.

Sports agents must understand the sport that the athletes they represent play, and they must be aware of the talent and records of upcoming college seniors and sometimes even elite amateur athletes. When sports teams pick their draft choices, sports agents persuade the draft choices to sign on with them as clients by convincing athletes that they will get them the most lucrative deals.

In addition to draft hopefuls, sports agents work with athletes who already play for pro teams by helping them to get book deals, television and movie appearances, and especially endorsement deals. As a sports agent you will do some or all of the following:

- Watch and evaluate young sports talents
- Keep up with changes in the sport and its governing rules
- Approach athletes to seek their commitment for representation
- Negotiate contracts with teams and management
- Seek out and negotiate media and endorsement deals for athletes

- Make statements to the public for your athletes when required
- Network to build relationships that will help you promote your athletes

Who is Likely to Succeed

The most important thing you need to be a sports agent is superb interpersonal skills. You must be able to convince people to talk to you — from athletes and their parents, to giant corporations — and you must know how to move conversations from "just talk" into negotiations for giant salaries and other contractual deals.

If you love sports, or are extremely knowledgeable about at least one sport, and you consider yourself a great communicator and expert salesperson, you may find that a career as a sports agent is perfect for you.

How to Learn It

While some sports agents are retired professional athletes or attorneys who specialize in sports law, there are no special educational or background requirements to be a sports agent. Many sports agents get into the business with just a love of sports, their great negotiating and sales skills, and their networking ability.

However, even if you are a rookie when it comes to being a sports agent, there are a number of ways you can learn the business, including some accredited college courses that specialize in teaching sports agents how the business works and what they will need to learn and do to get started.

Begin tuning up your talent by reading up not only on the business of being a sports agent, but also the sports that you hope to focus on when you become an agent. Start at your local community college by taking sales, communication, or sports history courses.

There are a number of courses available both online and in traditional classroom settings designed for those who wish to become sports agents, like those offered through the international sports management agency Sports Management Worldwide (**www.smwathlete. com**).

SMW has a program that allows agents in training who have taken their course to register to be "Agent Advisors," who act as quasi-agents and get to recruit and develop relationships while working in tandem with experienced agents.

Most professional sports leagues require you to register and pay fees to become a registered sports agent who is legally able to represent athletes in a league. Some leagues also require agent applicants to take and pass a test. Contact the league you are interested in for more details.

What It Pays

Salaries for sports agents are based on commission. When an athlete gets a contract, the sports agent takes a cut. The amount of the cut or commission increases based on the overall deal. Sports agents who work with NFL (National Football League) or NBA (National Basketball Association) athletes generally make more in commission than those who work with MLS (Major League Soccer) athletes, for example. The most successful sports agents make more than a million dollars per year.

Fab Fact: Many sports agents have made a name for themselves in their industry, such as Scott Boras in baseball; Bill Duffy, David Falk and Rob Pelinka in basketball; and Drew Rosenhaus and Leigh Steinberg in football. However, the most famous sports agent is still Jerry Maguire, the fictional character played by Tom Cruise in the movie of the same name. "Show me the money!" is the well-known quote from that movie.

HOW TO BREAK IN

To break into one of these careers, it helps to have business savvy, an understanding of office politics, connections, people skills, and the right image. Here's how to prove you are up to the task.

Be Business Savvy

Be an Industry Insider

In mover careers, you need to have an understanding of how things work in your industry — what you might call "knowing how the game is played." If you don't have a basic knowledge of how the work is done, how information and people are managed, or even the vocabulary associated with the career, you risk looking unintelligent, or at least uninformed.

One of the best ways to get business savvy is to make a connection with someone who is already working in the career. So long as you are respectful of their time, most people are happy to answer questions about a career they are passionate about. Make sure that you ask for insider information when you meet, though — not just whether or not they like their job.

You should also immerse yourself in the industry. Subscribe to newsletters, be a frequent visitor on websites, read books, and attend industry events. This will help you to learn the lingo and keep in touch with the latest happenings. Just make sure any sources of information you use are up-to-date.

No matter what mover career you choose, being in touch with the latest in communication technology will give you a competitive edge. Read the "Technology" or "Business" sections of your city's newspaper to keep your finger on the pulse of the latest in electronics so you can keep in touch with the best of them.

Depending on the career you are working towards and your background to date, you could also benefit from attending seminars or workshops in your area that pertain to the work you'll be doing. Workshops are usually geared towards covering issues that are hot or new to the industry, which will put you where you want to be — in the know.

Of course, no one can know everything there is to know about any particular industry. You'll find that the people who are most capable are not necessarily the people who know everything, but the people who are the best at finding information, using the Internet, information databases or other resources. Become familiar with techniques for tracking down information, and you could quickly find yourself a hot commodity.

Understand Office Politics

When someone mentions politics, most people usually think first of government politics. However, when you work in a variety of different offices and different jobs, you come to realize that every work environment has its own set of politics that affect how events play out within its walls.

In some jobs you can ignore office politics and get along okay, but in mover careers, everything from the type of chair in your office to the color of your tie or hair can be a political statement that can make or break your career. In order to avoid making the wrong moves, you need to learn the "politics game," and learn it fast.

Every workplace has a hierarchy in place of who reports to whom, who is on the same level, etc. While every workplace will be different, the important thing for you to know is that the hierarchy exists, and that as an employee, contractor, or applicant, you have to go through the correct departments and channels to get what you want.

For example, if you skip over the deputy director and go right to the director with a concern, you risk damaging your relationship with both of these people. The deputy will feel like you went "over his head" for some reason; and the director will feel like you wasted her time by not screening your idea through the deputy first.

TIP: When you are first starting a job, make it a point to ask questions about the office hierarchy. You can accidentally anger someone who is valuable to your career by not realizing that they should have been consulted first.

Still, there will be occasions where you might have to decide whether it's worth jumping the chain of command if you feel like your ideas are being ignored or someone is taking credit for them.

When this happens, make sure you weigh the reward of being noticed or getting your idea implemented against the chance of damaging relationships with your co-workers or supervisors. Good relationships in the workplace are one of the most valuable assets you have in your quest for success.

Like the hierarchies in office command, there will also be policies and procedures that you need to learn and follow. Again, ask questions until you are sure, and ask more than one person if possible when it comes to following procedure.

Dress the Part

According to Brian Tracy, bestselling author of *The Psychology of Achievement,* "many capable men and women are disqualified from job opportunities because they simply do not look the part." Although we can't tell you exactly how to dress for your career, since you are unique and so is the career you are pursuing, we can give you some guidelines that you can adapt to your situation and personal style.

The most important thing to remember is that clothing is not just about protection from the elements — it is part of the overall message you are sending about yourself, and you want it to be calculated and controlled (in a good way).

First, think about your current personal style. That is, what look do you generally go for when you shop for clothing? Then think about whether or not that look is a fit with the career you have in mind. You might like the sporty look, but if you want to work as a political aide, you will stand out among the business wear of your colleagues. You don't have to sacrifice your individuality, but you should modify your wardrobe to match your career goals.

If you have a closet full of sweatpants and no idea where to start, you may want to hire a wardrobe consultant to help you shop smart. A good consultant should not cost you too much in the long run, since they save you from buying items that you would not get good use of, and may be able to get you discounts at their preferred vendors. And you benefit by pulling together a look that projects a consistent, positive image.

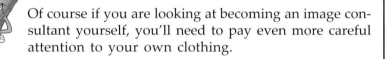

TIP: Of course if you are looking at becoming an image consultant yourself, you'll need to pay even more careful attention to your own clothing.

Here are some other tips on dressing to impress in your career:

- Buy the best quality clothing you can afford, and keep all your clothing clean and in good repair.
- What you wear to work should never be sexually suggestive or revealing unless you want to send the message that your skills and talent are not really your number-one selling points.
- Makeup for women should be worn in moderation and should look natural in the workplace.
- Color has a psychological effect on the person viewing it. For example, red conveys power and energy, while green radiates harmony and calmness. Try to match your color to your personal or daily message.
- Avoid strong perfumes or colognes, which can offend sensitive noses.
- If you want to stand out from the crowd and show your creative side, choose a single unique accessory (or tie) to go with a more conservative outfit. Avoid overdoing it.

Dealing with People

Making connections with people who work in your industry is a great way to get a foot in the door or find potential clients, and a great boost to your career once you are in.

Remember that when you are building networking relationships, the partnership should be mutually beneficial. This means that you should offer some value to the other person as well. When you are low on the totem pole you might wonder what you have to offer, but there is almost always a way to make yourself useful to someone.

For example, consider volunteering to help someone out on one of their pet projects in exchange for a recommendation or referral. When you work with this person and their team, find ways to make them look good in front of their colleagues, and you're likely to earn their appreciation.

The rest of this chapter offers advice on how to have positive relationships through diplomacy, building trust, and earning respect as a leader. For more information on how to effectively network to build your career, see Chapter 13, "Make Friends."

Be Diplomatic

Diplomacy is a skill that you likely use every day, although you might not actually call it that. Any time you communicate with the purpose of helping people to see things in a different way, you are using diplomacy.

There's no question that being diplomatic can be a challenge in certain circumstances. Many mover careers involve working with sensitive topics, a team of people (either colleagues or business associates) and ever-changing agendas, so you can bet that your diplomacy will be put to the test. You may even have your diplomacy challenged in an interview with a hypothetical situation, so you should be prepared to use it right from the start.

The key to being diplomatic is to present your views in a way that makes them appealing to others, by being non-confrontational and friendly. If you have to disagree with someone, explain the ways that you do agree with them first, or at least summarize their position so they know you understand where they are coming from.

When forced to make a tough call between offending someone and making your opinions heard, try to find solutions that accommodate the greatest number of people, or at least the key decision-makers. In some cases holding your tongue will be the only option — don't sweat it, there will be more chances to get ahead in your future if you avoid big confrontations early on.

If this is an area you want to improve in, a great resource used by many professionals is the book *How to Win Friends and Influence People*, by Dale Carnegie. Another valuable book for movers to read is *Get Anyone to Do Anything and Never Feel Powerless Again*, by David J. Lieberman.

Education and Training

2003-2004
Amundus College, Business Management program
Courses included Management, Accounting, & Entrepreneurship. Volunteered as a teaching assistant in second year (up to 40 students per lab). Graduated in top 5 percent of class.

2001
St. Stephen's High School
Graduated with honors.

Related Skills and Experience

- Conversational Spanish skills
- Current member of Toastmasters International

Build Trust

Building trust is an excellent way to make yourself a player in any organization. Start by not gossiping about or bad-mouthing your previous employers, competition or co-workers — ever. It might seem like a good way to gain an edge, but the person you are speaking with might wonder what you say behind his or her back. And if your insults ever get back to the person you are gossiping about, you've got a whole new world of trouble to deal with.

It's important in mover careers to understand what information should be kept confidential and what can be relayed. If you have a tendency to blurt things out without thinking, start practicing a count to ten before you reveal your thoughts. Take this ten seconds to think about whether what you are about to say is appropriate for a) the listener and b) the situation. In time you may not need a full ten seconds to do this, but it's a good way to practice editing your speech.

Another way to build trust is to create real relationships with people you work with. See a certain amount of socializing as part of your job, and allocate part of your day to learning more about other people, their interests, and their goals. When you know more about the people you work with or hope to work with, it's easier to spot when you may have goals in common, and then you can team up for greater success.

Share information about yourself, too, but keep it limited and career-based, or light personal topics — it's safe to assume people don't want to hear about your health problems or relationship troubles.

Earn Respect

The following tips can help you earn respect and be seen as an effective leader:

- Give credit to others where appropriate. Expect the same in return.
- Confront challenges and problems head-on; don't let misunderstandings or bad feelings linger. A face-to-face discussion is better than an email, which opens the door to misinterpretation of your message.
- Be aware of the power of your words and communicate respectfully with everyone regardless of race, gender, sexual orientation, etc. The "How to Break In" section in chapter 8 has more dos and don'ts for speaking effectively.
- Also be aware of email etiquette. For example, you should not forward any emails that have questionable content — even if you didn't write the words, you are responsible for the message.
- Accept that in some positions you may have to make decisions that are unpopular. Take responsibility for your actions, and don't try to blame "upper management" or outside forces.
- Don't disrespect someone because their position is "below" yours. Everyone can be a helpful ally at some point, and people can move up and down the ladder, too.

Once you are confident in your business savvy and people skills, it's time to get the job of your dreams. Read on to discover how to make it happen.

Part Three
Create

11

Make a Plan

How to Set Your Career Goals

You might have turned to this chapter because you know which career you want to break into and want some techniques to help you achieve it. If so, you can jump ahead to the goal-setting worksheet on page 300.

Or you might be here with several possible careers in mind, hoping we'll help you decide which one to go after first. After all, you can have many different careers in your lifetime, but you can't have all of them at the same time! Although only you can choose which career to start with, the information in the next section might help you make a decision.

If You're Finding It Difficult to Choose Only One Career

Are you hoping to "keep your options open" and make a career decision "later"? In fact, feeling like you are unable to choose among several careers can be a way to procrastinate and avoid pursuing any of them. You might think you can wait until you know "for certain" which career is best for you to go after right now, but the reality is that you might never be absolutely certain. Some of the negative beliefs we discussed in chapter 4 (such as "I might choose the wrong career... I might not be good at it... It will probably turn out to be something I don't like...") could keep you from ever pursuing a new career, unless you take action in spite of them.

So for now, just choose one career that you want to pursue — any one. Remember, you can change your mind later. The idea is to get in the habit of choosing, so you don't get stuck in procrastination. Here's a technique that might help you make up your mind. Write each of the careers you want to pursue on a separate slip of paper. Then mix up the slips and choose one at random. If you don't like the one you get, choose another, then another if necessary. As you do this, you might be hit by the realization that you really hope one of the careers is on the piece of paper you choose. If so, congratulations, that's the one for you to go after first.

As you go through the goal-setting worksheet later in this chapter, and start identifying the steps you'll need to take to break into that career, you will have an opportunity to decide whether this is the career you really want to go after right now.

There is a popular myth that the reason most people don't succeed is because they fail to set goals. Some authors actually say that only 3% of the population sets goals. That would mean 97% of us are walking through life aimlessly.

Nonsense! You have set and achieved thousands of goals in your life. In fact, every day of your life you are setting and achieving goals. If you doubt this, just think about what you do during a typical day.

Do you sleep until sometime in the afternoon, then get up and wander around your home until it's time to go back to sleep again? No, you have goals and you have plans. You may set an alarm clock so you can achieve the goal you've set about the time you'll wake up. Then you decide what you'll eat, where you'll go, and what you'll do — and you do it. All day long you make decisions and take actions. You envision a goal and you achieve it. If you change your mind, you are essentially setting a new goal to achieve.

Using the same basic techniques, you have probably also set and achieved some more important life goals as well. Have you ever...

- Taken a class or earned a diploma?
- Applied for and been hired for a job?
- Overcome a habit?
- Saved enough money to buy something you wanted?
- Found someone to love?
- Started a business?
- Planned a vacation?

- Moved to a new home?
- Gotten married and/or started a family?

If a biographer were looking at your life they would probably find many examples of times when you have successfully set and achieved goals. Each time, you saw something that you wanted, and you took the actions necessary to make your vision a reality. Where you are right now in your life is a direct result of all the thousands of goals, both large and small, that you have set for yourself and achieved so far. You know how to make things happen and achieve your goals!

So if you are not where you want to be right now in your life, isn't it possible that the only significant difference between you and someone you consider more successful is that you may not have set your sights high enough yet? If so, you can change that starting now.

Setting Your Goals

Putting your goals in writing can help you make your dreams a reality. On page 300 you will find a goal-setting worksheet. Create a worksheet for your career goal, and refer to the information below if you need help filling it out.

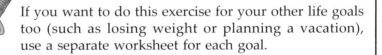

TIP: If you want to do this exercise for your other life goals too (such as losing weight or planning a vacation), use a separate worksheet for each goal.

Statement of goal

Must be specific, measurable, stated positively and simply. Remember to think big.

Priority

How does this goal rank compared to your other goals? Is your career goal #1, #2, #3, etc.

Term of goal

Short (within 3 months), medium (within 3 years), or long-term (over 3 years)

Goal-Setting Worksheet

Statement of goal:

_____

_____

_____

Priority: _____   Term of goal: ❏ Short-term (within 3 months)
                                     ❏ Medium-term (within 3 years)
                                     ❏ Long-term (over 3 years)

Life area: _____   Target date: _____

Obstacles: Solutions:

_____   _____

_____   _____

_____   _____

_____   _____

Action steps to achieve it:	Target date for step:	Reward for completing step:
_____	_____	_____
_____	_____	_____
_____	_____	_____
_____	_____	_____
_____	_____	_____
_____	_____	_____
_____	_____	_____
_____	_____	_____
_____	_____	_____

Is it worth it to me?   ❏ Yes   ❏ No

What achieving this goal will mean to me:

_____

_____

_____

Life area

As mentioned, in addition to using this goal worksheet for your career goal, you can create separate worksheets for your goals in other areas of life, so indicate if the life area is: career, financial, physical, mental, emotional, spiritual, family and friends, community, etc.

Target date

This is the date the goal will be accomplished.

Obstacles

What currently and potentially stands between you and this goal? Include both tangible and intangible obstacles such as lack of money, time, support, or education, fear, etc.

Solutions

How will you overcome the obstacles? Include both tangible and intangible resources you can use to help you pursue your goal, such as self-confidence, support from other people, education, time, money, etc.

Action steps to achieve it

Break your goal down into smaller tasks. Remember to include steps for handling obstacles.

Target date for step

It may help to work backwards from your target goal date.

Reward for completing step

It is important to give yourself the positive reinforcement of rewards. You can do this for each step or for selected steps.

Is it worth it to me?

Are you really willing to do what it takes to achieve this goal?

What achieving this goal will mean to me

How will achieving this goal benefit you? Include any benefits for your family, the other people in your life, and the community.

Taking Action

For your action steps, it may help to realize that there is more than one way to achieve what you want.

Years ago we tried to help our friend "Jo" see that she could quickly raise $20 if she really wanted to. That $20 was the cost of a seminar she wanted to attend, but to her it might as well have been $20 million dollars.

In her mind, the only way to get $20 was to wait until she received her next monthly paycheck from her part-time job. To help Jo see that she could come up with the money right away if it were important enough to her, we asked, "If someone you love needed money for an operation to save their life, do you think you could come up with $20?" Jo's reply was amazing: "Not for at least three weeks," she said.

Our friend "Lisa" overheard our conversation and laughed at Jo's reply. Lisa said, "If someone I love needed a life-saving operation, I would apply for help from foundations and charities, I'd arrange for a bank loan, I'd ask for help from all my friends and relatives, I'd apply for assistance from government agencies, I'd take my story to the news media to ask for donations from strangers, and that's just for starters. I would raise a million dollars if I had to."

So while you are determining your action steps, be open to the possibility that there may be a number of ways to accomplish them. For example, taking a college course is one way to learn a job skill, but as Part 2 of this book shows, there may be many other ways to learn a particular skill, including volunteer work, a part-time job, an internship, reading a book, researching on the Internet, taking an online class, etc.

The key is to take action. We recommend taking at least two steps toward your career goal every day. Complete two phone calls, write two letters, take any two actions that will get you closer to your dream. On those days when you feel tired or discouraged — and there will be days like that — take two steps anyway. Every morning, remind yourself of a time you achieved success and remember what it took for you to get there.

Whenever you must choose between two courses of action, let your choice be guided by your answer to the question: "Will this help me move closer to achieving my dream career?"

Making It Happen

While taking specific action steps will help ensure you keep moving toward your goal, you can achieve your dream much more quickly and with much greater success if you harness the power of your subconscious mind.

There are three ways to do this. The first is to use the power of your imagination the way professional athletes do. Every day, visualize yourself reaching your goal. Create a picture in your mind of you getting hired or actually working at your dream career.

The second technique is to imagine how it feels to have achieved your dream. As you visualize your goal you may experience a feeling of excitement, happiness, or even some fear. Let yourself feel those emotions as if you are actually experiencing the event.

Finally, we recommend using a technique known as affirmations, and telling yourself what you will achieve. We're not talking about trying to change your beliefs (although that may eventually happen). We're talking about changing another aspect of your behavior: replacing negative messages you tell yourself with positive messages.

For example, just because you believe "I'm not the right age," "there's too much competition," or "if I get an interview I'll say or do something to mess it up," doesn't mean you have to keep reminding yourself.

There is a wonderful children's story called *The Little Engine That Could*, about a little train engine that agrees to haul a cargo of toys to a group of children after several other engines refuse the job. Faced with the seemingly impossible task of getting over a mountain, the little engine is nevertheless determined to succeed. As it starts its slow climb the little engine says to herself, "I think I can... I think I can... I think I can..."

Even if you haven't heard this story before you probably know the ending: the little engine does indeed get over the mountain. It's a technique human beings can use too. Any negative beliefs you have can be restated positively and used the way the little engine did. You can repeat affirmations to yourself over and over again by:

- Silently reciting them in your head
- Saying them aloud while you're looking in the mirror
- Writing them in a notebook
- Recording them on tape and playing them back as you're falling asleep (your subconscious mind will hear them even if your conscious mind dozes off)
- Singing them in the shower
- Anything else you can think of to help you reinforce them

In his book *The Dilbert Future*, Scott Adams describes how he used affirmations to become a syndicated cartoonist and have the most successful comic in the world. He recommends writing your affirmations 15 times per day in the following form: "I, Joe Blow, will be a famous jazz musician." Check out his book to read more about how affirmations have worked for him.

To make your affirmations work in your favor, it's a good idea to make sure they're worded positively. Whenever an affirmation is worded negatively (e.g., "I won't mess up the interview"), the unconscious mind seems to miss the disclaimer and concentrates instead on what you're trying to overcome. For example, if as a child you often said, "Sticks and stones may break my bones, but words can never hurt me," you may actually have been reinforcing the belief that "words can hurt me." So leave out the "nevers" and the "nots."

The more you continue all three of these behaviors — affirming, visualizing, and imagining how it feels to have achieved your dream— the less reinforcement your old beliefs will get. These techniques will help you remain focused on your goal and remind your subconscious mind to do what it takes to make your dream a reality.

People who use these techniques are often surprised to discover how many opportunities suddenly appear. There's a scientific reason for this. Each of us is bombarded with thousands of pieces of information every day. Think of how many things compete for your attention on any given day: television, radio, websites, newspapers, magazines, books, billboards, newsletters, phone calls, emails, street signs, flyers posted on bulletin boards, people passing you on the street, casual conversations you might overhear at the coffee shop, and so on. Your brain would be overloaded if you tried to pay attention to everything, so you are selective. You pay attention to what you're interested in and what you need to know.

Once you start programming your brain about your new career, chances are you will start noticing what you need to help you achieve your dream. What was once just "background noise" will become messages about upcoming auditions, companies that are expanding, or whatever particular information you need to know.

Once you hear about those opportunities, you can use the information in the next few chapters to help you land the job.

Did You Know? Comedian Jim Carrey used the power of his subconscious mind to achieve his goals of becoming rich and famous. While living in poverty as a teen, Jim wrote himself a check for $10 million and kept it in his wallet. Each day he would take the check out of his wallet, look at it and visualize himself as a big star. Jim was successful! Not only did he receive a $10 million check for a movie role, but he surpassed that by becoming a $20-million-per-movie man.

12

Make a Move

How to Get a Dream Job the Traditional Way

It might surprise you to learn that even dream jobs are advertised to the public in traditional ways. But it makes sense when you consider how often life demands change — people choose new careers, start families, or move away. Businesses are starting up and growing all the time, opening up positions for fabulous jobs in all sorts of careers.

This chapter will cover each of the following components of finding a dream job the traditional way:

- Where to find jobs advertised
- How to apply for an advertised job
- How to create a stand-out resume
- How to draft a cover letter
- How to shine during the interview
- What to do afterwards to boost your chances of getting hired

Starting a job search can be overwhelming, but it doesn't have to be. If you use the systematic approach explained in this chapter, you may find yourself employed in your "field of dreams" more quickly and easily than you think. To start, first you'll need to know where to look.

Where to Find Jobs Advertised

Most people begin their job hunt with a coffee and the local newspaper. The fact is that certain kinds of dream jobs rarely, if ever, are advertised in the newspaper, but this doesn't mean you'll never stumble across a gem.

If your region has more than one major newspaper, read each of their career sections for about a week and compare the number of positions advertised, as well as the types of positions in each. You will likely find that one paper caters more to your dream career than the other, or that one simply has a better selection of jobs. Many newspapers publish a beefed up "Careers" or "Working" section one day a week that has more ads than usual (and career advice too), so take note of which day this is for each publication.

Some newspapers also post their content online for free or for a subscription rate, although if it is not posted at the same time the print edition is published, it's probably worth paying to get the earlier edition. This way you can get a jump on writing your resume and cover letter when you spy an attractive ad.

Trade magazines are another way to look for job openings. These industry-specific publications frequently contain a classified section where people can find a targeted audience of viewers. Do a keyword search on the Internet to see if your dream career has a few industry associations that publish trade magazines, or ask anyone you know in the industry which ones are worth picking up. As an added bonus, you'll be keeping up with the latest happenings in your new field of employment.

General job websites are also a good stop on your job-hunting journey. The most popular sites like Monster.com, Careerbuilder.com, and HotJobs.Yahoo.com have databases where you can type in the job you are looking for and search across the country or around the world.

TIP: It's not enough to simply post your resume on these sites, unless your profession is in high demand — you may be waiting a long time for an employer to find you. Instead, try searching the boards for jobs.

Many types of careers have a centralized or popular online job board where people who are interested in the profession can look for job openings. While some of these boards are run by associations or publications, others are independent, so you may need to search around the Internet a bit to find them.

Try typing "jobs" or "careers" and different variations of your dream career's name into a search engine to see what comes up, and bookmark the best to return to frequently. The individual career write-ups in this book might also have a few leads for you to start with.

If you already know of a few employers you'd like to target in your job search, you can add their company website to your list of online favorites. Most employers have a website these days, and many of them post an online career page where you can find job openings and contact information, or submit your resume using an online form.

You may also find jobs advertised at career centers, which are central agencies that help employers spread the word about job openings, and may also provide career counseling services. Your community may have a career center open to the public, and if you are attending college or university you will certainly have a student career office where you can access these job postings.

TIP: The great thing about jobs posted at colleges or universities is that the employer will be looking specifically for someone with enthusiasm and great ideas, not someone with a list of experience as long as their arm.

Many schools or communities also host job fairs where employers will come looking for prospects. While they will not be "advertising" a single open position, the fact that they have a presence at a job fair means they are growing rapidy, have frequent turnover, or a bunch of new positions are opening up soon, and you can fill out an application or submit a resume right on the spot.

How to Apply for an Advertised Job

So you're scanning the ads looking for that perfect job when all of a sudden, your stomach lurches and you feel your spine tingle — you see a job that's perfect for you. You read the details of the position thinking... yes... YES... YES! Now the challenge is — how do you go about convincing the employer you are who they are looking for? Here are five steps to follow in applying for any advertised job.

1. Research the company.

Start online, and take note of the company's mission statement. Read the background of their leaders and/or current staffers, which will give you insight into what they truly desire in an employee. You can also visit a research library to access information databases with archived news material, which may contain recent news about your potential employer. And if all else fails, try being a "lurker": go by or hang out with a coffee near the office or business, and observe current employees to get a sense of the company ambiance.

2. Prepare your materials.

If the job posting doesn't state what to send, you can try contacting a receptionist at the company for clarification. Expect to assemble items such as a resume, cover letter, samples of your work, letters of recommendation, and names of references. This may be a good time to call your references and make sure they are still at the same number, and are still willing to say positive things about you — if your reference says, "who?" when the employer calls, or worse, the number is disconnected, that doesn't make you look good.

3. Get contact information.

This may be provided in the ad itself, but in some cases employers will not print contact names or addresses. If you can dig up this information on your own, you showcase your ability to go one step beyond the competition. If you can't find a company website, try searching the Internet for any mention of the details that were provided in the ad, such as a fax number, a company name, or the names and email addresses of the people you'll submit your resume to. At best you'll dig up pertinent information you can use in your application, or at worst you'll discover weird special-interest message boards where they've posted comments in the past.

4. Submit your materials.

Sometimes the ad will specify a preference for submitting these in person, fax, or email, and sometimes you'll have a choice. If it's possible, in person is the best option. You get to see the place and people, and they get to put a face to your name and credentials. You can ask to see the decision-maker, but be aware that this can backfire if they are busy — you become not just an applicant, but the rude applicant who interrupted their lunch.

Emailing your materials is a good choice to show you know your technology, so long as you make sure you follow the etiquette described later in this chapter. Faxing is also attractive since the recipient doesn't have to print anything out, although the drawback is that your materials will end up on whatever cheap fax paper the machine spits out.

If you do submit your materials by email or fax, it is a good idea most of the time to also send a hard copy by mail that is printed on good-quality paper for better presentation. However, this isn't recommended for compaines only to business online.

5. Follow up.

If you have not been called for an interview by the deadline specified, it is okay to call or email and ask if the applicants have been selected. Your follow-through may even be the element that bumps you to the top of the "yes" pile. When you follow up, don't demand that they review your resume on the spot, or ask for detailed reasons why you haven't been called yet. Simply inquire politely if the selection process is complete.

To follow up in a timely fashion, it's important to keep track of where and when you've applied. You can do this by hand, or there is software you can purchase that will track your applications for you.

Writing Your Resume

Your resume is the way you communicate your skills and experience to a potential employer. But remember, your resume is not just a list of facts and dates, it is a form of communication with a message you control. The wording of your resume, the information you choose to include, the way it is arranged, and the style it conveys are all going to act as subtle clues to your ability.

We could write a whole book on resumes — and of course, many have been. You can find a list of some of the best resources at the end of this guide. In the meantime, here are some basic tips to get you started on the art of resume writing.

What to Include

Once you've typed your name, address, phone number and email address onto your resume-to-be, you may end up sitting and staring at the page for some time, perplexed about where to start, and how to fill all that blank space.

Luckily, resumes are one of those cases where sometimes less is more. When sifting through a bunch of applications, employers are looking to make a match quickly between their needs and your skills.

They may make a decision about a resume within seconds, so if your resume contains too much irrelevant information, it could be rejected before the employer has even finished reading it.

For this reason, you won't list every job you've ever had. Instead, pick and choose the ones that have best prepared you for this particular job. As introduced in Chapter 2, a useful technique is to create one "master resume" that has every single work-related experience in your past on it, from high school jobs to current ones, including unpaid and volunteering positions.

Don't expect to develop your master resume in one sitting. Instead, start with what you can remember, and go back to it and add on when you remember something else. You can keep a notepad handy to jot down ideas when they come to you, and call friends and family who might be able to jog your memory. This master list can be as long as needed, since you'll never be sending it out to anyone as is.

Every time you apply for a job you will cut and paste only the relevant experience and skills onto a new, custom-created resume. Don't forget to rearrange or reword information to highlight the aspects of your career history that are most in step with the open position, and use a final proofread to remove anything that doesn't help "sell" you to the employer.

TIP: As a general guideline, you should try to keep your resume to a page or two unless you have extensive relevant experience.

Be sure to include any special accomplishments, such as rewards, promotions, and achievements. Use action verbs to spice up your descriptions of the duties and responsibilities of each position, like: initiated, launched, activated, designed, conceptualized, implemented, expanded, increased, etc.

Styles to Choose From

Most resumes these days come in two formats: traditional, and functional. The traditional resume is the one you are likely used to reading or using. In it, you list your experience and education from most recent to most dated, as well as detail your relevant skills, and perhaps include a career objective to introduce yourself. (You can see an example of a traditional resume at the end of Chapter 8.)

While this style of resume can be very effective for some job applicants, for some it can lead to preconceptions based on gaps in your work history, or the passage of time. For example, if you had experience in a design field but it was 20 years ago, the employer could question whether you are capable of using the latest in computer design programs.

If you were working in advertising but took 10 years off to raise children, employers may wonder if your sense of what's "hot" will be a decade behind, or if you'll fit in with the hip and trendy culture in the office. In fact, most employers consider any skills you learned more than 10 years ago to be out of date.

To counter these preconceptions, some applicants are now using what is called a functional resume style instead, focusing on the skills and experience the employer is looking for.

To create a functional resume, start by listing all the skills you have that are relevant to the job you're applying for. Beneath each skill, list the ways you developed that skill (experience) at different jobs, volunteering, or through life experience. Steer clear of using dates or names of supervisors unless they are going to help you sell yourself more effectively.

When Your Experience is Limited

Here's some good news: even if you have never been paid to work in the career you are applying for, you can still write a powerful resume that can help you get hired. In order to do this, you will need to get some related experience through being an assistant or intern, or by volunteering.

You don't have to list these experiences as unpaid even if they were — if you did the work, it doesn't matter what you were (or weren't) paid to do it. After all, it's not like you list the pay for any other jobs you have held on your resume. The key is to present your volunteer experience in a way that is attractive to employers.

A functional resume is often a good solution for people with limited experience in the field, since it helps the employer make connections between what you did in seemingly unrelated jobs, and how those skills will transfer over into the new one.

You can beef up your resume with life skills and experience unrelated to employment, such as the negotiation skills you learned chairing the PTA, or the Internet research skills you developed by investigating your family's ancestry.

In addition to your skills, you can summarize your education, and briefly itemize your work history. By using this format, you are drawing attention to the skills you have, not when you learned or applied them. (You can see an example of a functional resume near the end of Chapter 9.)

The danger in preparing a functional resume is ending up with a disorganized list that is only going to make the employer's job harder, so once you have a list of your skills, group them into categories such as "technical," "leadership," "sales," or whatever applies to the job you are applying for. You can use the same master resume technique described earlier to whittle down your experiences to include strictly the ones that sell you best for the job at hand.

The E-Resume

Let's face it: it's a lot easier to attach your resume to an email and click "send" than to drop off a resume in person, or track down a fax machine to send from. For this reason, job applications sent by email come in by the hundreds or thousands. In many cases the applicants are too lazy to write a cover letter or personalize their resume, but are sending their application on the off-chance that no one better applies.

It's nice to think that every application will be opened, read carefully, and weighed according to merit, but in the real world, this is not always the case. The person in charge of receiving and evaluating the applications may have their regular job to do as well, and may not have the time to give every applicant a fair shake.

So there's your personalized resume and well-thought-out cover letter, sitting in the crowded inbox among the mediocre applicants. How can you make sure it gets the consideration it deserves?

Tip #1

Make sure your emailed materials are easy to open and print. This may mean sacrificing fancy layout and fonts to use a simplified file format such as .txt. You can also cut and paste the content of your attachment into the body of your email to make sure it arrives in at least some format, especially since many people are hesitant to open attachments from people they don't know.

Tip #2

Consider using a creative subject line to stand out. What is appropriate will vary depending on the culture of the workplace, but highlighting your best quality or years of experience in the subject line is pretty safe. "Re: job opening" or "job application" is what everyone else will use, so stay away from these ho-hum lines. Keep it professional, though, or it may be deleted as spam.

Tip #3

The email address you send from will also be scrutinized. Email addresses from a reputable Internet service provider using your real name are ideal; free email providers are acceptable if the username is not too quirky or risqué. You can sign your cover letter "Yours truly" with all the professionalism you can muster, but if the email is coming from VampireLover32 or BigSexyMama, you can bet it will raise a few eyebrows.

Tip #4

Install and use a virus software program on whatever computer you are using to send job applications. This is more than a courtesy — consider it a requirement.

Tip #5

According to Washington, DC journalist Paul Armantano, an estimated 80 percent of large and medium-sized organizations now rely on resume-scanning technology to screen job applicants. This software counts "keywords" from incoming resumes, and then ranks the resumes according to the number of "hits" they receive. Armantano suggests that including a list of keywords and phrases you think will be appropriate, separated by a comma or period immediately below your contact information will help your e-resume make it past the screening process.

Other Resume Tips and Ideas

- If you are going to start with a career objective or summary statement, make it interesting and relevant to the position you are applying for. Use language that speaks to the employer's needs and the value you will bring them; don't just state what you want.

- Do not include references on your resume unless you are asked to do so. It will be assumed that they are available on request, so you don't need to write that either. To spice things up, instead consider using quotes from your references like a testimonial or movie review to catch the decision-maker's attention — sprinkle them throughout your resume, or use them at the beginning or end.

For example: "Brenda was the best team leader our company ever had. Her insight and accuracy were stunning. — Jane Employer, ABC Co."

- Use language that mimics the job description you are applying for so the employer can quickly scan your resume and evaluate whether you are a match. For example, if they ask for someone with "expert presentation skills" in the ad, state exactly that in your resume: i.e., not "great" or "wonderful," but "expert."

- There are a lot of different opinions out there on what makes a perfect resume, so in the end it's best to use your own judgment, and tailor it to the field of work and position you are applying for. The perfect resume is of course the one that gets you called in for an interview, and it will be a bit different for each job and each individual.

- Appearances count. Choose an attractive paper stock, lay it out nicely on the page, and make sure there are no typos.

Cover Letters

Some people wonder why they need a cover letter at all, when all the pertinent information is included in the resume — but cover letters are an important chance to let a little of your personality shine through. Think of your cover letter like an attractive book cover that entices readers to take a look inside.

Your cover letter should be personalized, and explain why you are a good candidate for the job. Most people find that a balanced amount of polite self-confidence in bringing your best skills to the forefront is convincing and effective.

Make your cover letter as easy to read as possible, or it may not get read at all. This means using an adequate-sized, non-decorative font for the bulk of the writing; and laying it out with an eye for ease of reading. This doesn't mean you can't be creative, but don't sacrifice readability for a zany look.

Be aware that "personalized" does not mean "personal"; you don't need to talk about your hobbies or interests, give the details of your recent divorce, or tell the story of your life. Maybe you have wanted to be a (insert your dream career here) since you were six years old, but save those personal details for your friends and family.

Cover letters can also damage your candidacy for a position if they contain faux pas such as the ones in the sample cover letter on the next page.

Sample Letter #1

Dear Sirs:

I saw you're ad. This is the kind of job I've been looking for. I'm pretty sure I would enjoy it and it would be good experience for me. I've wanted to do this kind of work since I was 10 years old and now that I'm middle-aged it's about time I got a job I like. I've already sent out a bunch of resumes without much luck so I hope you'll hire me. I don't know what the job involves but it's got to be bettter than sitting around the house in my underwear. As you can see I have everything your looking for. It's your loss if you don't hire me. Call me at 5555-1212. If my mother answers don't tell her I applied for this job. She wants me to become a doctor.

Andy Applicant

In the cover letter above, Andy has done a number of things wrong. See how many of these mistakes you noticed.

Incorrect Salutation

Andy could make a better impression by addressing the letter to the appropriate hiring manager by name. If you don't know who to send your letter to, you can access the company's website and look for the appropriate person, or call and ask.

Even if the advertisement reads "send letters to human resources," don't address the letter to "Human Resources." Send it to the decision maker, because 9 times out of 10 the decision maker is going to be the person you would work for if you get hired. The worst that can happen is that the manager of the department will forward your materials back to human resources, so it's worth a shot.

If there is no other way but to address your letter to human resources and you don't know the gender of the person you're sending the letter to, then at least avoid gender salutations such as "Dear Sirs," and instead write "Dear Hiring Manager."

What's the Position?

The letter doesn't state what position Andy is applying for. Many companies advertise more than one position at a time. Omitting the position shows lack of attention to details.

Typographical and Grammatical Errors

Letters must be proofread before being sent. You'll never hear a compliment on an error-free resume or cover letter; they're supposed to be perfect. While there's no correlation between good spelling and intelligence, few things turn off a prospective employer more than a sloppy resume. The attitude is that a sloppy resume equals an employee who does sloppy work.

Furthermore, don't rely too heavily on your word processor's spell check since it won't catch mistakes such as using "two" instead of "too" or including an inaccurate phone number. Ask a friend to read the letter for you — the most difficult part of proofreading is catching your own mistakes.

Disclosing Personal Information

Employers may assume an applicant who gives "too much information" will show poor judgment in other areas as well. So don't disclose personal information about yourself such as: anything you did as a child, your age (including saying you are "young" or "middle-aged"), your health, your family, your hobbies, your talent for writing poetry, or anything else not directly related to the position you're applying for. (By the way, if anyone in your household won't respond professionally to an employer's call, get yourself a cell phone.)

Failing to Address the Company's Needs

The letter doesn't address the company's needs. Andy writes that he wants to "enjoy the job and get experience," instead of directly addressing what the company wants. Employers want to know what value you will bring to them.

Failing to Mention the Company by Name

Andy could make a much better impression by doing a little research in order to say something flattering about the company. You can find out what a company prides itself on by checking its website. The best place to start would be in the "About Us" section of the site. This will reassure them that you are serious about wanting this job, not just any job you can get.

Negativity

By stating, "I've already sent out a bunch of resumes without much luck," and "I hope you'll hire me," Andy sounds desperate. Employers may wonder if there's a good reason why no one else has hired him. And as you can imagine, writing something like, "It's your loss if you don't hire me" does not make a good impression.

Sample Letter #2

Ms. Jane Doe
Vice President, Personal Shopping Division
Sunstrum's Department Store
(Address)
(Date)

Dear Ms. Doe:

Re: <u>Assistant Personal Shopper Position</u>

I was thrilled to see your company's recent advertisement in the Tribune for an assistant personal shopper with Sunstrum's Department Store. I am contacting you to let you know I am available to step in and fill this position for you quickly and professionally.

When I read the mission statement on the Sunstrum's website, I realized that our professional goals of top-notch service, dedication and excellence are closely aligned. I am more than familiar with Sunstrum's selection of superior products, having frequently shopped for myself and others in your store.

I started my own personal shopping service, Fabulous Shopping, just over a year ago, and have worked at developing a client base through networking, personal contacts, and of course providing excellent service and value. As a result, I have doubled my clientele in the last six months.

This hands-on shopping experience, combined with my part-time studies in fashion merchandising and my previous employment in a retail boutique, create a strong recipe for my success with Sunstrum's. I excel at customer service, have a keen fashion sense, work hard to get repeat business, and have numerous letters of recommendation from my satisfied clients.

Thank you for taking the time to review the attached resume, which has a more detailed description of my skills, education and experience. I look forward to meeting with you or one of your associates to discuss my candidacy for assistant personal shopper with Sunstrum's at your earliest convenience.

Best regards,

Andrea Applicant

If you were an employer, wouldn't you be more impressed with the second cover letter (shown on the previous page), in which the candidate is applying for a personal shopper position?

Your own cover letter will of course depend on the position you are applying for, and the company you are applying to. It should also include your name and contact information at the top of the page to make you easier to contact, or in case it gets separated from your resume.

Interviews

Most employers are looking for something simple but rare in a job candidate: someone with a positive attitude, and excellent interpersonal skills, who will do a good job. And for many decision-makers, the order these qualities are listed in is the order they are valued. The challenge of interviews lies in showing the employer in such a short period of time that you are those three things, and more.

Three Qualities to Demonstrate

In this section we will focus on the art of interviewing and the importance of making a great first impression. We will start by discussing the three most important qualities to exude in an interview: enthusiasm, interest and a positive attitude.

Enthusiasm

You want the employer to sense that you will bring energy and ideas to the position, and that you are eager to do whatever it takes to step in and make yourself part of the team. You can communicate enthusiasm with the tone of your voice, your responses to interview questions, and your body language, as we'll explain in a bit. Note that there is also a fine line between being enthusiastic, and seeming desperate.

Interest

Letting your eyes glaze over while the employer gets nostalgic about the history of the company is a definite no-no. Even if you have little interest in the topic at hand, try to stay engaged. (Then again, if you're not interested in the history of the company, maybe this isn't your dream job after all.) You can best demonstrate your interest in the company and the position by asking intelligent questions, and reading about the issues affecting the industry and/or the company in the few days before the interview.

A Positive Attitude

When an employer sees your signs of a positive attitude, you will be a much harder candidate to resist. While skills can usually be learned on the job or in training, it's much harder to try to instill a positive attitude in someone who is lacking it. The sample interview questions in this section will give you some examples of ways to express yourself in a positive way.

Once you have these three important qualities in mind, it's time to start preparing for the interview. And although good advice, there's more to it than laying out your clothes the night before and getting a decent night's sleep, so read on.

Researching the Company

Once you've received the call and scheduled the interview, it's time to learn as much as you can about the employer and the industry in the amount of time you have.

Chances are, most of what you learn will not become a topic of conversation during the interview, but as the interviewer is telling you something about the company, you may have the chance to say, "Yes, I read about that on your website," or "I noticed that in your annual report." This is always impressive because it shows the employer you took the time to learn about the company on your own. Beware of spouting off too much about what you learned, though. After all, you are not there to prove you know more about the company than the interviewer.

Just as when you researched the company to prepare your application, your first stop for company information should be the company's website. How they present themselves on the website will also tell you something about them. If possible, try to find some information about the person who will be interviewing you.

If you are hungry for information about some of the bigger players in the industry, check out websites for company overviews and histories, key people, financial information, and industry news and trends. Some of these websites include Hoovers Online (**www. hoovers.com/free**) and Inc.com 500 (**www.inc.com/inc500**).

> **TIP:** Don't forget that interviewers can research *you* online just as easily as you can research them. Do a Google search of your name to see what comes up, and make sure you take down anything embarrassing that you've posted at sites such as **MySpace.com**.

Preparing to Answer Interview Questions

In addition to researching the company, you should also take time to think through your answers to some common interview questions. Don't memorize them — your answers should sound natural — but have an idea of what you want to say. If you get the chance, do a little role-playing with a friend in advance of your interview day to practice answering the inevitable tough questions with poise.

There are two basic styles of interviewing today. The behavioral interview asks about specific past behaviors in an attempt to gauge how well you would perform on the job. "Tell me about a time when you experienced conflict at work," is a good example of a behavioral question.

The interviewer will not be satisfied with a hypothetical answer about what you "would" do in such a situation. They want to hear about an actual time you experienced conflict. The purpose is not to see if you have ever had a conflict (they expect you have); the purpose is to see how well you resolve difficult situations and, if something did not work out in the past, what you learned from it.

You can expect to hear behavioral questions such as: "Describe your most successful project so far. What did you do to make it a success?" and "Describe a project where something went wrong. How did you solve the problem?" When confronted with these types of questions, always be sure to describe the situation, tell what you did, relate the outcome, and finish with what you learned from it.

The traditional interview uses broad-based questions, such as "Tell me about yourself," or "Why do you want to work for our company?" How you respond to these open-ended questions tells the interviewer how well you communicate.

- Does your answer sound pat and rehearsed?
- Do you go on and on?
- Can you be succinct yet interesting?

Below are 10 traditional interview questions, with tips on how to answer them, and some sample bad and better answers.

1. Tell me about yourself.

Bad Answer: "I'm a 36-year-old Pisces who likes knitting and long walks in the park. Dislikes include my ex-husband and his new trophy wife."

Avoid giving information that is irrelevant or too personal in your answer. Instead, prepare a one-minute "personal commercial" that you can relate, which focuses on the education and experience you have to offer. This should not sound rehearsed, but should be conversational, with words you use normally.

Better Answer: "I started off in this business as an assistant's assistant, and learned the ropes the hands-on, unglamorous way. But it helped me get to know the job inside and out, and I loved the work. I decided to take night courses last year to learn new skills and reconnect with trends in the industry. When I completed the additional training, I moved to the city and was immediately hired by JB and Associates. There I was doing..."

2. Why are you looking for a new job?

Bad Answer: "My boss is a jerk and the customers are hard to deal with."

Keep the answer positive, in terms of where you want to go, not what you want to get away from. Resist the urge to bad-mouth your current employer, even if it is a truly horrendous place to work.

Better Answer: "I have been promoted as far as I can go with my current employer. I'm looking for a new challenge that will give me the opportunity to use my skills to help my employer's business grow."

3. What are your strengths?

Bad Answer: "I can burp on demand and keep a straight face when telling a lie. Plus, as you can see, I have a great sense of humor."

Discuss three or four of your strengths as they relate to the position you are interviewing for, and give examples of times they have helped you do your work.

Better Answer: "I have a really good eye for detail, and in the past, I have caught critical mistakes for employers before they happened. When I worked for ABC Company, I helped the company avoid a few catastrophes this way, so they started routing orders through my office to check even though I wasn't working in the ordering department.

321

Of course, I'd be happy to apply this skill in any way you feel is suitable in this company. Another strength I can offer an employer is..."

4. *What is your greatest weakness?*

Bad Answer: "Gee, it's hard to pick only one. I'm usually late, I have trouble getting along with co-workers, I steal office supplies, and I nap at my desk when no one is looking. Wait a minute, you're trying to trick me into saying something bad about myself. I meant to say that I'm a perfectionist workaholic."

If you think a good answer is that you're "a perfectionist who won't quit until the job's done right," think again. Chances are the employer has heard that one before, and you'll sound like you're hiding something. Be honest, but don't confess something big. Instead, admit a minor weakness that can be fixed.

Or consider this tongue-in-cheek response from Danny Kiss, a New York lawyer: "My biggest weakness? I would say chocolate, especially milk chocolate. A nice piece of milk chocolate makes me weak in the knees."

Better Answer: "I'm not a very speedy typist, but I've been completing one of those online typing courses, and I've already improved by 10 words a minute." (Of course, if typing is a major requirement of your new job, choose a different weakness!)

5. *Why have you had so many jobs?*

Bad Answer: "I get bored easily."

Give acceptable reasons (frequent moves, changes in personal goals, etc.), but focus on the fact that you're ready for a permanent position now, which is what they are really concerned about.

Better Answer: "When I was younger, I decided to sample a wide variety of careers. That way, when I was ready to choose a career path I would be absolutely certain that I had found the right one for the long-term future. Now I'm committed to this industry, and that's why I'm here today."

6. What are your short-term and long-term goals?

Bad Answer: "Considering how hung-over I am, my short-term goal is to make it through this interview. Long-term, I hope to quit my job within a couple of years and become a ski bum."

Sometimes employers ask this because they want to know whether you are looking at their company for long-term employment or simply a short-term job until something "better" comes along. Other employers want to judge your ability to plan for the future. Most employers do not want to hear that in five years you hope to be retired or plan to start your own business. Your short-term goals should involve getting hired into the right position (that's why you are there); long term is where you want to go within your profession.

Better Answer: "Short-term, I'd like to find a position where I can build a solid clientele of return clients. I enjoy building relationships with clients who come back year after year for service and advice. Long-term, I can see myself taking some additional training over the next few years, and applying for a more senior position here once I have the right combination of experience and education."

7. What kind of salary do you expect?

Bad Answer: "Anything's better than what I'm making now."

Tell them that you would prefer to delay a salary discussion until you've been offered the position. If pressed, you can ask them to give you a range of what the position pays first, and indicate that somewhere in that range would be acceptable. Or you can say you would expect to be paid a rate in keeping with your experience. You do not have to give a dollar figure at this time.

Better Answer: "I think I would be in a better position to quote you a figure once the interview process is complete and an offer is on the table, so I can weigh all the factors involved appropriately."

8. Describe your ideal supervisor.

Bad Answer: "Someone who is never around and doesn't bother me or notice when I mess up."

Once you are called in for an interview, chances are the employer already feels your skills are up to par. The real question being asked here is, "Can you work with me?" Avoid launching into a diatribe against a former supervisor, and focus on the positive qualities that you appreciate in a boss.

Better Answer: "For me, the ideal supervisor is a leader with a vision of where the company is headed. They make you feel valuable and that your ideas really count. But they're human, too — able to admit the occasional mistake."

9. Why do you want to work for us?

Bad Answer: "I'm desperate and no one else will hire me."

This is your chance to reveal the research you did on the employer before the interview. Focus on one or two flattering items, and connect them to how you like to work or do business, or to your overall philosophies of life.

Better Answer: "When I read the mission statement on your website about giving back to the community, I felt really inspired. I was also impressed with the facts about your growth in the past three years — three new locations, and a 45% overall sales increase. That's really something to be proud of. I think it would be rewarding to be part of a company that is such a leader in their industry and in the community."

10. Why should I hire you?

Bad Answer: "I need the money to pay off my gambling debts."

This is an opportunity to reiterate your skills and relate them to the position you are applying for. If you are confident about your skills, it will show.

Better Answer: "When I read your ad, I couldn't have imagined a better match for my skills and experience than this job. Now that I have spoken with you, and learned more about your needs, I'm even more certain that I'm the right candidate. I know that I can hit the ground running and exceed your expectations because of my experience with..."

Other Tips for Getting Ready

In addition to preparing your answers, you'll want to spend some time preparing your "look" too. While the image you should project will vary depending on the environment you are coming into, the best across-the-board advice is to dress like you already work there (within reason).

If you get a chance to observe other employees before the interview (perhaps while "lurking" or dropping off a resume), make sure that you take note of what employees are wearing, and mimic this look when you come in for your interview. This will position you in the decision-maker's mind as someone who is a natural fit with the company.

If you are still unsure what to wear, think about the qualities you want to project, and match the clothes to complete the look. If you are trying to look professional, wear something similar to what professionals in the industry wear. If you are trying to look fashionable and creative, put together an outfit that is trendy and unique.

You should ask when the interview is scheduled if there is anything specific you should bring with you. If in doubt, bring:

- Any proof of licensing or qualification you need
- Background checks, if required
- Samples of your past work (or photos)
- Any tools or props you need to demonstrate your abilities
- Letters from past employers or clients
- Any articles that you have published or that have been written about you
- An updated list of references
- A cell phone, map, and the employer's phone number and address

Most job applicants also bring a few copies of their own resume in case the employer has misplaced their copy, and so you can follow along as they ask you questions about your experience.

Ideally you should show up at least a few minutes before your interview time — make sure you are not late.

If the interview is going to take place in a part of town you are not familiar with, try to find time to go by the place in advance, so you can get a sense of how long it takes to get there, and be able to arrive on time. Nothing will frazzle you more than driving through a maze of one-way streets and dead-ends with two minutes to get to your interview. If this does happen, though, take a few seconds to compose yourself before walking in.

During the Interview

When you arrive for your interview, you should be outgoing and enthusiastic from the minute you step through the door. Your attitude and ability to get along with people are being judged by everyone from the receptionist to the other employees peering at you as you are led in. Shake hands, smile and make eye contact with each person you meet — you should also jot down the names of the people you interview with to help you remember them during the interview, and later when you are following up.

During the interview, relax and try to be yourself as much as possible. Of course this isn't always easy because interviews tend to make people nervous, which usually means they smile less and act more formal. A good piece of advice is to act how you would if you did not feel nervous. This may sound strange, but consciously behaving like you were not nervous can actually make you start to feel more confident! If you can, find ways to genuinely connect with the interviewer, and you'll likely sense both of you relaxing.

Remember that your tone of voice and body language communicate more than words alone. Speak with a moderate tone and speed. Loud talkers may be perceived as insensitive or domineering, soft talkers as self-effacing or shy, and fast talkers as shifty or untrustworthy. While these may be far from the truth, the perceptions are common and ones you want to avoid.

A UCLA study found that non-verbal forms of communication such as posture, gestures, facial expressions and eye contact are particularly powerful in face-to-face communication. If there is conflict between the words being said and the message communicated by the body, the body is more likely to be believed, so make sure that your body is in step with your language. Sitting up straight and leaning forward in the chair shows that you are interested, engaged, and involved in the conversation. Eye contact establishes rapport and trust, while crossed arms can signify fear or disagreement.

TIP: If you are interested in learning more about gestures and their meanings, the book *How to Read a Person Like a Book* by Gerald I. Nierenberg and Henry H. Calero describes the message conveyed by numerous gestures commonly used in business settings.

Here are a few other Dos and Don'ts you should keep in mind for any interview. They may sound strangely like your mother's advice on manners, but common courtesy goes a long way in an interview setting, and the lack of it can be a major turn-off for employers.

Do:

- Arrive about ten minutes early
- Speak up and make eye contact
- Turn off your cell phone
- Wear clean, pressed clothing that fits well

Don't:

- Chew gum
- Sit down until you are offered a chair
- Use offensive language or tell off-color jokes
- Come in reeking of cigarette smoke
- Fidget or tap a pen

Questions You Should Ask

Don't forget that you should ask questions in an interview as well. After all, you have a legitimate reason: finding out if this is a place you would want to come to every day to work!

Asking questions demonstrates your interest in the company and the job, and makes you a proactive (not a passive) job seeker. It gives the interviewer a sense that you are not just a doormat to hire and use, but an intelligent individual with desirable skills. Following are some good questions:

- What is a typical day for someone in this position?
- How will my performance be measured? By whom? How often?
- How would you describe the company's management style?
- What challenges will the company face in the near future?
- Does the company support ongoing training and education for employees to stay current in their fields?
- How does this department fit in with the organization? How is it perceived by the rest of the company?

Demonstrating Your Skills

For some dream careers it will be necessary to demonstrate your skills during the interview. This may be in the form of a standardized test, a performance, a tryout, or some other hands-on demonstration of you performing the tasks that would be expected in the job.

Alternately, you may be asked to supply a recording of your abilities (written, filmed, recorded, photographed, etc.) for the interviewers to review at a later date. Part Two of this book has more details about what to expect that are specific to each type of career.

You can inquire in advance if there will be a need to demonstrate your skills, so you can be mentally prepared, as well as physically prepared with any props or supplies you need to do the job. Ask how long you should take to do this demonstration, so you won't be suddenly cut off due to time limits. It's also a good idea to be well practiced in whatever tasks you will perform, so that you can perform them under the pressure of scrutiny quickly and without error.

Ending the Interview

You'll want to end the interview on a high note. This can be in the form of a summary statement that reiterates your key skills or your interest in the position, or even an anecdote that ties in to something discussed in the interview. If you feel like things have gone well, you can pull out your list of references and briefly go over the people you have listed and why.

Some employers will use the end of the interview as a chance to chat in a less formal way, by asking you if you drove or rode the bus there, if you enjoy baseball, etc. This can be a good time to forge a connection with the interviewer, but make sure that you don't get too personal, and only chat as long as they seem to want to — chances are they have another interview scheduled shortly after yours.

Following Up

The decision-making process doesn't end when you shake hands with the interviewers and walk out the door. Many job candidates are taking the time to contact the employer soon after the interview to thank them, and to make one last push to land the job. In fact, it's become such a common practice that even strong candidates who don't follow up with the interviewer can be overshadowed by the "thoughtfulness" of the candidates who do.

You can follow up with the interviewers by phone, email, or by hand-delivering a note. Whatever method you choose, you should thank each person you interviewed with separately, and address them by name. Your thank-you should come within a day of your interview, since you can never be sure about the pace of the hiring process.

In your note or phone call, you will thank the interviewer for their time, and confirm your interest in the position. You can also answer any questions about yourself or your skills you felt were not adequately covered during the interview. Conclude by saying that you will follow up again in about a week (or another appropriate amount of time) to find out if a hiring decision has been made — although by following the advice in this chapter, you'll make yourself much more likely to hear from them first.

When that phone call comes in to offer you the job, this is the time to discuss salary. Many people wonder, when the salary offer is not what they imagined, if they should negotiate. The answer is "yes." A 2005 survey by **CareerBuilder.com** found that 58% of hiring managers say they leave some negotiating room when extending initial offers. To negotiate a higher salary you'll need to prove your value to the employer. See chapter 14 for advice.

TIP: To prepare yourself with an idea of what will be offered, check out the national and local averages in your field at **http://fabjob.salary.com**.

If you are an entry-level applicant, realize that your true benefits may not be in monetary remuneration, but in experience, which is often much more valuable. Once you have a certain level of experience, you will be in a better position to negotiate salary.

If you are stuck on more money but know there is not a lot of wiggle room, you can also ask about non-monetary rewards in lieu of cash, such as additional paid sick days or time off, flexible hours of work or working from home, bonus structures or commission, shares, health benefits, contribution towards training you wish to acquire, or anything else you can dream up. If it's not cash out of hand, your future employer will be more likely to oblige.

Turning Interview Rejection Into Success

If the employer tells you "we've selected another applicant," take the opportunity to thank them again. On the next page is an excellent response in the form of a follow-up letter.

If the new hire doesn't work out, a letter like this could result in you getting the job you thought you had lost. Or it could lead to other opportunities.

Sample Follow-Up Letter

October 12, 2006

Ms. Veronica Employer
ABC Company
(Address)

Dear Ms. Employer,

    Thank you for advising me of your decision. I am writing to thank you and let you know how much I appreciated the opportunity to meet with you. I continue to be impressed with your professionalism and (insert nice things about the company and the interviewer personally).

    If you ever have a need for someone with my skills and experience, please do keep me in mind as I would love to work with you and (insert something the interviewer mentioned about what they are looking for such as "help ABC company expand into new markets").

    All the best for your continued success.

Sincerely,

Jennifer Jobseeker

If another position at that company opens up, you could get that job. If the employer has a friend who's looking to hire someone for a similar position, you could be recommended. (Tag once got a fabulous job when a friend of someone who had interviewed her — and received a thank you letter after rejecting her — phoned and said "Joe recommended you. Are you available to start Monday?") They might even decide to create a new position for you.

Of course there are no guarantees. But in these days when there may be hundreds of skilled applicants for the fabulous job you want, going the extra mile by thanking an interviewer after a rejection could help you stand out as someone worth hiring.

13

Make Friends

How to Get a Dream Job through Word of Mouth

Think back to the last time you watched the Academy Awards or any other awards show. As each of the winners got up to accept their award, did you hear anybody say:

"The reason I'm here is because of how hard I alone worked to get here. I did it without any help from anybody else. There's nobody I want to thank."

That doesn't sound familiar, does it? Instead, you probably heard the winners thank their families and many other people who have supported them along the way.

You will find similar expressions of gratitude if you watch interviews with athletes after they have won an Olympic medal, or if you read the biography of any successful business person.

In this chapter you will find a variety of ideas to help you get others to support you in achieving your dream career, such as joining professional associations, attending networking events, going on information interviews, or asking for advice on Internet message boards. Other people are an often untapped source of career information, leads on work, and even job referrals.

Some people, particularly those who are quiet or shy, have a negative first reaction to the idea of networking. If you are one of those people, then to help you warm up to the concept we'll start by taking a closer look at what the word actually means.

There are different definitions of networking, but a particularly useful definition is the one given in the *American Heritage Dictionary of the English Language*:

"To interact or engage in informal communication with others for mutual assistance or support."

As you will see from this definition, two keys to networking are that it is "informal" and "mutual." That means that you are not begging people for work, forcing favors, or aggressively shoving your business card into the reluctant palms of everyone you meet.

It does mean, however, that you will be constantly alert to the possibility that everyone you know could help your career, and could possibly use your help as well. Remember, those who succeed in life do not do it alone!

Informal Networking

Have you ever heard of a theory called "six degrees of separation"? Based on the play and film of the same title, the theory is that every person in the world is connected to every other person through only six (or fewer) steps.

For example:

1. You know Bob
2. Bob knows Carrie
3. Carrie knows Dave
4. Dave knows Emma
5. Emma knows Fred

Fred is therefore "connected" to you through only five degrees of separation. Now, what if Fred is someone with influence and power, who could recommend you for a job where he works or with one of his associates? Or maybe he could be in a position to regularly refer clients to your business, since he works in a related career.

What you need to do is break through the "degrees of separation" by spreading the word about who you are and what you can do, until you connect with the right people like Fred who can advance your career in some way. Here's how to do it.

Who to Start With

To start your informal networking, think about all of the people you know, family and friends alike. In that vast network, is there anyone who is working in a field where they could connect you with someone who could advance your career?

The answer is almost certainly "yes." Remember, you don't need to know someone who is working in the job you want to pursue; all you need is to know someone who knows someone who knows someone, etc.

There are usually a number of people who, because of their careers, are separated from someone working in or hiring for what you want by just one degree. Trying to connect with these people can seem much less overwhelming than trying to connect directly with a total stranger.

The first key to using your own network is to start getting the word out that you are looking for work in your field, and that you want referrals to people who might be able to hire you or refer you to clients.

For example, perhaps your brother-in-law is a lawyer at a firm that represents some famous clients, and you're interested in becoming a personal assistant to a celebrity. Call him, and he may have some advice or even a few leads for you. In fact, many of the lawyers at that firm will more than likely talk to assistants and publicists on a day-to-day basis, so they'll be one of the first to know if a position will be opening up.

Not sure who to ask for contacts? Start with your parents, brothers, sisters, aunts, uncles, in-laws, other relatives, friends, acquaintances, spouse's friends, relatives' friends, neighbors, customers, co-workers, former co-workers, people you attended school with, people you meet at parties… in other words, ask everyone.

Why Some People May be More Helpful than Others

The first person you network with will be someone who knows and trusts you, and will help you out simply for that reason. But from that point on, each person who agrees to refer you or interview you will do so because they know and trust the person who has mentioned you to them.

This can feel like a pretty big risk to the person agreeing to take a chance and recommend you. And when you think about it, they have very little to gain for putting their reputation on the line. When was the last time you heard that someone got a raise or promotion because they recommended the perfect person for a job? They'd probably be lucky if they got a thank you from the person they recommended, or from the company whose need they filled.

The challenge of having little to gain is added to by the fact that the person who is being asked to refer you does have something important at risk: if you end up doing a bad job, their judgment skills will look poor, and their reputation will be tarnished.

With all this uncertainty and little reward, then why does anyone recommend anyone else at all? Usually, it goes back to the reason we mentioned right off the top: because someone they know and trust asked them to, and they want to help a friend out. But now you understand that a simple recommendation isn't always that simple after all!

Additionally, as you go about asking for referrals or leads you will find that there are certain types of people who may be more willing than others to go out of their way to help you (e.g. to pick up the phone and call an employer on your behalf). While this is partly based on how well you know them, surprisingly enough their gender may factor into the equation as well.

Many men are comfortable promoting only close friends, and are often reluctant to take a chance on a stranger simply on the basis that they have been referred by a friend of a friend. It's not that both men and women don't want to help people out. In fact, a man might help a close buddy even if he knew the buddy might not be the best pick for a job. However, our experience suggests that women are more likely to help someone they barely know simply because they like him or her.

However, if you are a woman who is seeking a job on the same level as the woman you're approaching for help, don't be surprised if that help is not forthcoming. Several new books examine how women compete with each other in the workplace, including *I Can't Believe She Did That! Why Women Betray Other Women at Work*, by Nan Mooney and *Tripping the Prom Queen: The Truth About Women and Rivalry*, by Susan Shapiro Barash.

An episode of *Survivor* reflected the type of competitive behavior that often happens among women in the workplace. When separated into tribes on the basis of age and gender, the group of older women found themselves with a member named Tina who was clearly the star. She made fire, found water, and caught fish – all the essentials for survival at a stage in the game when tribes need to keep their strongest players. Yet when the tribe was forced to vote off a member, Tina was the first to go. If you think people don't act like that in "real life," think again.

The lesson is to be cautious of asking for help in your job search from women who might view you as potential competition, and focus instead on getting help from people who are not in a position to feel threatened by you. If a woman is a star herself, she is less likely to feel threatened and therefore more likely to help you.

To keep being referred by contacts who don't know you, be professional and try to "fit the part" of whatever position they recommend you for. Each person who recommends you must see you as a serious potential candidate — there should be no doubt that you will reflect well on them. When they recommend you and you do a fantastic job, then they'll be able to take the credit for seeing your potential in the first place.

Saying Thanks

Always remember to thank the people who make introductions for you. A "thank-you" email or card is appropriate for anyone who makes a referral; for someone who is especially helpful, consider showing your appreciation with a gift basket, a flower arrangement for their office or another thoughtful gift.

While wine or other forms of alcohol are often used in this manner, this is a potential pitfall if you don't know the person's favorite social drink, or even whether they drink at all. The same goes for chocolates or rich foods — your recipient may be struggling with a diet and resent the temptation. Play it safe if you don't know for a fact what your recipient may like. You can always discreetly ask one of their associates what they would consider to be an appropriate present for the person you want to thank.

Networking Activities

While tapping into the contacts you already have and doing some informal networking is a great way to start looking for work, it is a good idea to also take action in expanding your network of contacts through meeting and interacting with people at social and business events.

While some of the people you meet may have an immediate job opening or need for your services, in many cases you are laying the foundation for future business. By establishing relationships through networking, you can be the one people think of when the need arises down the road.

So who should you try to connect with? It might be tempting to approach everyone, but you simply do not have the time to network with everyone who might possibly ever have a need for your services or your talent. Instead, you need to think about what events and groups are most likely to attract people who could help your career, and focus your efforts where they are likely to be the most productive.

This section offers a variety of ideas, but you don't have to pursue all of them. Choose a few to begin with, based on the dream career you have in mind. If the first ones you try don't turn out to be great networking opportunities, scratch them off your list and try something else. You'll eventually hit on what works for your business or career.

Networking Clubs

Valuable networking time can be spent in a well-balanced networking club. Some of these are general business groups, but many have a target group of clients and include one member from different industries (e.g. insurance, financial planning, law, professional photography, real estate, etc.) to reach those in the target group. Each member of the club is expected to bring a certain number of leads to the group each week or month.

Fees will vary, but can be as low as the cost of breakfast once a week or breakfast plus a membership fee. You may also be required to serve on the executive board after a time. In addition to the self-marketing opportunities, benefits of joining networking groups may include discounts on services provided by other members of the group.

To become a member you are either recommended to the group by an existing member, or you might approach the group and ask to sit in as an observer for a meeting or two, and get accepted from there. Most groups will allow a trial period before you join. You may be required to give a short presentation about your own business or career, and the business and personal skills you can bring to the group.

The types of participants will differ with every group, so don't settle for the first one you visit. Check around first before deciding which one to join. Consider their professions, their average incomes, their levels of education, and anything else that defines them as a group. Make sure the members represent the kind of people who might become clients or who would know others who could benefit from your services, or who work in positions of influence in the industry you want to break into.

One way to find a good networking club is through word of mouth. You can ask individuals you know or do business with who hold sales jobs (such as insurance agents, financial planners, computer sales professionals, car salesmen, or travel agents) what groups they belong to, and if they have been effective for them.

You can also look for networking groups online. Business Network International (**www.bni.com**) has more than 2,300 chapters in cities around the world.

Membership Organizations

Another excellent way to network is by joining associations that prospective clients or decision-makers may belong to. Some examples include:

- Civic and service clubs (such as Rotary Club or Kiwanis Club)
- Business organizations (such as your Chamber of Commerce)
- Clubs that attract the wealthy (for example, golf, polo, yachting, and country clubs)

Membership fees may vary from $20 to hundreds or even thousands of dollars (the latter if you want to join an exclusive country club or private golf club). The more exclusive clubs usually require current members to introduce you and put you up for membership, so you may have to join some less exclusive clubs in order to meet people who might also belong to the more exclusive ones. Many less exclusive clubs will let you attend a few times for a nominal fee so you can decide if you really want to join.

You can find organizations by asking your friends and colleagues what they are involved in. You can also find them in your local telephone directory or online.

If you simply attend club functions without getting involved, the value of the membership will not be as great as if you truly pitch in. What sorts of things can you do to help out and gain the attention of others whose goodwill can help your career or business grow? Here are some suggestions:

- Serve on a committee
- Write articles for the association newsletter
- Volunteer to help out with the organization's events
- Run for election to the Executive Committee

Industry Events

The industry you are trying to break into is likely to have one or more large trade shows a year, as well as smaller workshops or seminars that you, as a newcomer, could attend. While you will likely have to pay a fee, these industry events put you in touch with the movers and shakers, suppliers, and big names in your field.

These events are usually put on or sponsored by professional associations, so once you identify those, take a look on their website or give them a call and ask when the next annual conference is scheduled for. Industry publications or websites may have ads for upcoming events, and even your local newspaper or large conference center might be a source of event information. The earlier you look into these the better, since if you miss a show the next one may be a year away.

If the event is a smaller one, take advantage of the chance to meet with the presenter or speaker at the conclusion of the event or on a break. Introduce yourself, explain that you are a newcomer to the industry, and ask for a business card so you can contact them later when they are not so busy. Perhaps they may be open to meeting with or mentoring you, as we'll discuss a bit later in this chapter.

You should also chat socially with other attendees and people at the event. If you get the chance, you can print up some business cards for yourself before you attend, so you can fit in with those already working in the career, and show you are serious about pursuing your dream.

If you are looking at a dream career that includes starting a business, don't limit yourself to events targeted only to people in your industry. You should also attend events that are geared towards people who are likely clients, or who may be able to refer clients to you. For example, a wedding planner could attend (or even set up a booth at) a bridal expo, but might also benefit from attending a florists' conference or a jewelry-makers' seminar.

> **TIP:** One way to attend trade shows for free is to volunteer to help the organizer put the event on. See if you can arrange to work two days of a three-day event, setting aside the third day to attend seminars or wander through the booths, for example.

Information Interviews

Another way to meet people in your industry face to face is to request a short meeting with them to discuss their (and your) career. These career-oriented brief meetings are called information interviews, and serve the double-purpose of expanding your knowledge of the career, and establishing some personal connections in the industry.

Use a polite letter or phone call to explain to the person you'd like to meet with that you are new to this particular field, and that you would like to arrange a 15- or 20-minute interview to discuss how they achieved success in their career, and what they think might be your next move.

TIP: While you aren't specifically coming in to ask for a job, it's best to arrange information interviews with people who are in a position to hire at some point, or who may be able to refer work to you when they get too busy.

It's important to not try to bluff your way through an information interview. You should have specific questions prepared, which may include:

- What do you like best about your job?
- What are the three things you look for when you are hiring for this company?
- What do you wish you had known when you were first getting into this business?
- What has been your biggest professional challenge to date, and how did you overcome it?
- Based on a quick review of my experience to date, what training or experience do you think I should pursue next?
- Is there anyone else you can refer me to who is looking for someone with my talents and abilities, or who might be willing to meet with me?
- Anything else specific to the interviewer or the company that you are curious about.

Respect the time limits you have set for your information interview, and let the person know when the time limit is up. If they are willing to continue that's fine, but if you get the impression you should wrap things up then do so. Thank them for their time and any referrals they were able to provide.

Most importantly, this is not the time to ask for a job. A direct request puts the person who has done you a favor by meeting with you in an awkward spot. You can, however, ask if they will keep a few copies of your resume to pass along to colleagues and keep on file for future job openings. You can also ask if they mind if you keep in touch with them from time to time to see if they know of any job openings.

Remember that you are laying the groundwork for the future, and building relationships. Like your other forms of networking, you may not see immediate results from information interviews, but making these key contacts will pay off in time.

Internet Message Boards

Many professions now have online forums where people who are working or interested in a particular career can post questions and have them answered by other people who have ideas or advice on that issue. These message boards can be public, which means anyone can post on or read them, or private, which means that you will need to apply to join.

These forums are a valuable source of information to newcomers, since you can go from post to post and read a variety of opinions on the very issues that you are dealing with, or will be dealing with once you are working. You may even establish a real trust with one or more of the posters on the site, and be able to turn to them for career advice whenever you need it.

To find Internet message boards, type the name of your dream career and the words "forum," "message," "chat," or "board" into a search engine. Some professional associations have boards that they moderate that you will gain access to once you purchase your membership.

Before you post on these boards, get familiar with the board and the types of questions that are asked. There may be a separate area for questions about getting started, or your question may have already been answered numerous times in the past. And remember to take any advice you get on a message board for what it is — just one person's opinion.

In some professions, people who consult for a fee will be frequent visitors to these kinds of message boards, so don't be surprised if you receive a message from someone asking you to contact them privately for more career-related information. We'll talk about paying for career advice in the upcoming section on finding a mentor.

If you are starting your own business, Internet message boards can also be a great source of clients. Just be aware that most message boards do not tolerate direct solicitation of their membership.

If you see a post from someone looking for a service you think you can provide, you can answer their question and include a link to your website or your email address. When people see proof that you know what you are talking about and are providing some helpful free information, they are more likely to inquire about paying for your services.

Why People in Your Dream Career Might Discourage You

When you're thinking of entering a new career, talking to people currently working in that career can be a huge help. They can give you the inside scoop on the job and the industry, refer you to people looking to hire, send clients your way, and as we'll discuss a bit later in this chapter, may even become a personal mentor who will guide and advise you like a friend.

However, if you are hoping that everyone who works in the industry will welcome you and be willing to help, you may be disappointed. Instead of getting fabulous career advice or job leads, you may get the message that there is no room for you in the industry, or that the hours are long and the job is unrewarding. You may be left feeling discouraged about the career, and even start to think you should consider giving up on your ambitions.

Don't believe it. If you are left feeling less than excited about a career after speaking with someone working in it, you are probably talking to the wrong person. People working in a career may have a hidden reason for being unhelpful to newcomers such as any or all of the following.

They want to feel special

Many successful people got where they are today because of their talent and effort. When asked how they did it, however, their story may sound like the one that parents used to tell about walking in the snow for miles every day to get to school and home again — uphill both ways. In other words, they make it sound much more difficult than it is. And while it's possible it really was difficult for someone else, you might have what it takes to achieve success in your chosen career more quickly.

Few people will tell others that it's easy to break into their career or that almost anyone with determination can do it, even if that's true. By saying that it takes a rare ability or many years to succeed in a career, those who are already working in that career validate themselves and what they have achieved.

Keep this in mind when speaking with someone working in the career, and don't say you hope to get a job like theirs right away. If you acknowledge their success and show respect for their achievements they may be more willing to assist you.

They are struggling

Someone who is struggling in a career may have spent years in the profession without achieving the kind of success they had hoped for. This type of person may try to "help" you by pointing out the "reality" of the profession you want to work in. They will tell you that at least 80% of those who enter their field will drop out or never achieve great success.

But that's true for the vast majority of careers. In a recent issue of *Harvard Magazine*, Michael Shinagel, Harvard's dean of continuing education, said that the average person will have six different careers in their lifetime — which means the average person will leave five careers. Why let that stop you from following your heart now?

Another reality is that virtually every career, from acting to real estate, has only a few people who reach the top. It is insulting for someone to assume you will not be one of the successful ones. However, someone who has personally not made it to the top after years of struggle simply may not be able to see how a newcomer can.

If you can overlook their discouraging attitude, this person may actually be able to help by filling you in on industry jargon, types of employers, and other career information. Just don't waste your time trying to convince them that you will succeed where they haven't.

They have a scarcity consciousness

People who have what's called a "scarcity consciousness" believe there will be less work for them if more people enter the profession. They see newcomers as potential competitors and will do what they can to discourage others from entering the field.

As an example, the moderator of a message board for a dream career mentioned in this book stated in response to a posting that if everyone who wanted to enter the career actually did so, "it would stop being a fab job for everyone else, as there would be very few who could ever make a living doing this."

Fortunately, there are people in every industry who have not only achieved success, but are willing to help others do the same. As Mark Twain said, "Keep away from people who try to belittle your ambitions. Small people always do that, but the really great ones make you feel that you, too, can become great."

On that note, let's now take a look at how you can find the opposite of a naysayer: a really great mentor to guide you, inform you, and inspire you to become one of the great ones.

Finding a Mentor

Wouldn't it be helpful to have someone to call when you were having a career crisis? Someone who had experienced the same challenges you are, learned their lessons the hard way, and was willing to save you time and effort by showing you how to do things right the first time?

Well, here's some good news: these fabulous people do exist, and they are called mentors. A mentor is someone who is willing to give you personal training and advice about breaking into a particular career, either for free, for money, or for an exchange of services.

As discussed, informal networking is a great way to start off building relationships with people who can help you along in your career. While developing these relationships, you will likely come across some people who are extra friendly, extra helpful, or just someone you click with right away. These people are likely candidates for being willing to take the relationship to a more personal level and becoming a mentor to you.

TIP: Ideally your mentor will be working successfully in the career themselves, so that they can share with you the "how to" instead of just the "how not to."

While books and courses will get you so far, the great thing about a mentor is that their advice is up-to-the-minute, personalized to your situation, and interactive — as in "you ask, they tell." And if you play your cards right, you could have a person to turn to for help making career-related decisions for years to come.

How to Approach a Potential Mentor

If you don't identify a suitable mentor in your early networking, you may need to start looking more aggressively. An excellent way to connect with professionals in an industry is to visit them where they work, if possible. This is of course most practical if they work with the public in some way.

Just seeing them at work is a great way to learn, but beyond that, take the opportunity to introduce yourself on a break or quiet time, ask for their business card, and let them know you will be calling to invite them for lunch or coffee in a few days. You don't have to get into all the details on the spot; save it for when you have their full attention.

If it's not possible to connect with a mentor in person, you can look for suitable professionals on the Internet, in the phone book, or in industry directories. Internet message boards often have resident experts who answer questions from newcomers, and they may be open to starting a personal mentoring relationship with you.

Especially when you are planning on starting a business, it's actually to your advantage to approach a mentor who is not in the same town as you, so that they know you won't be competing for the same clients. Also, it gives you an opportunity to look for true experts in the field, as opposed to connecting solely on the basis of who is located nearby.

To make the most of your relationship, look for a mentor who, as much as possible, shares your intended specialty (if you have one in mind), your values, and your way of doing business. If you can't find all this in one person, you may want to approach more than one mentor to round out the advice you receive.

Once you have identified one or a few potential mentors, approach them with a written letter or email of introduction (a sample is included on the next page). Or you can use these same notes as conversation points when you meet with them for coffee or lunch.

- Explain why you selected them as a potential mentor. This may be their success within a specific industry you are interested in, or it may be that you admire their skills. Whatever your reason, let your potential mentor know why you chose them out of all the professionals in North America or your region.

- Make a specific request. Don't just say you want them to be your mentor; explain what you are asking. Do you want to talk with them on the telephone once a week for 20 minutes? Do you want to meet with them once a month over lunch? Do you want to communicate with them on a weekly basis via email? Also, be open to their offer of an alternative method of contact, as you are the one asking for a favor. Some people shy away from mentoring because they fear it will take too much time or energy. Assure your potential mentor this isn't the case.

Sample Mentoring Request Letter

Jones Etiquette Consulting
Attn: Judy Jones
123 Any Street
Lincoln City, ME

December 1, 2006

Dear Ms. Judy Jones,

I recently had the opportunity to attend your seminar on communication etiquette at the Hanover House in Lincoln City. I was very impressed with your presentation and your ability to make the subject fun and entertaining. I have read about your success as an etiquette consultant and this is the reason for my letter. I am beginning an etiquette consulting business in Jackson City, about 150 miles from your city. I would like to ask if you would be willing to mentor me in this new career.

I know that you are very busy and very involved with your work with Children's Hospital, which is one more reason that I wanted you to be my mentor. You have such a heart for the community and manage to handle a successful business and still have time for civic work, which is something I strive to achieve as well.

I want to assure you that being my mentor will not require an exhaustive effort on your part. I would like to be able to communicate with you via email — this would be only when I had specific questions or concerns about the business. I would also like the opportunity to call on you once a month to discuss business issues or, if your schedule allows, we could meet for lunch once a month for these discussions.

In exchange for your information and time, I have experience as a specialist in computer systems, and would be happy to offer my services to get your computer running smoothly.

Thank you and I appreciate your consideration of this proposal. I will follow up with you next week.

Warm regards,

Polly Proper
Proper Etiquette Consulting

• Offer something back. While some professional mentors charge a fee for mentoring (see below), others will provide the service at no charge. However, there may be many demands on their time, so think about what you can offer in return. A free lunch is a start, but it's better to volunteer your services or share information. Maybe you are a computer whiz and can offer to set up her new computer network. Or maybe you can write great advertising copy, and offer to write his next brochure.

If they are located reasonably nearby, you could also propose an unpaid internship where you would help out in the professional's office on a part-time basis at no charge to them. This can be a win-win for both of you — they benefit from your help while you learn from their experience.

Mentoring for a Fee

In industries that are notoriously challenging to break into, some professionals make a living by mentoring others. They sell their consulting services to you, as well as accompanying products, books, or seminars, for a fee.

You may find that it is faster for you to look for someone who is already working as a mentor rather than approach people who may be unfamiliar or unreceptive to the idea. Again, this comes down to which you have more of: time, or money.

In the case where you are paying a mentor, you need to make sure you are getting value for your money. Ask lots of questions up front about their specialty and what their availability will be like, and ask if you can speak to other people they have mentored to ensure that they were satisfied with the results.

TIP: Your mentor should be currently working in the industry, or else they may be out of touch with today's market. If you have any doubts, keep shopping around until you find someone who has the right credentials and reliability.

For personal one-on-one mentoring, you should expect to pay the going rate for expert consultants, which is anywhere from $30 to $75 an hour, or more. For example, one mentoring program we found related to one of the careers in this book cost $3,000 for three months of contact or $5,000 for a 10-day hands-on internship.

> **TIP:** To quickly learn about your dream career from an experienced mentor check out **www.VocationVacations.com**. For a fee typically ranging from about $350 to $1,000 (not including travel expenses), you may be able to spend time with someone who is currently working in your dream job. Most VocationVacations last from one to three days, with hundreds of mentors in careers from A (actor) to Y (Yoga Studio Owner).

To find paid mentors, you can contact the professional associations in your industry and ask them for a referral, or look in the classified section of industry-related magazines.

You can also type the career name and the words "training" or "coaching" or "personal training" into an Internet search engine. If you have already bookmarked some of the websites of the top professionals in your industry, look for a tab or link to "coaching," "internships" or "training."

More Thoughts on Word-of-Mouth Job-Hunting

If you are looking for work, you want to show up on as many radar screens as possible when that signal goes out that an employee or contractor is needed. Word of mouth is a great way to establish your presence as a job seeker or service provider.

Remember, many employers find employees through word of mouth. Hiring managers pass resumes around — they may ask friends, business associates, and current employees if they know anyone who might be suitable for the job.

If you can network with and impress Employer A, who may not have an opening at any given time, they may be willing to pass your resume along to a company they know that is hiring. And of course, referrals to new clients go a long way when you are trying to start up a new business.

Being well connected might even help you identify an opportunity to create a job for yourself where no position previously existed. Sound impossible? Find out how it has worked for other people (and can work for you too) in the next chapter, Make It Happen.

14

Make It Happen

How to Create Your Dream Job

It would be wonderful if you could just open the want ads in your Sunday paper and see columns and columns of advertisements for your dream job, but that isn't likely to happen. With so many people trying to break into dream careers, and so many positions being found through word of mouth, many dream job openings are filled immediately with no need to advertise them.

So if there are no jobs "available," what can you do? It may surprise you to learn that even if the job you want doesn't currently exist, you might be able to get it anyway. How?

By creating it.

Every job that exists today was created when a company decided someone was needed to fill that role. Of course most new positions are initiated within a company, but some are created when job-hunters persuade employers to hire them for a brand-new position. Many of the careers listed in this book are relatively new, meaning that an employer may have a need for your services and not even know it until you make them aware.

This chapter will explain how to create a job with your current employer or how to create a job with any company by providing more value than you cost. You can also create a job for yourself the

348

more obvious way, by starting your own service business, which we will also explain in this chapter.

Bringing Value: The Secret of Creating a Job

The secret to creating a job for yourself is really quite simple: you need to show an employer that you will bring them value that will outweigh the costs of hiring and employing you.

In fact, many services are sold based on this equation. For example, although you can book a vacation yourself using the Internet, you may hire a travel consultant to do this for you because they bring you value that outweighs their fee, such as:

- Reduced flight and/or accommodation costs
- Inside information about accommodation
- Saving you the time of booking
- Peace of mind that the trip has been booked by a professional

The Costs

To start thinking about how you can bring value to an employer, you should first understand what things employers see as "costs" when they hire a new employee. You might be surprised at the length of this list — it's not as simple as what they pay you once you are hired. Here are some examples:

- Time communicating and meeting with you
- Time spent deciding whether or not to hire you
- Your salary
- Your benefits
- Resources you'll need to do your job (e.g. computer, supplies)
- Time and cost to create a workspace for you
- Time to complete hiring paperwork
- Time of other staff members to train you and answer your questions (the more training you need and the more questions you have, the more you "cost" to hire)
- Time of your supervisor to oversee your work
- Time or business lost due to errors in your work
- Insurance to cover you in the workplace
- Employer government costs, such as Social Security and Medicare contributions in the U.S., or CPP payments in Canada)
- Time and cost to handle payroll regarding your employment

> **TIP:** 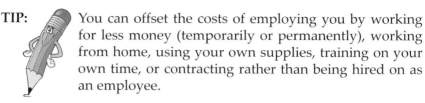 You can offset the costs of employing you by working for less money (temporarily or permanently), working from home, using your own supplies, training on your own time, or contracting rather than being hired on as an employee.

The Value

As you can see, you will need to demonstrate to an employer that you would bring them more value than simply covering the cost of your salary. Value is perceived a bit differently by each employer, depending on where they need assistance, but it boils down to solving problems and typically involves saving time or making money.

Here are some examples of things employers may see as valuable:

- Increasing profits by getting more sales (this could be done through training sales staff, bringing new clients to the business, or expanding awareness of the company to new markets)
- Increasing profits by reducing costs (preventing lost sales, doing work for less than they are currently paying to have it done, or finding better rates from suppliers)
- Freeing up your boss's time so she can do more important work and/or make more money (taking over some of her tasks, or helping her get better organized)
- Reducing your boss's frustration by doing tasks he doesn't like doing himself (common examples include filing, making coffee, responding to emails, returning phone calls, typing, etc.)
- Increasing profits by promoting awareness of the company or individual (tapping into new markets, or innovative public relations or marketing ideas)
- Increasing profits by making the company or person more productive (helping get more done, or streamlining processes)
- Providing a valuable or unique service or talent that is hard to find (certification or training, or a particular talent that allows them to offer more value to clients)
- Providing a solution to a current challenge (low productivity, high expenses, unmotivated employees, or low sales)

Find out what the company or decision-maker's needs are, so you can be certain you are offering things that are valuable to them. You can do some research in advance, and also ask this question in an information interview, by email, or by telephone.

To create a job, it's important to be proactive. Many job-seekers miss the opportunity to create the job of their dreams by simply telling employers what their skills are then leaving it up to the employer to figure out where they might fit into the company. You are much more likely to create the job of your dreams if you tell them exactly what you can do for them that will solve their particular problems.

It's also important to focus on what they perceive as their needs, and not what you think they need to improve. It is a waste of time to try to convince them that you can solve something they don't consider to be a problem.

For example, one job-seeker who applied to FabJob had only one idea of what he could do for us. He said he would change our slogan from "Got a drab job? Get a FabJob!" because he said "clearly, few people understand the word 'drab'." The problem with this was that not only had no one else ever told us they didn't understand our slogan, but we have spent thousands of dollars trademarking it, and we like it!

We'll explain some more dos and don'ts of what to say when you approach someone who can hire you in the upcoming sections of this chapter.

Create a Job With Your Current Employer

You don't necessarily have to leave your current employer to get a chance to do work you love. Instead, you can investigate how you can actually start "doing" your dream job part-time with your current employer, and then possibly move into a full-time position, either with that employer or another employer.

> **TIP:** Staying with your current employer while you build experience for your dream career is a good idea if it's possible. If you haven't quit your job yet, remember that it's usually a good idea to line up a new one first!

For example, Jacqueline Whitmore, who is a Florida-based etiquette consultant, created her own job when she was working at the famous Breakers Hotel in Palm Beach, Florida. At that time, the hotel did not employ anyone to consult on protocol and etiquette issues.

Whitmore obtained etiquette training certification on her own. Then she petitioned her boss to become the first protocol officer of the Breakers, and succeeded in being convincing that this position had a value that outweighed the cost. Whitmore launched her career as an etiquette consultant, and is now the founder and director of The Protocol School of Palm Beach.

Break In By Volunteering

If you are currently employed, think about the different offices or departments where you work. Even if you work for a small business, your company very likely has one or more people working in customer service, sales, or human resources, for example. Chances are that someone in your current place of work is currently doing tasks that are relevant to your dream career, or even doing your dream job.

But you can't just walk into the marketing department, for example, and say, "Step aside, Tim. I've got your job covered for the day." Nor will your supervisor take kindly to you telling them that you are abandoning your current responsibilities to fill a need for another department, or even better, a need they have yet to identify. So what are your options?

One solution is to volunteer to help the department you want experience with. Although not everyone will accept an offer of help (some people are territorial, afraid of training someone who might take over their job, or simply don't want to share work they enjoy), you might be surprised at how many people will jump at the opportunity for assistance. As a result of downsizings, many departments are short-staffed and could use a hand.

Your offer is much more likely to be accepted if you state your willingness to do the work that other people dislike doing. If you are willing to file, photocopy, make coffee, or do whatever is needed, say so. There are plenty of people who want to do fun tasks, making it tough for someone without experience to break in. You will have very little competition if you offer to do the work others are not willing to do.

One caution: unless you are able to persuade your employer to transfer you to that department immediately, you will still be expected to do your regular job. If you are not willing to work for the other department on your own time (lunch hours, evenings, or even weekends), getting work experience in this way is probably not an option for you.

How to Move Into a Full-Time Job

Once you are volunteering in the department or area of work that is closer to what you want to transition into, it's time to put your investigative mind to work and look for where you might fit in as a full-time employee there.

You can do this by identifying what needs the department or individual have that are not currently being met. Speak to the right person. In some cases it will be the head of the department. In other cases it will be someone who is currently doing a particular task you want to get experience with. Ask questions like:

- What are some current challenges you are experiencing?
- Are there any areas you feel are being overlooked right now?
- If you had two weeks with no other projects to get done, where would you start?
- What areas do you see yourself expanding into in the near future?

When you have identified what needs the department or person has, then you can propose to the head of the department or the person you are assisting how you can help them meet these needs with a value that outweighs your cost, as explained. Show that you have a positive attitude and are willing to do what it takes to get the job done. If you provide excellent value to the department, you could be offered a job doing what you want.

If most of the positions in your desired field require previous experience or a degree and you don't have or want to get that level of education or experience, consider creating or suggesting an entry-level position for yourself. Many fabulous positions are filled by individuals who started as administrative assistants or executive assistants and worked their way up in the organization.

Even if you aren't offered a full-time position where you are volunteering, you are still gaining valuable experience that you can use to sell yourself to a totally new employer, as explained in the next section of this chapter.

Create a Job with a New Employer

Creating a job with a new employer can be a bit trickier than trying to set something up with your place of work, simply because you don't have the same connections in place as a current employee. You will have to investigate the company's needs more formally, by setting up an interview with a decision-maker and selling yourself to them using the cost-value equation explained earlier.

For example, if you want to get a job in wedding planning, a company that occasionally provides services for weddings (such as a caterer, florist, or resort) might hire you to set up a new "wedding department" if you explain how you could increase profits by getting more clients for the company with your new department.

Who to Contact

To decide which companies to apply to, keep up with local news. Read the business pages of daily newspapers and watch the TV news to find out what companies in your area need, so you can determine how you can fill that need.

Is there a fast-growing company in your area? These companies are usually looking to be the best and the brightest in the field, and may be open to adding that little something extra that makes them stand out in a crowd. Is there a company that is focused on offering the best customer service? Is there a company that is gearing up to expand? You may find these employers most open to adding a new position to maintain or build on their reputation.

Remember when you contact an employer that you need to deal directly with someone who has the authority to hire new people. Despite what you might think, this doesn't mean contacting the human resources (HR) department of a large company, unless that is the department you want to work with. HR fills positions that already exist.

If you want to create a new position, you will need to speak with the appropriate department manager or, in a smaller company, the owner. You will need to meet with this person and learn what they need to be able to figure out how you can create value for them.

It's best if you can establish a relationship with someone through networking. However, you may even be able to create a job through cold calling. For example, here is the type of message you might leave on someone's voicemail:

Hello (name of potential employer), this is Annie Assistant. I am an experienced employee trainer, and would like to meet with you to discuss how I could help (insert name of potential employer's company) increase profits by having me train sales and customer service staff. Please call me at (insert your phone number) so we can schedule a time to meet. (If you actually reach the person, simply change the last sentence to ask when would be a good time to meet.)

If the company is looking to increase profits, as many companies are, this call is more likely to get returned than a call simply asking if there are any job openings. You may need to be persistent and make a lot of calls, but if what you are offering is something that will bring a company more value than it costs, you can create a job.

How to Sell Yourself

During a meeting with the employer, you will need to provide convincing answers to questions such as:

- Why should this company create a job just for you?
- How will you and this job benefit the company?
- What do you bring to the table?

Your answers should directly address their needs, such as explaining that your skills will help this company and its employees be more competitive in a very competitive industry. Review the section earlier on the cost-value equation for some ideas of what employers may need or value.

You should make an effort to match your skills and talents to the employer's needs. For example, perhaps you are a dynamic trainer who can create and present training programs on a variety of subjects, and you are also able to do one-on-one training for executives who need special attention.

Close the meeting on a high note, and don't forget to follow up. Even if they can't find a way to create a job for you right away, you will have planted the seed of an idea that might grow into an opportunity in six months or a year.

Other Options

While it can be a fun challenge to create a job for yourself working for a company or assisting an individual, some of you may be thinking, "I really don't want to sell myself to any employer. I just want to start doing what I love right away."

For many people, a key component of their dream job is being their own boss, setting their own hours, and choosing their own salary. The last section of this chapter on creating jobs has to do with taking it all into your own hands and creating a job for yourself running your own service business.

Create a Job by Starting Your Own Business

Rather than trying to get hired by a company and work your way up the ladder, you can make a lot more money, have a lot more freedom, and do a lot more of the interesting work right away by starting your own business from home (or otherwise), offering services directly to clients.

A service business can be started small, with little or no upfront investment. If you don't think you have the resources to start your own business, think again. As long as you have access to a telephone and a means of transportation (even public transit) you can start your own service business. You can ask clients to pay you in advance for any upfront expenses, as we'll explain in the fees material a bit later in this section.

The information provided here is a basic outline for those who want to start a home-based service business. If you are interested in starting a retail or other type of business instead, you can re-read Chapter 7 (Fab Merchants). And for lots of detailed information specific to your dream career, you can visit FabJob.com to find a full length FabJob guide with industry specific information about how to start the type of business that interests you.

Why a Service Business?

Many of us have been raised to believe that the "best jobs" are those that involve working in an office. In 1959, the term "knowledge worker" was coined by management consultant Peter Drucker to describe someone who works primarily with information.

However, we believe the 20th century's demand for knowledge workers is giving way to an increasing need for "service workers" in the 21st century. And the result is a dramatic shift in both the nature of work and the types of employers.

The service workers we traditionally think of are those who sell us our coffee, wait on our restaurant tables, deliver our newspapers, serve us in retail stores, drive the taxis or buses we take, and so forth.

While the need for these types of service workers is greater than ever before, there is also a growing demand for new types of service workers, particularly in areas with a booming economy. In this era of the service worker, you can create your own job providing personal services to members of the baby boomer generation who have more money than time, or who place value on the unique service you offer.

To understand why there is a growing demand for personal services, consider how the baby boomer generation is changing the world. As baby boomers age, they start to get a sense of how precious time is. They want to spend it doing things they enjoy. And if they don't enjoy running errands, organizing closets, grocery shopping, maintaining the home, or cooking dinner, they want to find someone else to do those things.

At FabJob.com, we have received numerous emails from people throughout North America asking us if we can help them find a personal shopper or professional organizer to hire. People are desperate for these types of services, and if you are willing to provide them you can earn a very good income.

Planning Your Business

As soon as you have decided to go into business for yourself it's time to start planning what your business will be, if you haven't already determined that from Part Two of this book. Even if your only experience is as a homemaker or volunteer, you have probably gained a wealth of experience providing exactly the types of services that many people would love to pay someone to do for them. You could start a business providing services such as any of the following:

- Personal Assistant
- Personal Shopper
- Personal Chef
- Interior Decorator
- Butler/Household Manager
- Party Planner
- Professional Organizer

These are just a few examples. Anything that some people would prefer not to do themselves, from bookkeeping to packing a household for a move, can be turned into a business.

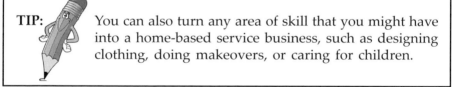

TIP: You can also turn any area of skill that you might have into a home-based service business, such as designing clothing, doing makeovers, or caring for children.

When you have narrowed down an area of interest, there's still more planning to do. Sure, you may know that you want to be a personal shopper or a party planner, but what items will you shop for, and what kind of parties will you plan?

Have a few informal brainstorming sessions with your business partner, spouse, family or friends, and really get creative. Remember, brainstorming is about sharing any and all ideas, regardless of how impractical or odd they might sound. You may hit on a hidden gem if you keep an open mind.

While you'll definitely come up with some great ideas for names, your website, or even themes and colors, what you are trying to pin down are the basics: what services you will offer, who will be your clients, and how you will stand out from the crowd.

It's important to choose a specialization so that people can understand what you are offering. Although it's tempting when you start a new business to say that "everyone" will be your target market, the most successful businesses have a clear vision of what they are offering, and who will be paying for it. In fact, people are more likely to hire you if they see you as an expert who specializes in what they need.

Finding Suppliers

Service business owners may need to identify and build relationships with industry-specific suppliers or vendors in order to offer their services. For example, a party planner will need sources of decorations, locations for parties, favorite caterers, and many other people in place before they can jump into planning parties.

Don't let this intimidate you — in fact, suppliers can also give great advice about using their products, and may even end up referring business to you if you are someone they like and trust.

A great way to find suppliers for your business is in your networking. Ask your mentor and other professionals working in the industry what suppliers they use. People are usually willing to give glowing recommendations and anecdotal warnings alike.

You can also check industry publications where suppliers are likely to advertise. And if you are interested in a particular dream career already, each FabJob career guide includes resources and hyperlinks you can use to connect with suppliers immediately.

A note on purchasing supplies: in many jurisdictions, if you are purchasing wholesale items to resell to clients, you won't pay your tax to the suppliers on items you buy from suppliers. But don't think that this gets you out of paying tax altogether!

Instead, you will pay the tax directly to the government, and collect it from the client, based on the price you sell the items for, not the price you paid. When you register with your local and/or federal agencies, they will supply you with the details you need to know about collecting and submitting sales tax.

How to Get Clients

To get clients you can start with word of mouth, and ask people to spread the word that you are available for hire. Chapter 13 will help you figure out ways to use networking to tell people that you exist and do great work.

Getting your first few clients will probably be your toughest challenge, so to get over this hump, consider doing a few jobs at a reduced rate or even for free while you gain skills and confidence. Friends and family are most likely to be willing to take a chance on you, and if you document the work you do for them, then you can build on that experience with paying clients down the road.

Volunteering is also a good way to promote yourself. If you can find ways to donate your services to worthy causes, you increase your exposure to clients who may be taking an interest in that cause as well. For example, if you are an image consultant and you offer free one-hour consultations to women with breast cancer, you are benefiting the community, and have great material for a press release to send to the media as well.

On the topic of the media, you will want to get in the habit of sending information to them regularly in order to build awareness of your business. The "media" are magazines, newspapers, radio, and television. When a business gets positive coverage in a magazine article, newspaper story, radio or television talk show, it can result in a tremendous amount of new business.

Most magazines and newspapers publish contact information for their editors. Find out the editor's name, and send a brief letter by email, fax, or snail mail saying what your business is doing, what's unique about it, and why it would be a great idea for a story (i.e. why it would interest readers). Local TV or radio talk show producers can be approached in a similar way.

Being seen as an expert in your industry is also a great way to build confidence in your services and spread the word about what you do. One of the best ways to establish yourself as an expert is to write articles or even a column for a newspaper, magazine, or newsletter. You can share aspects of your knowledge with the readers, and pique their interest in you and your business. You can also be seen as an expert if you host a seminar, give a speech, or teach a class on your area of expertise.

While word of mouth and networking can be particularly effective ways to get business for yourself, you may also be able to attract some clients through advertising. Consider the Yellow Pages if you are specializing in a service that seems compatible with them. To minimize your risk, you might want to start with a small display ad, such as a 1/8 page ad.

If you choose to buy advertising, it will probably be most cost-effective to place ads in small local magazines read by your target markets. The publications you advertise in will usually design your ad for an additional cost, and give you a copy of the ad to run in other publications.

A website is another excellent marketing tool. Although it won't necessarily generate much business itself, your website can complement your other marketing efforts. When someone sees your web address on your business card, in a Yellow Pages ad, or elsewhere, they can visit your website 24 hours a day to learn more about your services.

Setting Your Fees

Service businesses are a smart way to make money on a flexible schedule. Even if you charged only $20 per hour plus expenses, you could earn over $3,500 per month before taxes if you worked 22 eight-hour days per month. And if you charged $40 per hour you could earn more than $5,000 per month — and even choose to take more time off.

When setting your prices for your services, the most important thing to consider is the difference between the price you charge versus how much it costs you to provide it. This difference determines your profit (or loss), and will determine whether you make enough money to not just cover your costs, but make a living with what you do.

Your pricing must also reflect what the market will bear — or what clients are willing to pay. This may be affected by what the perceived value of your service is, and what price clients are paying for the same service in your area. It may also be influenced by whether your market is residential or corporate.

There are different types of fee arrangements you can choose from, as we'll detail below. Each industry is likely to have somewhat of a standard format, so ask your mentor and other professionals what has worked for them in the past, and why.

Hourly:	You bill the client per hour or portion of an hour that you are working for them. In some service businesses you might have different hourly rates for different components of the service, such as a certain rate for hands-on work, a slightly reduced rate for consultation, half-rate for time spent traveling to meet clients, etc.

Daily:	For projects that will run over several days, you may want to quote the client a daily rate that covers a set number of hours or certain services. This is a more common fee arrangement when you are working for larger clients or corporations.
Per Project:	In this type of billing you quote the client a flat fee that covers the whole project. Clients often prefer it when you can quote them a flat project rate, so that they won't be surprised by the final bill.
	Per project fees are most appropriate for small jobs where it's easy to see what's involved. With bigger jobs you need to be careful that you can quote accurately and fairly to protect yourself.
Cost-Plus for Supplies:	If you will be purchasing discounted wholesale supplies for your clients, you can use a cost-plus fee structure, when you purchase items at wholesale discount, and then mark them up closer to retail cost for your clients. While your clients will still save a bit of money from the retail cost, you make money as well.

When it comes to charging for an initial consultation with a prospective client, most service providers are like lawyers and other professionals: they offer a free initial consultation. In most cases, this first meeting is simply an opportunity to learn more about what the client needs and explain how your services can benefit them. You will not actually be doing any actual hands-on work in this meeting.

At the end of your initial consultation, if the client wants to go ahead, you can ask the client for a deposit to start getting ready to work — buying any supplies, preparing planning materials, or developing a budget or cost estimate, for example.

Once the client has approved your plan and cost estimates, have the client sign a contract or letter of agreement that sets out a payment schedule, with your final payment due upon completion of services. Jobs with individuals may be paid up front and/or on completion of the work, while businesses you do work for will likely require you to invoice.

15

Resources

Where to Get More Information

Career Assessments

There are many resources available to help you identify your ideal career, including the following online career assessments. Some are free, while others charge a fee. Please note that inclusion on this list is not an endorsement.

- Career Test by CareerFitter.com
  www.careerfitter.com

- The CareerLink Inventory
  www.mpc.edu/cl/climain.htm

- Career Liftoff
  www.careerliftoff.com

- Career Maze Career Guidance Assessment Report
  www.careermaze.com/sample/cawebsamplereport2.asp

- CareerPlanner.com
  www.careerplanner.com

- Focus Career Planning System
  www.focuscareer.com

- iVillage Ideal Job Test
  http://ivos.ivillage.com/assessment/exec/idealjobindex

- Kiersey Temperament Sorter
  www.advisorteam.com/temperament_sorter/

- LiveCareer.com
  www.livecareer.com

- Motivational Appraisal of Personal Potential
  www.assessment.com

- The Princeton Review Career Quiz
  www.princetonreview.com/cte/quiz/career_quiz1.asp

- The Testing Room
  www.testingroom.com

- Tickle: Career Personality Test
  http://web.tickle.com/tests/classiccareer

- TypeFocus Careers
  www.typefocus.com

For an excellent overview of career assessments, Quintessential Careers rates a variety of services in their 'Online Career Assessment Tools Review' at **www.quintcareers.com/online_assessment_review. html**.

General Job Sites

- CareerBuilder.com
  www.careerbuilder.com

- FabJob.com
  www.FabJob.com

- Government Job Bank (Canada)
  www.jobbank.gc.ca

- Monster.com
  www.monster.com

- Wetfeet.com: internships
  www.wetfeet.internshipprograms.com

- Workopolis.com (Canada)
  www.workopolis.com

- Yahoo HotJobs
  http://hotjobs.yahoo.com

Starting a Business

- Government Services for Entrepreneurs (Canada)
  http://canadabusiness.gc.ca

- Internal Revenue Service
  www.irs.gov

- National Association for the Self-Employed
  www.nase.org

- Nolo Legal Resources
  www.nolo.com

- SCORE "Counselors to America's Small Business"
  www.score.org

- U.S. Small Business Administration (SBA)
  www.sba.gov

TELL US WHAT YOU THINK

Please contact us at **www.FabJob.com/feedback.asp** to tell us how this guide has helped prepare you for your dream career. If we publish your comments on our website or in our promotional materials, we will send you a gift certificate for **50% off** your next purchase of a FabJob guide.

 **Order Form**

Ways to Order

Fax   Complete the form on this page and the next 3 pages, cut it out, and fax it to **1-403-949-2080**.

Mail   Complete the form on the next 3 pages, cut it out, and mail it with a Visa or MasterCard number and expiry date or an **international money order** (we don't accept personal checks) to our Canadian processing center:

FabJob Inc.
23 Sunmeadows Road S.E.
Calgary, Alberta T2X 2M2 Canada

Phone   You can phone in your order 24 hours a day to **1-403-949-4980**. Then press 1 to place an order. Be ready to provide the following information to our automated system: your name, email address, mailing address, **Visa** or **MasterCard** number and expiry date, and which guides you are ordering. (Please note that calls can only be returned to bulk buyers purchasing a minimum of 5 guides. All other customer correspondence is by email.)

Online   To get your guide(s) immediately, place your order at **www.FabJob.com**.

Purchaser Information

First Name: _____

Last Name: _____

Email: _____
Include your email address if you want a receipt.

Address: _____

_____

City: _____

State/Province: _____

Country: _____

Zip/Postal Code: _____

continued on next page

Your Order

Select your guide(s) from the list below. All prices are in U.S. dollars. Shipping and handling charges for CD-ROMs and print books are $5 additional per guide.

FabJob Guide to...

The following include an e-book.
(Price is same without an e-book.)

Become an Actor	❏ Ebook ($14.97)	❏ CD-ROM ($19.97)
Become an Advertising Copywriter	❏ Ebook ($14.97)	❏ CD-ROM ($19.97)
Become an Archaeologist	❏ Ebook ($14.97)	❏ CD-ROM ($19.97)
Become an Art Curator	❏ Ebook ($19.97)	❏ CD-ROM ($24.97)
Become a Bed & Breakfast Owner	❏ Ebook ($19.97)	❏ CD-ROM ($24.97)
Become a Book Editor	❏ Ebook ($14.97)	❏ CD-ROM ($19.97)
Become a Bookstore Owner	❏ Ebook ($29.97)	❏ Print book & CD-ROM ($39.97)
Become a Boutique Owner	❏ Ebook ($29.97)	❏ Print book & CD-ROM ($39.97)
Become a Business Consultant	❏ Ebook ($29.97)	❏ CD-ROM ($34.97)
Become a Butler	❏ Ebook ($19.97)	❏ CD-ROM ($24.97)
Become a Cartoonist	❏ Ebook ($9.97)	❏ CD-ROM ($14.97)
Become a Caterer or Personal Chef	❏ Ebook ($29.97)	❏ CD-ROM ($34.97)
Become a Celebrity Personal Assistant	❏ Ebook ($29.97)	❏ CD-ROM ($34.97)
Become a Children's Book Author	❏ Ebook ($19.97)	❏ CD-ROM ($24.97)
Become a Coffee House Owner	❏ Ebook ($29.97)	❏ Print book & CD-ROM ($39.97)
Become a Day Care Owner	❏ Ebook ($14.97)	❏ Print book & CD-ROM ($24.97)
Become a Doula	❏ Ebook ($29.97)	❏ CD-ROM ($34.97)
Become an Etiquette Consultant	❏ Ebook ($29.97)	❏ Print book & CD-ROM ($39.97)
Become an Event Planner	❏ Ebook ($29.97)	❏ Print book & CD-ROM ($39.97)
Become a Fashion Designer	❏ Ebook ($29.97)	❏ Print book & CD-ROM ($34.97)
Become a Flight Attendant	❏ Ebook ($14.97)	❏ CD-ROM ($19.97)
Become a Florist	❏ Ebook ($29.97)	❏ Print book & CD-ROM ($39.97)
Become a Food Critic	❏ Ebook ($14.97)	❏ CD-ROM ($19.97)
Become a Funeral Director	❏ Ebook ($19.97)	❏ CD-ROM ($24.97)
Become a Human Resources Pro	❏ Ebook ($19.97)	❏ CD-ROM ($24.97)
Become an Image Consultant	❏ Ebook ($29.97)	❏ Print book & CD-ROM ($39.97)
Become an Interior Decorator	❏ Ebook ($29.97)	❏ Print book & CD-ROM ($39.97)
Become a Jewelry Designer	❏ Ebook ($29.97)	❏ CD-ROM ($34.97)
Become a Landscape Company Owner	❏ Ebook ($14.97)	❏ CD-ROM ($19.97)
Become a Life Coach	❏ Ebook ($29.97)	❏ CD-ROM ($34.97)
Become a Makeup Artist	❏ Ebook ($29.97)	❏ Print book & CD-ROM ($39.97)
Become a Management Consultant	❏ Ebook ($29.97)	❏ CD-ROM ($34.97)
Become a Massage Therapist	❏ Ebook ($19.97)	❏ CD-ROM ($24.97)

Become a Model	❏ Ebook ($14.97)	❏ CD-ROM ($19.97)
Become a Motivational Speaker	❏ Ebook ($29.97)	❏ Print book & CD-ROM ($39.97)
Become a Movie Reviewer	❏ Ebook ($14.97)	❏ CD-ROM ($19.97)
Become a Mystery Shopper	❏ Ebook ($19.97)	❏ CD-ROM ($24.97)
Become a Mystery Writer	❏ Ebook ($9.97)	❏ CD-ROM ($14.97)
Become a Party Planner	❏ Ebook ($29.97)	❏ Print book & CD-ROM ($39.97)
Become a Personal Shopper	❏ Ebook ($29.97)	❏ Print book & CD-ROM ($34.97)
Become a Personal Trainer	❏ Ebook ($14.97)	❏ CD-ROM ($19.97)
Become a Private Investigator	❏ Ebook ($14.97)	❏ CD-ROM ($19.97)
Become a Professional Golfer	❏ Ebook ($14.97)	❏ Print book & CD-ROM ($24.97)
Become a Professional Organizer	❏ Ebook ($29.97)	❏ Print book & CD-ROM ($39.97)
Become a Public Relations Consultant	❏ Ebook ($19.97)	❏ CD-ROM ($24.97)
Become a Published Writer	❏ Ebook ($14.97)	❏ CD-ROM ($19.97)
Become a Recording Star	❏ Ebook ($14.97)	❏ CD-ROM ($19.97)
Become a Restaurant Owner	❏ Ebook ($19.97)	❏ Print book & CD-ROM ($29.97)
Become a Romance Writer	❏ Ebook ($9.97)	❏ CD-ROM ($14.97)
Become a Super Salesperson	❏ Ebook ($9.97)	❏ CD-ROM ($14.97)
Become a Secondhand Store Owner	❏ Ebook ($19.97)	❏ Print book & CD-ROM ($29.97)
Become a Screenwriter	❏ Ebook ($14.97)	❏ CD-ROM ($19.97)
Become a Songwriter	❏ Ebook ($14.97)	❏ CD-ROM ($19.97)
Become a Spa Owner	❏ Ebook ($29.97)	❏ Print book & CD-ROM ($39.97)
Become a Stand-up Comic	❏ Ebook ($14.97)	❏ CD-ROM ($19.97)
Become a Technical Writer	❏ Ebook ($9.97)	❏ CD-ROM ($14.97)
Become a Television Producer	❏ Ebook ($14.97)	❏ CD-ROM ($19.97)
Become a Television Reporter	❏ Ebook ($19.97)	❏ CD-ROM ($24.97)
Become a Travel Consultant	❏ Ebook ($19.97)	❏ CD-ROM ($24.97)
Become a Travel Writer	❏ Ebook ($14.97)	❏ CD-ROM ($19.97)
Become a Video Game Designer	❏ Ebook ($14.97)	❏ CD-ROM ($19.97)
Become a Web Developer	❏ Ebook ($14.97)	❏ CD-ROM ($19.97)
Become a Wedding Planner	❏ Ebook ($29.97)	❏ Print book & CD-ROM ($39.97)
Become a Yoga Teacher	❏ Ebook ($19.97)	❏ CD-ROM ($24.97)
Get a Job on Capitol Hill	❏ Ebook ($19.97)	❏ CD-ROM ($24.97)
Get a Job on a Cruise Ship	❏ Ebook ($9.97)	❏ CD-ROM ($14.97)
Get Your Child into TV Commercials	❏ Ebook ($19.97)	❏ CD-ROM ($24.97)
Ultimate Guide for Pro Organizers	❏ Ebook ($34.97)	❏ CD-ROM ($39.97)

Shipping & Handling $5 per CD-ROM or print book/CD $ _____

Total $ _____

continued on next page

❑ Check the box to subscribe to the **FREE FabJob newsletter** with valuable tips on how to break into the career of your dreams. Delivered every other month by email with discounts on FabJob guides. You can unsubscribe at any time.

Payment Information

See page 365 for information on how to order by phone, fax, or mail.

Payment by: Visa ❑   MasterCard ❑   Money Order ❑

Payment must be included with order. If paying by money order make sure it can be cashed **internationally** and make it payable to **FabJob Inc**.

Credit Card Number: _____

Visa or MasterCard only

Expiry Date: Month: _____   Year: _____

Signature: _____

Canadian orders include GST (registration number 86995 1327 RT0001). Customers from all other countries acknowledge that they are purchasing products only for use outside Canada.

Delivery Information

❑ Check the box if the delivery address is the **same** as the purchaser's address. Complete the following if you want delivery to a different address.

First Name: _____

Last Name: _____

Email: _____

Include the email address if you want an e-book.

Address: _____

_____

City: _____

State/Province: _____

Country: _____

Zip/Postal Code: _____

E-books will be delivered by email within 24 hours of receipt of your order. If you have ordered a CD-ROM or print book (where available), please allow 2-3 weeks for delivery in North America and several weeks longer for overseas orders.